Champions For Zion

Remarkable Teachings on Building Zion by Early LDS Leaders

by

Jesse F. Fisher

2nd Edition

Copyright 2018 by Jesse F. Fisher

All rights reserved.

CHAMPIONS FOR ZION

Dedication

To

Barry Eaton

- my first and best Ziontist friend -

Save me a seat, my brother.

- and -

To

Joyce Gunther

- my first and only sister! -

Thanks for sparking in me a love of Zion.

CHAMPIONS FOR ZION

Contents

	Introduction	1
1	Building Zion was Central to the Gospel	8
2	What IS Zion?	25
3	God's Will	36
4	Prophecies about Zion	48
5	Our Obligations Regarding Zion	56
6	The Saints were Actively Building a Zion in Utah	63
7	What is Required of Us to Establish Zion?	75
8	Building Zion Is Spiritual AND Temporal!	98
9	Babylon, Zion's Opposite	108
10	Building Zion Includes Achieving Economic Independence	122
11	Zion Requires Economic Unity	135
12	Cooperation is a Stepping Stone to Zion	159
13	Afterthoughts: Zion Shrugged	177
14	Objections & Rebuttals	186
15	No Need to Wait	191

Appendix A: Additional Quotes

Chapter One	198
Chapter Two	206
Chapter Three	209

Chapter Four	216
Chapter Five	224
Chapter Six	232
Chapter Seven	241
Chapter Eight	254
Chapter Nine	260
Chapter Ten	266
Chapter Eleven	275
Chapter Twelve	283

Appendix B

The Signs of the Coming of the Son of Man—The Saints' Duties. - Wilford Woodruff	296
Cooperation - Brigham Young	310
United Order—Tithing—Cooperative Labors in Brigham City – Lorenzo Snow	317
Revelations Pertaining To Being One In Temporal, As In Spiritual Things – Orson Pratt	332
Our Traditions—Receiving Counsel – George Q. Cannon	350

Appendix C

An Encyclical Letter Upon Co-operation and the Social System. - First Presidency & Quorum of the Twelve, 1875	363

About the Author	370

Introduction

"Love God, Love Others".

This book reviews the teachings of early LDS apostles and prophets about establishing Zion. Both their society and a few others have enjoyed various degrees of success in applying the First and Second Great Commandments, to love God and one's fellowman, to their day-to-day lives. While reviewing these teachings, I hope to fill the reader's heart with confidence that we Latter-Day Saints can all take personal responsibility for moving our society off of Babylon's path to inevitable destruction, and onto Zion's path to societal peace and prosperity for all.

I propose that by picking up where our LDS ancestors left off in their efforts to establish City-of-Enoch-style Zion communities, we would all "prosper in the land" and experience the joy for which we are designed. Building the type of society God wants for his children would also spare us and our families from most of the personal and social muck we have to wade through in today's world.

Recently, I was saddened by a very despondent phrase written on a Facebook meme which declared, "Human life is existential horror". With the LDS concepts of Babylon and Zion in mind, I replied, "I'm thinking it's more, 'We have made human life into an existential horror.' Doesn't have to be this way."

Had that meme been posted in an LDS forum, I might have continued, "As a culture saturated with the worldly values of 'Babylon', we Americans (and others) have inadvertently reaped the whirlwind and turned human life into an existential horror. In sharp contrast, were we to apply the root core of Christianity to our social institutions (businesses, schools, clubs, etc.), remaking society in a way which institutionalizes Christ's directives to love God, and, love our fellowmen, human life could become an existential *joy* instead. Others have done it. So can we."

Yet, sadly, we drift along in the filth of the river Babylon—waiting for someone else to take the initiative to begin building the prophesied Zion society of the Last Days; complaining all the while that our children and other loved-ones are being spiritually swept away out into the mists of darkness.

It does not have to be this way.

In his General Conference address of October, 2008, "Come to Zion", Elder D. Todd Christofferson said that "The *antithesis and antagonist* of *Zion* is *Babylon*". I propose that we can free ourselves and our fellowmen from all the yuck Babylon spews on us in today's world by working individually and together to take up the charge to build Zion to whatever extent we are able, and, that the Lord will bless us <u>as promised</u> as we do so. (1 Nephi 13:37)

How this all started.

A few years back, I had the opportunity of teaching my High Priests group in our ward every quarter or so. Having been enamored with the LDS concept of Zion since my teenage years, decades ago, it was natural for me to teach about building Zion.

Yet, every single time I taught (and, every time our Stake President's vision of establishing Zion was mentioned), a well-respected, retired Institute teacher in our ward would interrupt and say, and I quote, "<u>We</u> can't build Zion, only *Jesus* can build Zion". What he said was *technically* true, we limited mortals can't build Zion without God's wisdom to guide us. But this well-meaning brother's statement felt like he was suggesting we sit around and wait for Jesus to do all the work, or, to at least wait to be "commanded in all things" Zion.

Brigham Young strongly refuted this attitude. He said in 1870, with emphases added:

*Are we prepared now to establish the Zion that the Lord designs to build up? . . . "Well," says one, "I thought the Lord was going to do this." So He is, **if** we will let Him. That is what we want: we want the people to be willing for the Lord to do it. But He will do it by means. He will not send His angels to gather up the rock to build up the New Jerusalem. He will not send His angels from the heavens to go to the mountains to cut the timber and make it into lumber to adorn the city of Zion. <u>He has called upon us to do this work</u>; and if we will let Him work by, through, and with us, He can accomplish it; otherwise **we** shall fall short, and shall never have the honor of building up Zion on the earth.*

This is one of my greatest concerns, that we American Latter-day Saints will lose the honor of building the New Jerusalem Zion through our disinterest and resulting inaction. An early apostle shared this concern, as we'll show at the end of Chapter One.

Teaching our High Priests group prompted me to search through all the records of talks given by modern apostles and prophets to find quotes about Zion that were *irrefutably* clear, and, to see exactly what *they* believed and taught about the subject. And so I did. I found there were 3,907 uses of the term "Zion" in the Journal of Discourses, which covers the 40 year time period between 1849 and 1889. Not having the patience to sift through all those, I limited my search mostly to those quotes that speak of "building Zion" or "establishing Zion"—I found over 700.

In that search, I discovered some real jewels that I used during my lessons, and, started sharing those quotes on my blog, BuildingZion.org. More importantly, I discovered that the early LDS leaders were *determined* to lead the Saints to build a real-live, brick and mortar, City-of-Enoch style Zion society here in Utah. Without exaggeration, I discovered they were truly grand champions for the cause of Zion.

As I read, categorized and sub-categorized these hundreds of quotes, a very clear <u>*and startling*</u> picture began to come into focus. I was *amazed* to discover just how central the building of Zion was to the early LDS Church: their missionaries preached it, their leaders taught that it was God's will that they build it, and they even taught that having the priesthood **obligated** us to build Zion.

I came to see that they saw building Zion as being much, much more than the spiritual goal of becoming pure in heart, which is, of course, crucially important. To them, building Zion was as much an <u>economic</u> effort as it was a spiritual one, if not more so. They worked diligently to make Utah's economy independent and self-sufficient and they referred to this same effort as "building Zion". They also referred to America's economy as "Babylon", and they worked tirelessly to create a literal, brick and mortar, here-and-now Zion economy in Territorial Utah and saw it as the alternative to Babylon prophesied by Isaiah and Jeremiah. As we will see from the quotes in later chapters, building Zion was the goal in the Church then, and Babylon's values of individualism, wealth-seeking, and materialism were strongly rejected.

Zion Shrugged

Leonard J. Arrington, who was later called as Church Historian, reported in his landmark book <u>Great Basin Kingdom</u> how the LDS Church abandoned its focus on establishing Zion. Unfortunately, due to political, economic and social forces, the US Government literally conquered the Mormons in the late 1880s and put an abrupt end to their Zion-building efforts, forcing them by necessity to integrate into America's capitalistic economy.

In a heavy-handed way, the United States Government dis-incorporated the Church, seized nearly all its assets, jailed its leaders, and up-ended the lives of numerous men and women who were living in plural marriages at the time. This resulted in the abandonment of all the social mechanisms LDS leaders had created to integrate the love of God and fellowman into the economic organization of the Saints.

Arrington went on to report that having been conquered, "the church no longer offered a geographic and institutional alternative to Babylon . . . Individualism, speculation, and inequality—once thought to be characteristics of Babylon—were woven into the fabric of Mormon life." *Ouch.*

Our modern Babylonian captivity has had some sad consequences for us as modern Israel. We LDS have become a little too fixated on the "delicacies" of Babylon which prevents most of us from having any interest at all in fleeing Babylon and in building Zion now. It's certainly possible that we LDS here in America have been "blinded by the subtle craftiness of men" (D&C 123:12) as we have been well integrated into Babylonian social and economic systems.

Elder David R. Stone of the Seventy, in his 2006 General Conference talk titled, "Zion in the Midst of Babylon", explained how we have become blind to Babylon's culture that pervades our daily lives and lures us away from the values of Zion:

We see Babylon in our cities; we see Babylon in our communities; we see Babylon everywhere.

And with the encroachment of Babylon, we have to create Zion in the midst of it. We should not allow ourselves to be engulfed by the culture which surrounds us. We seldom realize the extent to which we are a product of the culture of our place and time . . .

People in every culture move within a cocoon of self-satisfied self-deception, fully convinced that the way they see things is the way things really are.

Our culture tends to determine what foods we like, how we dress, what constitutes polite behavior, what sports we should follow, what our taste in music should be, the importance of education, and our attitudes toward honesty. It also influences men as to the importance of recreation or religion, influences women about the priority of career or childbearing, and has a powerful effect on how we approach procreation and moral issues. All too often, we are like puppets on a string, as our culture determines what is "cool" . . .

Seduced by our culture, we often hardly recognize our idolatry, as our strings are pulled by that which is popular in the Babylonian world.

Having been first conquered by the US Government in the late 1880s, then swallowed up by America's culture which is so thoroughly saturated with the values of Babylon, we modern LDS naturally see Babylon's skewed values as "normal" and many see the pursuit of Zion as fanatical, which is 180 degrees opposite of the case during the mid- to-late 1800s.

It's no surprise that the Church and its members became very gun-shy about doing anything out of the ordinary economically. The Church today is in a very precarious position, under the close scrutiny of the

United States government, therefore it is understandably hesitant to restart its earlier efforts to build independent Zion communities and/or Zion-preparatory cooperatives, as it did in the mid-1800s.

That being said, we rank-and-file members probably only see a fraction of the Church's efforts to move its members back towards Zion. Establishing the Perpetual Education Fund was a grand step in that direction, as was the recent Self Reliance program. I have reason to believe, which I outline in Chapter 13, that when the members are ready, Church leaders will be directed to ramp up their efforts to establish Zion, because at that point, they will have a much more willing audience. I also suspect that, for whatever reason, the powers-that-be will become unable or else lose interest in controlling the Church.

"Says Who?!"

While reading a recent book about Zion by a well-known LDS author, I wrote many times in the margins, "Says who!?"—more than I have written in any other book I've ever read. Over and over and over again the author would make assertions about the latter-day Zion with no scriptural or authoritative support. This feels irresponsible and potentially doctrinally dangerous.

My intent in <u>Champions For Zion</u> is to *report* to the reader what the early LDS leaders **themselves** were actually teaching and *then* draw conclusions based on those specific teachings. I rarely include points that were made by one or two people once or twice, but when I do, I label them as such. All of the assertion-making section headings in the first twelve chapters are based squarely on multiple statements made by multiple apostles and prophets, with one easily-justified exception. I left out a fair number of quotes that were "one-offs", where the speaker shared a unique idea about establishing Zion of which no one else spoke. They might have been true and valid points, but because no one else "backed them up" in the matter, I excluded those statements.

We seek the truth. We can safely trust authoritative statements saying the same thing from different leaders over time; which demonstrates a unity of thought and belief. In some chapters, I do make some logical deductions based on concepts well outlined by our early LDS leaders. And, occasionally, I'll point out related historical realities as reported by a legitimate historian.

My Agenda

Although I am reporting what early LDS leaders taught, I do have an agenda in doing so, which I freely admit:

1. According to Moses 7:62, Christ won't return until at least one Zion society is built—the New Jerusalem. I want to live in such a society. I find living in "Babylon" <u>so</u> <u>very</u> <u>tiresome</u>.

2. As members, waiting to be "commanded in all things" pertaining to Zion is probably not a wise strategy—in light of D&C 58:29 which states, "But he that doeth not anything until he is commanded . . . the same is damned." Apparently, God prefers we take personal initiative in doing good.

3. Since "Practice makes perfect", getting some practical experience in building and living in Zion-like social organizations (businesses, schools, clubs and, perhaps eventually, communities), might be a great way to prepare ourselves and our children for building the official Zion society, when the Lord so commands it through His prophet.

4. I truly believe in my heart that God would smile upon such an effort, and would see it as our doing "many good things of their own free will, and to bring to pass much righteousness. For the power is in them, wherein they are agents unto themselves. And inasmuch as men do good they shall in nowise lose their reward" (D&C 58:26-28). I can hardly imagine a better good we could do than building and participating in pre-Zion social institutions and communities as practice runs and learning experiences.

5. In regards to the last days, Christ said, "And blessed are they who shall seek to bring forth my Zion at that day" (1 Nephi 13:37). I seek the Lord's blessings for myself, my posterity, and my fellow Saints.

Chapter One - Building Zion Was Central to the Gospel

As I gathered the 700+ quotes mentioned in the Introduction, I noticed that they easily fell into a dozen categories. Ninety-two of those quotes fit into a category I labeled "Building Zion is Central to the Gospel". In gathering and reading all the quotes, I found many that contained concepts that were new to me. This was rather surprising as I have been a member since 1970 and a frequent reader of books about Zion.

I later noticed those same 92 quotes could be divided up into the following five subcategories. (Again, all numberings and emphases added to the quotes are mine, unless otherwise noted.)

1. Building Zion was taught by our early Missionaries.

This subcategory of quotes was one of those many surprises; I had no idea that early LDS missionaries were preaching that the Saints were building the long-prophesied Zion in the Territory of Utah, and, apparently, were inviting their investigators to join the cause. This message would appeal especially to those poor souls in the brutally-demanding factories in England at the time.

In 1860, President Brigham Young made a statement that clearly shows that building Zion was a central part of the early missionaries' message. Speaking from the perspective of a British convert, he said, "*You came to England and preached the Gospel, and told me not to trust in man, but to seek unto the Lord my God . . . and receive a witness for myself and know for myself that [1] Joseph Smith is a Prophet of God, that [2] the Book of Mormon is true, and that [3] God has set to his hand to gather the house of Israel <u>and build up Zion</u>.*"

The next quote, from 1862, shows that the early missionaries were using the Bible to show investigators the prophecies in it about what the Lord would do in the last days, and then testify that the LDS Church was actively working to bring those things about. Here's the quote:

"While the meek of the earth remain scattered among the wicked, the Elders of this Church can go forth with the Old and New Testament in their hands, and show what the Lord is going to do in the latter days, the great miracles he will perform, the gathering of his people, the saving of his Saints, **the building up of Zion,** *the redeeming of the house of Israel, the establishing of the New Jerusalem, the bringing back of the ten tribes . . . and this is proclaimed to both Saint and sinner."*

Ten years earlier, Brigham had said, *"When you had obeyed the first ordinances of the Gospel, [in other words, when you were first taught it by the missionaries] then you discovered that the Lord had set his hand to gather Israel, that Zion might be built up and Israel gathered from the four winds. These doctrines have been taught and re-taught again and again. I think there is not a man here who did not fully understand them while in his native country."*

Brigham Young, in 1853 stated, **"Let me refer your minds to the time that the Gospel was first introduced to you,** *and the light and glory of it opened up to your understandings; when eternity and eternal things reflected upon your benighted minds, and your conceptions were aroused to see things as they were, as they are, and as they will be. What were your feelings and meditations,* **when Zion and its glory burst upon your vision**? *[and] when the people of God appeared to you, assembled together, preparatory to the coming of the Son of Man?"*

Jedediah M. Grant, 1854: *"I am aware that some Elders who go forth and preach long and pious sermons, frequently represent Zion as one of the most delightsome places in the world, as if the people in Salt Lake City were so pure and holy that the flame of sanctity would almost singe the hair off a common man's head. Others suppose when they come here, that they are to be fed, clothed, and housed independent of their own exertions."*

From Apostle Grant's report, we can easily conclude that the missionaries' preaching about Zion was actually causing some problems when their converts arrived in Salt Lake City expecting to find a City-of-

Enoch-style Zion in full bloom. Three quotes by President Brigham Young from the 1850s show this as well:

You were annoyed with the ungodly conversation and filthy deeds of your neighbors, your peace was destroyed, and you could not enjoy that happiness held out to you in the Gospel; yet you felt the influence of the spirit of truth burning in your heart, which kindled in you a longing desire to mingle with the Saints; you would exclaim . . ."Oh! that I had means to gather up my little family, and journey to the place of the gathering of the Saints of the Most High." This was your feeling, and this your prayer. You anticipated deliverance from hell, to find a heaven with the Saints; **you expected to exchange confusion for a Zion of order and beauty** *. . . starvation for plenty . . . I think I have drawn a faithful picture of what were* <u>the thoughts of the majority of this people, before they were gathered to the body of the Church</u>. - Brigham Young, 1853

When you were gathered with the Saints of the Most High, and became associated as a brother, a sister, and a neighbour with that blessed society, **you expected . . . that you would be in heaven, and in the Zion of the Lord**. *These were your expectations.* - Brigham Young, 1853

<u>You hear brethren talk of coming to Zion</u> *to enjoy the blessings of this land; but do you not see that it is the short-sightedness of men which causes their disappointment when they arrive here? They read in the Bible, in the Book of Mormon, and Book of Doctrine and Covenants, about Zion, and what it is to be; but brother Park and others could not realize, before they came here, that they were the ones to help to build up Zion. They gather here with the spirit of Zion resting upon them, and* <u>expecting to find Zion in its glory</u>, *whereas* <u>their own doctrine should teach them that they are coming here to make Zion</u>. - Brigham Young, 1857

These three quotes make it clear that the early missionaries' converts had been taught that the Saints were building Zion in Utah and they expected to find a Zion in all its glory when they arrived. In fact, in 1860, Brigham Young appeared to want to stem the tide of convert immigrants with these unreasonably-high expectations when he said:

You need not teach that this place is Zion, or that Nauvoo or Missouri is Zion; but tell the people that North and South America are the land of Zion, and that our God will finish his work where he commenced it, where the Center Stake of Zion is, and where the Garden of Eden was. Say to them—"If you want to become as gold seven times purified, go up to Utah."

It appears that President Young was trying to get the missionaries to make sure their investigators' expectations of what they would find in Utah was more accurate when they preached about Zion. In the same paragraph he continues, *"Some must come here in order to apostatize. We have thought that we could try to stop that class in the States, and let them apostatize there; but we cannot. They think all things should be here now as they are in heaven."*

Had Brother Brigham changed the doctrine? Did he really mean that they weren't trying to build Zion in Utah? Apparently not. Because one year after Apostle Grant's quote above, Brigham said, *"When our Elders go out to preach the Gospel, they tell the people to gather to Zion. Where is it? It is at the City of the Great Salt Lake in the Valleys of the Mountains, in the settlements of Utah Territory—there is Zion now."*

Then the next year, 1856, Apostle Orson Pratt's comment shows the missionaries were still preaching Zion. He said, *"The Elders go forth in faith and with prayer for the gathering of Israel; to bring them to Zion, to plant vineyards, to build houses, to help build up the cities of Zion, and beautify the earth."*

Apostle Orson Hyde, in the October 1863 General Conference gave instructions to *"missionaries who go abroad to labor for the building up of Zion"*.

Then Brigham in 1867 said, *"I want the missionaries to remember this and lay it to heart, if they will. Go and preach the gospel, and help the honest-in-heart to gather, <u>that they may aid in building up Zion</u>, for that was the design of the Lord when He said, through the Revelator John, "Come out of her, my people, that ye be not partakers of her sins, and that ye receive not of her plagues."*

The skeptic reader may observe, "But these last three quotes don't specifically *say* the missionaries were preaching about Zion." True enough, but then in 1870 Apostle George Q. Cannon makes it clear, again, that the Elders were definitely preaching that the Saints were building Zion in Utah:

How was it with us when we first heard the truth? Oh! How sweet and delightful the sound of the Elder's voice when he proclaimed that God had spoken from the heavens; that angels had come to the earth again, and that the holy Priesthood was bestowed upon men! . . . When they heard the gathering preached they had the testimony that it was true; and some had it before it was preached. They knew it was from God and that God established His Zion, and their hearts burned at the thought that they would soon be with the Saints of God in Zion. They yearned for the land of Zion and for the society of the people of God.

2. **Building Zion Was Considered a Core LDS Doctrine.**

This second subdivision of the general category "Building Zion Was Central to the Gospel and LDS Church" was also a surprise to me. Until I read these quotes, I assumed that since the topic of building Zion is so infrequently mentioned in General Conference today, that it must not be a central doctrine of the Gospel. Yet, the quotes in this subcategory seem to suggest that, at least during the Utah Territory years, building Zion was front and center.

In 1867, President Brigham Young made a statement that illustrates this subcategory quite well. He said, *"A great many have said to you and me, 'Just leave out Joe Smith, the Book of Mormon, and modern revelations, and you will become popular.' . . . We are not going to leave out Joseph Smith, the Book of Mormon, nor the gathering,* **nor the building up of Zion.***"*

Five years earlier in 1862, he said, *"If I lay [aside] the Book of Mormon, I shall have to deny that [1] Joseph is a Prophet; and if I lay [aside] the doctrine and cease to preach [2] the gathering of Israel and [3] the building up of Zion, I must lay [aside] the Bible; and consequently, I might as well go home as undertake to preach without these* **three items.***"* If Brigham believed it pointless to preach the gospel without mentioning the building of Zion, then clearly he considered it a core doctrine.

In fact, it appears members would include Zion-building in the testimonies they bore. Both in the April 1860 General Conference, and again in a talk given in 1865, President Young comments on those testimonies, listing among the doctrines testified, the building up of Zion. Here are the two quotes:

Men rise up here and say they do know that this is the work of God, that Joseph was a Prophet, that the Book of Mormon is true, that the revelations through Joseph Smith are true, that this is the last dispensation and the fulness of times, wherein God has set to his hand to gather Israel for the last time, and redeem <u>and build up Zion on this land</u>.

There are persons who say they believe in Joseph the Prophet, in the Book of Mormon, in the gathering of the house of Israel, <u>in the building up of Zion</u>, and in all the blessings promised to the Church and kingdom of God upon the earth . . .

This idea that building Zion was a central tenet of the restoration endured past Brigham's death. In April Conference in 1882, President John Taylor reiterated, *"One part of the Gospel is that we should be gathered together to a land that should be called Zion. Have we been doing this? Yes."*

Brigham spoke frequently about building Zion, but interestingly, President John Taylor spoke about building Zion in just about every opportunity he had to address the Saints. I surveyed every talk he gave while prophet, of which there is a record. Surprisingly, of the 80 talks Taylor gave, he mentions Zion in 78 of them! Specifically, he spoke of gathering to Zion, or building Zion, in exactly 81.25% of his talks. *He often compared the Latter-Day Saints and their efforts to build Zion in Utah directly to Enoch's efforts to do the same.* He also quite frequently quoted Jeremiah 3:14 where the ancient prophet foretold, "I will take you one of a city, and two of a family, and I will bring you to Zion." If John Taylor, as prophet, seer, and revelator spoke of the subject of gathering and building Zion 81.25% of the time, isn't it a safe to say that building Zion is a core LDS doctrine?

3. Building Zion is Central to the Church's Mission

According to 17 of the 92 quotes covered in this chapter, building Zion was apparently one of the primary missions of the Church during Utah's territorial years. Remember back in 1981, President Spencer W. Kimball outlined very succinctly the three-fold mission of the Church? Unfortunately, no leader in the early days of the church sat down and took the time to outline its mission in such a clear and distinct way as did President Kimball. However, in reading these 17 quotes, it became very clear what that mission included. The first two of them clearly say that Zion building was central to the mission of the Church:

"Here is the Mission of the Saints to go and aid in the gathering of the poor, to labor here for the building of the Temple . . . and prepare to redeem Zion and to build up the waste places thereof, and to establish the principles of righteousness and truth upon the earth." - Elder Daniel H. Wells, April 7, 1862

"We are to build up and establish Zion, gather the house of Israel, and redeem the nations of the earth. This people have this work to do, whether we live to see it or not." - President Brigham young, June 3, 1860

"We have a mission to perform, and that is to [1] preach the Gospel and introduce correct principles, to [2] unfold the laws of God as men are prepared to receive them, to [3] build up his Zion upon the earth, and to [4] prepare a people for the time when the bursting heavens will reveal the Son of God . . ." - President John Taylor, April 8, 1878

The other fourteen quotes, which span a 26-year period, may not *specifically* state that the building of Zion is central to the Church's mission, as do the previous three, but you can see it is so by "reading between the lines". Here is a sampling of the remainder of the quotes; the rest are found in Appendix A:

There is no time allotted to us to use outside of the limits of duty. But in doing our duty, in serving our God, in living our religion, in using every possible means to [1] send forth the Gospel of salvation to the inhabitants of the earth, [2] to gather Israel, and [3] **establish Zion***, and [4] build up the kingdom of heaven upon the earth are incorporated all blessings, all comforts that men can desire.* - President Brigham Young, July 5, 1857

If the Twelve Apostles and the Presidents of Seventies and the High Priests will take the responsibility of [1] bearing off this kingdom and [2] sending the Gospel to the uttermost parts of the earth, of [3] gathering the poor, [4] <u>building up Zion</u>, and [5] doing all that is necessary preparatory to the coming of the Son of Man, Brigham is with you to labor with you all his days, and support himself. - President Brigham Young, September 23, 1860

We are called to set our hearts upon the living God, who has called us to be his people, and to worship him with full purpose of heart. If he gives us houses and lands, goods and chattels, gold and silver and the precious things of the earth, receive them with thanksgiving, and hallow and sanctify them and dedicate and consecrate them to [1] **the building up of Zion***, [2] the house of our God, [3] the gathering together of his Saints, [4] the preaching of his Gospel to the ends of the earth, and the accomplishment of the great work, whereunto God has called us in the latter days.* - Elder Erastus Snow, September 14, 1873

It remains for us to continue to [1] bear our testimony to the world, to [2] build our Temples, in which to perform the work for ourselves and our dead, essential to salvation and exaltation in his kingdom, and to [3] **build up a Zion to the glory of God***. That this may be our determined purpose to a faithful consummation, I humbly pray, in the name of Jesus, our Lord. Amen.* - Elder Franklin D. Richards, April 1882 General Conference

I fully realize what Elder Woodruff said this morning concerning the aged Elders of Israel passing away, and that **the responsibility and labor** *of bearing off this kingdom will soon rest upon the generation which is growing up in our midst, upon which will devolve* **the work** *of [1] carrying the Gospel to those who have not heard it among the nations of the earth, and [2] gathering Israel and [3]* establishing Zion *and [4] building up and maintaining the Kingdom of God upon the earth . . .* - Elder Erastus Snow, April 1883 General Conference

After reading and reviewing commonalities among the 17 quotes in this subcategory, it becomes clear that the Church's mission at that time included at least these three major elements:

- ⚜ Preach the gospel,
- ⚜ Gather the Saints, and
- ⚜ Build Zion, in that order.

4. Building Zion is Central to God's Last Days Plan to Prepare the World for Christ's Return

Not only was building Zion a central part of the mission of the early LDS Church, our leaders made it very clear that building Zion was a central element in God's over-arching, big-picture plan for the Last Days to prepare Earth for the Second Coming of Christ. Of the 24 quotes in this subcategory, we begin with four that are spread out over the 40 year span of Utah's years as a US territory.

On June 7, 1860, Brigham Young stated, *"The Latter-day Saints throughout the valleys in these mountains and throughout the world ought to be learning what they are on this earth for. They are here to increase and multiply, to enlarge, to gather the house of Israel, redeem Zion, build up the Zion of our God, and to promote that eternal intelligence that dwells with the Gods . . . until every obnoxious principle in the hearts of men is destroyed, and the earth returns to its paradisiacal state, and the Lord comes and dwells with this people, and walks and talks with them as he did with Father Adam. That is our business, and not to suffer all our energies to be expended in merely preparing to die [or, in our day, retire]."*

In 1879, one and a half years after Brigham passed, President John Taylor made it very clear that this doctrine had not changed. He said, *"[T]he time had come, in the councils of heaven, that it was necessary to start the latter-day work, and to prepare a people, gathering them together to build up Zion and establish the kingdom of God upon the earth, that His will might be done upon the earth as it is done in heaven."*

In 1883, Apostle Charles W. Penrose outlined God's big-picture plan for the earth in the most eloquent language. He said:

The Saints of God will be gathered, and there is no power [that] can stop their gathering. They will come to Zion, and build temples to the Most High God. They will unite together, and build up the Zion of God, and prepare the way for the coming of the Lord Jesus, whose right it is to reign; and every kingdom, every government, every society and every power upon the face of the earth that fights against Zion will become like the dream of a night vision . . . But <u>Zion</u> will arise and shine, and the glory of God will rest upon her; and all the kingdoms of this world will become the kingdoms of our God and His Christ. Then there will be liberty to all. Then the chains and shackles that bind the oppressed will fall to the ground, and light and truth will go forth until the whole earth is immersed in the spirit thereof, and every nation, kindred, tongue and people will sing praises to the Most High and to the Lamb forever.

In 1889, nearly two years after John Taylor's death, President Wilford Woodruff briefly summarized God's over-arching plan, and Zion's role in that plan, when he said "... *Joseph Smith was reserved to lay the foundation of this great Kingdom and dispensation of salvation to the whole human family in these last days, to build up Zion, to establish God's Kingdom, and to prepare it for the coming of the Son of Man.*"

If you're convinced already that the Brethren were teaching that building Zion was a key component of God's global Last Days plan, feel free to skip to the last subcategory, otherwise here are 19 more quotes as evidence. I would have included them in Appendix A, as recommended by my author friend, but I feel it is important that the reader see just how frequently and thoroughly the topic was discussed in earlier years. I know the more I read and re-read these quotes, the deeper my sense grows of their purpose and mission; I want to share that with you, the reader. Now, notice how nearly every year between 1853 and 1884, some apostle or prophet mentioned the idea, and sometimes during General Conference.

⚜ *It now remains with us to bear off this kingdom,* **build up Zion,** *and establish the law thereof, until Christ shall reign King of nations . . .* - Brigham Young, June 7, 1853

⚜ *They will then find out that the 'Mormons,' notwithstanding their curious bumps, for they have got some curious bumps, are authorized to preach the Gospel of God, gather Israel,* **build up Zion,** *bind Lucifer with a chain, and establish the reign of peace on earth.* - Jedediah M. Grant, February 19, 1854

⚜ *...we will roll on the Kingdom of our God, gather out the seed of Abraham,* **build the cities and temples of Zion,** *and establish the Kingdom of God to bear rule over all the earth, and let the oppressed of all nations go free.* - Brigham Young, July 8, 1855

⚜ *May we accomplish the great work thou didst commence through thy servant Joseph, that truth may reign on the earth, and righteousness predominate among all people. May we have power over the wicked nations, that* **Zion** *may be the seat of government for the universe, the law of God be extended, and the scepter of righteousness swayed over this wide world.* - Jedediah M. Grant, July 24, 1856

⊥ May the Lord God of heaven and earth bless you, and may He preserve us and all good men and women upon the earth, and give us power to blow the Gospel trump to earth's remotest bounds, and gather up the honest in heart, **build up Zion**, redeem Israel, rebuild Jerusalem, and fill the earth with the glory and knowledge of our God, and we will shout hallelujah! Amen. - Brigham Young, August 31, 1856

⊥ [W]e will go to work and labor with all our [might] to build up the kingdom of our God, to carry out the purposes of the Lord, in the **building up of Zion**, the establishment of his kingdom, and restoration, and salvation of the house of Israel. - Wilford Woodruff, February 22, 1857

⊥ It now remains with us to bear off this kingdom, **build up Zion**, and establish the law thereof, until Christ shall reign King of nations as he now reigns King of Saints. - Brigham Young, June 7, 1857

⊥ That we may be blessed, let us do our duty, gather the house of Israel, redeem and **build up Zion**, see Jerusalem established, and Jesus reign triumphantly upon the earth; which is my desire, in the name of Jesus Christ. Amen. - Brigham Young, September 2, 1860

⊥ I testify to you that we were . . . cast out for . . . believing, preaching, and practicing the doctrines of the New Testament; for believing in the events to take place in the latter days, as foretold by the ancient Prophets; and, for believing the declarations of Joseph Smith, that Jesus was indeed the Christ and the Savior of all men . . . and that he had set to his hand the second time to gather his people, to establish his kingdom, **to build up Zion**, redeem Jerusalem, empty the earth of wickedness and bring in everlasting righteousness. - Brigham Young, August 31, 1862

⊥ Have we learned how to handle the things of this life in the name of Israel's God to his glory, for the building up of his kingdom, for **the bringing forth of his Zion**, for the redemption of the earth, for the establishment of everlasting righteousness, and for the endless happiness of those who will thus be made happy? - Brigham Young, September 28, 1862

⊥ **The purpose of our life should be to build up the Zion of our God**, to gather the house of Israel, bring in the fulness of the Gentiles, restore *and bless the earth with our ability and make it as the Garden of Eden, store up treasures of knowledge and wisdom in our own understandings, purify our own hearts and prepare a people to meet the Lord when he comes.* - Brigham Young, April 1863 General Conference

⚔ *It is the kingdom of God or nothing with us, and by the help of the Almighty we shall bear it off triumphantly to all nations, gather Israel, **build up Zion**, redeem Israel, and Jesus Christ will triumph, and we shall reign with him on the earth, and possess it and all its fulness with him.* - Brigham Young, January 8, 1865

⚔ *In killing the Prophet Joseph Smith, they did not kill 'Mormonism,' and they cannot kill it unless they kill all the 'Mormons,' for if they leave a single Latter-day Saint living he will cry to the people to repent of their sins and return to the Lord, and the Lord will work with him to gather the righteous, build up His kingdom, **build up Zion**, and establish Jerusalem no more to be thrown down.* - Brigham Young, August 17, 1867

⚔ *Christ lives and is the Savior of the world, and has commenced His work in the last days, to gather His people, redeem and **build up Zion**, gather the remnants of Israel, bring the Gentiles into His covenant who will receive the gospel, restore the Jews to their land, and establish the New and Everlasting covenant, which He established with the fathers and ratified to the children. We are in this work; and we are called to be faithful and to sanctify ourselves as a people and prepare for the coming of the Son of Man. May God help us to do so. Amen.* - Brigham Young, May 10, 1868

⚔ *...the Saints, and although mixed like corn in a sieve among the Gentile nations they have been prepared from the foundation of the world to come forth as the sons of Jacob in these latter days, **to build up the Zion of God on the earth**. We have got to come to it.* - Wilford Woodruff, October 1873 General Conference

⚔ *Let them bring forth their wise men, if they have any, and tell us how we shall obtain an inheritance in the kingdom of God. This is something they cannot do. Why? Because they have not the Gospel; and it is the Gospel that brings life and immortality to light, and this is the kind of intelligence we are after. To redeem and save the living and the dead; **to build up the Zion of our God**, that a people may be prepared who shall* *be pure in heart, and prepared to associate with the intelligences around the throne of God.* - President John Taylor, January 6, 1879

⚜ *It is a day in which the Gospel is to be **preached** to every nation, tongue and people for a witness of what shall follow; a day in which the Israel of God who receive it in their dispersed and scattered condition are to **gather** together to the place appointed of God, the place where they will perform the "marvelous work and wonder" spoken of by the ancients who, in vision, saw our day; and where they will begin to inherit the promises made to the fathers respecting their children. The work that is to be so marvelous in the eyes of men has already commenced, and is assuming shape and proportions; but they cannot see it. It will consist in [1] preaching the Gospel to all the world, [2] gathering the Saints from the midst of all those nations who reject it; [3] **building up the Zion of God**; establishing permanently in the earth His kingdom; preparing for the work of the gathering of the Jews and the events that will follow their settlement in their own lands, and in preparing for ourselves holy places in which to stand when the judgments of God shall overtake the nations.* - Wilford Woodruff, January 27, 1883

⚜ *[F]or God . . . has chosen His own instruments to further His great purposes on the earth—the organization of his Church, the proclamation of the everlasting Gospel, **the establishment of His Zion**, and bringing to pass His wonderful works which He predicted by the mouths of the ancient Prophets.* - Erastus Snow, April 1883 General Conference

⚜ *The work before us is a great one . . . Israel is to be gathered, Jerusalem rebuilt, **Zion established**, the vineyard of the Lord pruned and the corrupt branches cut off and cast into the fire . . . .* - Erastus Snow, February 2, 1884

Phew! Did you really read *all* those quotes? Good for you! As I re-read them while adding them here, I marvel at what a global, big-picture view they had of the Church's role in the prophesied events of the Last Days. What vision! What glorious purpose! And, what a blessing to be part of this Gospel at this time in Earth's history. It is no wonder that missionaries like Wilford Woodruff were able to convert so many people when their message was so lofty and grand!

5. Building Zion Was a Primary Focus of LDS Leaders

The largest subcategory makes up nearly a third of the 92 quotes in this chapter's category. This includes quotes by prophets and apostles, spanning 33 years from 1854 to 1887, that clearly show that building Zion was a primary focus of the leaders of the LDS Church, and, that they expected it to be a primary focus of the general membership. Since you may have already gathered this fact from reading all the quotes in the four preceding subcategories, I won't bore you with all 33 of them . . . just eleven (though you can find the balance in Appendix A). The quotes are in chronological order showing a wide variety of speakers over a long period of time, thus assuring us that this Gospel tidbit was no fluke or flash in the pan.

Brigham, 1862, *"I have Zion in my view <u>constantly</u>"*. Pretty clear.

Heber C. Kimball, 1863, *"May the Lord multiply his blessings upon you, brethren and sisters . . . and may He bless all those who do good, who love righteousness and desire the welfare and building up of Zion"*.

Brigham, 1867, *"We have many duties to perform, and a great work is before us. We have Zion to build up, and <u>upon this we are all agreed</u> . . ."*

Apostle George A. Smith, 1867, *"I bear my testimony to the truth of the counsel and instruction that we have received this morning, and I trust they will be treasured up in good and honest hearts, and that men and women will consider these things and realize that **we have one great interest**, which is to build up Zion . . ."*

Brigham Young, 1873, *"The Lord has blessed me; he has always blessed me; from the time I commenced to build up Zion, I have been extremely blessed. I could relate circumstances of so extraordinary a character in regard to the providences of God to me, that my brethren and sisters would say in their hearts, 'I can hardly give credence to this.' But <u>my heart has been set in me</u> to do the will of God, to build up his kingdom on the earth, <u>to establish Zion and its laws</u>, and to save the people . . ."*

Wilford Woodruff, 1873, *"My brethren and sisters, we are commanded not to give the whole of our attention to the accumulation of earthly things; we are commanded also to lay up treasures in heaven. **We are required to build up Zion** on the earth . . ."*

1 - Building Zion Was Central to the Gospel

Apostle Joseph F. Smith, 1877, *"Then let us search after truth . . . that we may comprehend the Gospel, be able to sustain the hands of the servants of God <u>in their efforts to build up Zion</u>, and work out our own salvation."*

Apostle George Q. Cannon, 1881, *"It is probable that today Brother Orson Pratt is the oldest living member of the Church, and certainly there is no man in the Church who has labored longer and more diligently and with a greater spirit of self-sacrifice in proclaiming its principles . . . for I know that there is no desire so strong in his breast . . . [than] the desire to proclaim the truth, and to win souls unto Christ, and* **to help establish that Zion***, of which God has laid the foundation."*

President John Taylor, 1882, *"Some people think we are a set of ignorant boobies, who do not know what we are talking about, and they try to overrun the faith of the Latter-day Saints by sophistry, falsehood and folly. Whilst the fact is, we are in possession of the principles of eternal life, and are operating for eternity; and then <u>we are operating to build up the Zion of God</u>, where righteousness can be taught, and where men can be protected, and where liberty can be proclaimed to all men of every color, of every creed and of every nation."*

Elder Franklin D. Richards, 1887, *"We mourn President Taylor's absence. We will lose his counsel. We can not well spare such men.* **We need such men in the Church to establish righteousness and preach the Gospel and build up Zion on the earth***."* [Any volunteers?]

I skipped one on purpose because it expresses my feelings exactly, in fact, I can't read the whole quote without tearing up. John Taylor, 1874, *"I want to be the friend of God and God to be my friend; I want to help to roll forth the Kingdom of God and to build up the Zion of the Most High, and I want to see my brethren engaged in the same work, and we will do it. In the name of Israel's God we will do it."*

Summary

Let's review. We have 95 quotes from early LDS apostles and prophets that make it very clear that building Zion was central to the Gospel and the Church. By reading all of these quotes we come to see five things clearly:

1. Building Zion was taught by our early Missionaries, apparently at the direction of the Brethren;
2. Building Zion was considered a core doctrine of the Gospel;
3. It was central to the Church's Mission;
4. It was central to God's over-arching Last Days plan for Earth; and lastly,
5. Building Zion was a primary focus of LDS leaders who also encouraged the members to focus there as well.

Afterthoughts

Isn't that remarkable? When I began my search, I never suspected to discover that building Zion was so central to the Gospel in the 1800s. That was what they were doing, that was their objective, their vision, their destiny. *Is it ours today?*

We're 130 years down the road from these quotes . . . and still no Zion. We Saints are collectively wallowing in Babylon's culture of filth and corruption, complaining all the while how awful its influence is on our children. Yet here we remain as fully-engaged participants in Babylon's pride-based school systems, businesses, and other social institutions. How long will the Lord wait before He decides our chance is over and He finds someone else to fulfill His plan?

Then-Elder Wilford Woodruff expressed this concern when he stated:

*The Lord has had Zion before his face from before the foundation of the world, and he is going to build it up . . . The work is in our hands to perform, the God of heaven requires it of us and **if we fail to build it up we shall be under condemnation, and the Lord would remove us out of the way and he would raise up another people who would do it.** Why? Because the Almighty has decreed that this work shall be performed on the earth, and no power on earth or in hell can hinder it.* - Wilford Woodruff, January 12, 1873

Then again, the Father may just decide to run us all through the wringer of adversity, humbling us enough that we will finally reject the fleshpots of Egypt and seek to fulfill His will in regards to building Zion. Two years after President Taylor died, President Wilford Woodruff expressed concern about the afflictions that would haunt the Saints if they did not build Zion. He said:

I do not pretend to know how many tribulations or how much suffering we shall yet have to endure before Zion is established in her beauty and glory; but I do know that Zion is not going to be moved out of her place. The Lord, however, will chastise us until we become purified before Him. He will plead with His strong ones, and what He has said concerning Zion will come to pass. I hope that we may exercise wisdom in all things, that we may escape these afflictions. - Wilford Woodruff, 29 July 1889

Personally, I would rather try to please the Lord by not waiting to be humbled by Him. I have enough "afflictions" in my life. How about you?

Moses 7:62 suggests Christ won't return in His glory until _after_ the New Jerusalem is built. Maybe we Latter-day Saints should follow God's counsel to "flee Babylon" and build Zion. Are we willing?

Now, in the following chapters we'll see how our Champions for Zion were actively pursuing the goal of establishing Zion communities as a Priesthood obligation and in a very tangible and proactive way. We'll also see how they viewed building Zion as an economic effort as well as a spiritual one, and, that they diligently strove to become economically self-sufficient as a people. We'll see how these brick-and-mortar efforts at building Zion were meant to keep the Saints in food, clothing, and shelter when the prophesied fall of "Babylon" finally came.

Chapter Two - What *IS* Zion?

Among the members of the LDS Church, the word "Zion", like the word "love", has many definitions -- a glance at the Bible Dictionary entry for Zion clearly illustrates that. Even the Lord uses the term to mean different things. In Doctrine and Covenants 97:21 the Lord uses the term in spiritual sense. He says, "Therefore, verily, thus saith the Lord, let Zion rejoice, for this is Zion—the pure in heart . . ." We typically assume that purity of heart is a spiritual condition, which perhaps even non-members may enjoy.

In contrast, other of the Lord's uses of the term Zion are geographic. As the Bible Dictionary reports, D&C 58:49–50, 62:4, 63:48, 72:13, 84:76, and 104:47 all show the Lord using the term Zion to mean a specific geographical place—Jackson County, Missouri. Then in D&C 45:66–67, the Lord uses Zion to mean the New Jerusalem, a physical city to be built, likely by people with pure motives, in Jackson County at some future date.

Many Saints equate Zion in their minds with the LDS Church itself, to them "building Zion" simply means doing the work of the Church. When others hear "Zion", they think of the New Jerusalem. So, when they hear me talking about "building Zion" on Facebook or on my blog, BuildingZion.org, they get uncomfortable and falsely assume I am trying to start my own splinter group. To them, "building Zion" means "building the New Jerusalem" and they correctly assume that the New Jerusalem will only be built under the Lord's direction through his Prophet.

2 - What *IS* Zion?

When I speak of building Zion today, I'm talking about something different than the geographic uses of the term. There is one other definition used by the Lord, not mentioned above—I think of it as **the societal definition**—the use of the term Zion on a societal level. It's found in Moses 7, verse 18. It reads, "And the Lord called his people Zion, [why?] because [1] they were of one heart and one mind, and [2] dwelt in righteousness; and [3] there was no poor among them." Here the Lord uses the term Zion to refer to a *type* of society, a mode of living, a social organization that yields at least three specific society-level results: unity, righteousness, and economic abundance for all.

As I found and read through all the 700+ quotes mentioning building or establishing Zion, it became clear to me, based on the words of the apostles and prophets, that Zion in its general sociological use, is what most early LDS leaders were typically referring to when they used the term. So, the point of this chapter is to clarify in the minds of the reader what that definition was for the early leaders of the Church. That general, societal definition, not the specific geographic ones mentioned in the Bible Dictionary, is how the term "Zion" will be used throughout the rest of this book.

One Potential Source of Confusion About Zion's Definition

In March of 1872, Apostle Orson Pratt gave a talk entitled, "What is Zion?" Sadly, I am afraid it only added to the confusion about the definition of the term Zion among the Latter-Day Saints, when his intent was likely just the opposite. In his talk, Pratt himself was inconsistent in his use of the word. He used it in reference to the modern LDS Church, the Church of Jesus Christ of Former-day Saints, David's Jerusalem, the New Jerusalem, and "any church with revelation". But, after all that, he declares his allegiance to one specific use of the term; he clearly states that he believes Zion is the Church of God:

But perhaps strangers may inquire, How are we to know the period or age of the world when the Lord shall bring again Zion, <u>or in other words restore his Church</u> to the earth?

As he does here:

Go to the Latter-day Saints and inquire of them what Zion is, and they will tell you <u>it is the Church of the living God</u> wherever it can be found.

Consequently in order to ascertain what Zion is it is necessary for us to understand what the Church of the living God is, and try to distinguish between that Church and all other Churches. I shall endeavor, in a very few words, to mark out some of the distinguishing features between the true Church of the living God and Churches built up by human wisdom; and <u>when we have ascertained what the true Church is we shall then have learned what the true Zion is</u>.

And again here:

Before Zion, <u>or the Church of the living God</u>, can have any existence on the earth it is very important and necessary that there should be divine administrators. What I mean by this is, men having a divine mission, a divine call—being called of the Lord by the spirit of revelation to build up Zion on the earth.

Here's the thing, I didn't find a single quote by any other LDS leader from 1850 to 1889 that clearly expressed that idea that Zion is the same thing as the LDS Church; there may be some, but I didn't find any. Apparently, many LDS members today equate the two in their minds. Perhaps it is from the teachings of Elder Pratt that this idea originates. Elder Pratt started preaching this idea heavily in 1870 and did so nearly every year through 1876.

But, other early apostles and prophets clearly did *not* believe Zion = LDS Church. In fact, within days of Orson Pratt's passing, the definition of Zion preached by the Brethren changed, or rather, reverted. It almost seems like they wanted to spare Pratt's feelings from further hurt. Pratt had been publically and formally censured by the Twelve back in 1865 for things he had written before the Saints came to Utah. Maybe the Brethren, out of respect for Elder Pratt, waited until he passed on to correct his teachings about Zion.

The idea that the Church was not the same thing as Zion first surfaces among our Zion quotes back in 1862 by Brigham Young when there were around 150 wards in the Church. You'll see in this astounding quote, worthy of pondering in depth, that Brigham did not see Zion as the Church:

I sometimes think that I would be willing to give anything, to do almost anything in reason, to see one fully organized Branch of this kingdom—

one fully organized Ward. "But," says one, "I had supposed that the kingdom of God was organized long ago." So it is, in one sense; and again, in another sense it is not. Wheresoever this Gospel has been preached and people have received it, the **spiritual** kingdom is set up and organized, <u>but is Zion organized?</u> **No**. Is there even in this Territory a fully organized Ward? Not one. It may be asked, "Why do you not fully organize the Church?" Because the people are incapable of being organized. I could organize a large Ward who would be subject to a full organization, by selecting families from the different Wards, but <u>at present such a Branch of the Church is not in existence</u>.

He's saying the Church is "the spiritual kingdom" of God, but it is *not* the same thing as "Zion". If Brigham is right, Zion is not the *spiritual* kingdom of God. So, if it's not a spiritual organization, he must think of Zion as something temporal. More on this in later chapters.

Language used by John Taylor and Wilford Woodruff appears to suggest they agreed with Brigham. Here's the best example: John Taylor on 17 August 1884 stated, *"<u>In addition to</u> establishing His Church, He has told us to build up a Zion to His name, and we are gathering the materials together for that purpose."* The phrase, "in addition to" makes it clear that "building up a Zion" and "establishing His Church" were not considered to be the same thing. Two years earlier, Wilford Woodruff's use of the word "and" in this next quote seems to suggest he agreed. He said, "The Lord Almighty has set His hand to gather His people, ***and*** to build up his Zion ***and*** to establish his Church in these the last days . . ."

Zion as One of Three Foundations of a God-centered Society

Jumping to the meat of it, it appears the early LDS leaders, Orson Pratt likely excepted, saw Zion as one of three grand organizational foundations of the society of God. There was the Church, or "the spiritual kingdom", as Brigham called it. Then there was the political Kingdom of God, which was manifest in the Council of 50 during the 1800s. And third, there was the Zion of God, whose nature we'll discuss later on. These three foundational organizations of the people of God are like the three legs of a stool, you likely need all three for the society of God to function as the Lord would have it.

We come to this conclusion based on ten different quotes by three prophets of God, Brigham Young, John Taylor, and Wilford Woodruff. Here's the strongest example:

The Lord has sent forth angels out of heaven. He has delivered the fulness of the Gospel to Joseph Smith. He was raised up as a Prophet of God, by the power of God, **to lay the foundation of this Church** *of Jesus Christ of Latter-day Saints on the earth,* and **to lay the foundation of that kingdom** *which the Prophet Daniel and the other Prophets spoke of,* and **to build up that Zion** *which Isaiah, Jeremiah and Ezekiel said should be built up in the latter days.* - Wilford Woodruff, October 23, 1881.

As you see, Elder Woodruff spoke of three separate foundations. Notice in the following quotes, listed in chronological order, how the Church, the Kingdom, and Zion are all mentioned in a way that suggests they are indeed three different things:

We have the promise, if we seek first the kingdom of God and its righteousness, that all necessary things will he added to us. We should not be distrustful, but seek first to know how to please our Father and God . . . and learn how to save and preserve ourselves upon the earth, to [1] preach the Gospel [ie. build the spiritual kingdom], [2] build up the kingdom, and [3] establish the Zion of our God. - Brigham Young, December 18, 1859

This is [1] the work and **kingdom** *of God; [2] this is the* **Zion** *of God* and *[3] the* **Church** *of Christ . . . When I look at the history of the Church of God in these latter days I many times marvel at what has been done and how we have progressed, considering the traditions, unbelief, failings, follies and nonsense that man is heir to in the flesh. We have had a great many traditions to overcome and the opposition of the world to contend with from the beginning until today. Brethren and sisters, we should be faithful. The Lord has put into our [ie. the* **Church's***] hands the power to build up his* **Zion** *and* **kingdom** *on the earth, and we have more to encourage us than was ever possessed by any generation that has preceded us.* - Elder Wilford Woodruff, January 12, 1873

[W]e shall try, in the name of the Lord, and under His guidance and direction, to build up his Zion upon the earth; that there may be . . . a people who are engaged in rolling forth the work of God, and establishing not only *the* **Church** *of Christ, but His* **Zion** and *the* **kingdom**

of God upon the earth. This is a work that is not popular among men. They want their ideas, their theories, and their notions; we want the ideas and theories, the word and will, and the guidance and direction of the Almighty; and if we are connected with his kingdom, if there is such a thing as the kingdom of God upon the earth, it means the rule and government of God. - President John Taylor, October 9, 1881.

And finally:

We are here really to build up and purify the **Church** *of the living God. We are here to build up and establish the* **kingdom** *of God. We are here* <u>also</u> *to build up <u>a</u>* **Zion** *unto our God . . . Let us observe the laws of God, and keep His commandments, and the blessing of God will be with us. We will go forward and build our temples and labor therein. We will go forth and build up the* **Kingdom** *of God; we will go forth and purify the* **Church** *of God; we will go forth and establish the* **Zion of God.** - John Taylor, November 30, 1884

Three legs of the same Society-of-God stool: The Church, The Kingdom, and Zion.

So, what *IS* Zion?

Generally, Zion is a Society Under God's Direction

Two quotes from both Brigham and John Taylor tell us that they saw Zion generally as a society under God's direction, or, a society where the inhabitants were primarily concerned with doing God's will and not their own.

President Young's two quotes come from the same talk given January 16, 1853:

Admit that the Spirit of the Lord should give us understanding, what would it prove to us? It would prove to me, at least . . . that Zion is here. Whenever we are disposed to give ourselves perfectly to righteousness, to yield all the powers and faculties of the soul . . . **when we are swallowed up in the will of Him who has called us***; when we enjoy the peace and the smiles of our Father in Heaven, the things of His Spirit, and all the blessings we are capacitated to receive and improve upon,* *then are we in Zion, **that is Zion**. What will produce the opposite? Hearkening and giving way to evil, nothing else will.*

*. . .**if every heart were set upon doing right**, **we then should have Zion here**. I will give you my reason for thinking so. It is because I have had it with me ever since I was baptized into this kingdom. I have not been without it from that day to this. I have, therefore, a good reason for the assertion I have made. I live and walk in Zion every day, and so do thousands of others in this Church and kingdom, they carry Zion with them, they have one of their own, and it is increasing, growing, and spreading continually. Suppose it spreads from heart to heart, from neighborhood to neighborhood, from city to city, and from nation to nation, how long would it be before the earth would become revolutionized, and the wheat gathered from among the tares?*

John Taylor's two quotes showing that Zion is a society under God's direction both came from when he was president of the LDS Church. The first was from a talk given August 8, 1880:

*And I would further remark in relation to these matters, that **this is the Zion of our God**; that <u>we are gathered here **not** for the purpose of seeking to do our own wills or to carry out our own designs, our own ideas or theories; but to be subject to the law of God, to the order of God and to the priesthood of God</u>; and that our greatest safety and happiness, under all circumstances, is in rendering strict obedience to His law, and to the counsels that may be given from time to time through the Holy priesthood. We are today a kingdom of priests holding to a very great extent the holy priesthood; and it is essential that we submit ourselves to the laws of that priesthood and be governed by them in all of our actions.*

Then in October of the following year, Taylor repeated the idea:

*Then again, did Enoch build up a Zion? So we are doing. What is it? **The Zion of God. What does it mean?** The pure in heart in the first place. In the second place those who are governed by the law of God—<u>the pure in heart who are governed by the law of God</u>. Shall we build up a Zion? We shall; but we shall not, every one of us, have our own way about it. We shall feel that we need the will of God; and we shall feel that we require the Priesthood, under His direction, to guide and direct us, not men who are seeking to aggrandize themselves; but men who are seeking to build* up the Church and Kingdom of God upon the earth; men of clean hands and pure hearts, every one honoring his Priesthood and magnifying it . . .

Specifically, Zion is the God-given, True *Economic* Organization of Society

In our three-legged stool metaphor, it appears that the Zion leg represents the economic organization of God's people. I suspect this idea may be a shock to many. <u>Stay with me and you'll see an enormous body of evidence that this is the case</u>, mostly in chapters to come. In the meantime, consider the following:

Apostle George Q. Cannon, over a period of 25 years (during most of which he was in the First Presidency), repeatedly commented on how all the misery and destitution in the world is a result of "the incorrect organization of society". In an 1869 General Conference talk entitled, "The Order of Enoch", Elder Cannon stated:

The evils that have flourished so long in what is called the Old World have been transplanted to this land. If Western men travel through the Eastern States they are struck with the great distinction of classes that exist there. There is an aristocracy of wealth fast growing up there; and at the same time there is another class in degradation and poverty, utterly unable to obtain the blessings and comforts of life. This is owing to various causes, the chief of which is <u>the incorrect organization of society</u>. It is so in Europe and in Asia, and, in fact, wherever wealth abounds.

In contrast, during the same talk, Elder Cannon points out that all the First Presidency's efforts to get the Saints to fully embrace the cooperative economic system they had set in place, was simply to try to move them in the direction of living in the same "organization of society that exists in the heavens". He said:

As a people we are expecting the day to come when Jesus will descend in the clouds of Heaven; but <u>before</u> this day comes we must be prepared to receive him. The organization of society that exists in the heavens must exist on the earth; the same condition of society, so far as it is applicable to mortal beings, must exist here. And for this purpose God has revealed this Order; for this purpose He is bringing us into our present condition. A great many of the Latter-day Saints scarcely understand the persistency with which the Presidency of the Church has labored to bring about the oneness of the people in <u>temporal things</u>; and this **cooperative movement** is an important step in this direction and is designed to prepare them for the ushering in of this Order to which I have been alluding. It has already produced greater union, and it will produce still greater union than anything that has been witnessed among us; and if we carry it out in the spirit in which it has been taught to us it will produce immense results.

Notice his point about the goal being a "oneness of the people in temporal things". The Saints during Utah's territorial years apparently never used the term "economic" in the same sense we do today. In every instance of the term in the Journal of Discourses, "economic" is used to mean thriftiness and frugality. Today, we use the term to mean something pertaining to our system for the production and distribution of goods and services. In reading all the 700+ quotes about building Zion, it became clear to me that when early LDS leaders spoke of "temporal matters", they meant what we think of when we say "economic matters"—matters dealing with the production and distribution of goods and services.

Back to our main point, Elder Cannon ties Zion to the God-given, economic organization of society again in 1883 when he says:

[W]hen **Zion** is organized properly, it will be found to be as admirably adapted to the [economic] wants of the children of men as the organization of the Church is today to the [spiritual] wants of the people. There will be nothing lacking. In every particular it will be found adequate to the wants of humanity. The evils under which mankind groan today, are attributable to the false organization of society. The evils under which we groan as a people and from which we suffer are not due to any lack of knowledge as the method or the means that will correct these evils, but they are due to the fact that we ourselves fail to conform to **the organization which God has prescribed**, which God has revealed.

Did you also notice how this quote also suggests that Zion and the Church aren't the same?

So, as we've seen in the statements above, the early LDS leaders understood Zion to be the economic organization of God's people, under His direction, whereas the Church is the spiritual organization, or, in other words, the organization of God's people to govern themselves in regards to spiritual matters. Zion, then, would be the organization of God's people to govern themselves in economic matters. Not only does this perspective agree with the few quotes above, but you will see in later chapters numerous other apostolic quotes that confirm this definition of Zion by its Champions during the mid-to-late 1800s.

Why It Matters How We Define Zion in Our Minds

In my discussions with my fellow Saints online, I've noticed that often people get nervous when I talk about "building Zion" today. If they see "Zion" as the New Jerusalem, they think I'm nuts because they know (and I agree) that the New Jerusalem will be built by commandment from God to his servant the Prophet. They see a desire to build Zion *now* as running ahead of the caravan, and they wonder if I'm trying to start my own splinter group. Neither could be further from the truth.

Others, those who see Zion as identical to the LDS Church, think I'm silly for even bringing it up. In their minds, "building Zion" simply means working to help the Church achieve its current mission of Preaching the Gospel, Redeeming the Dead, and Perfecting the Saints. In their minds, by simply being an active member, we "build Zion".

However, if we define Zion the way God defines it, as recorded in Moses 7, then we are empowered as His children to seek to bring about the type of society where we are of one heart and one mind, where we dwell in righteousness, and where there are no poor among us. And, according to 1 Nephi 13:37, we are promised great blessings, if we seek to "bring forth my Zion at that day."

In addition, if we see Zion as being the solution to all the misery and destitution endured by the people under Babylon's "false organization of society", then we can all take personal responsibility and do our part to begin to build the economic foundation of the type of society God wants for all his children. The societal definition of Zion allows us to be proactive in bringing it about.

Afterthoughts

The most compelling connections I made in regards to this chapter are these:

1. That Zion is the type of society God wants all his children to enjoy while here in mortality.

2. That Zion is the organization of society in Heaven, and we need to be moving in that direction while here, if we are to have a hope of being able to live in it there.

3. That Babylon is a false economic organization of society, and eventually results in abundant prosperity for some and misery & destitution for many, and

4. That how we define Zion in our minds either paralyzes us, or empowers us. Our choice.

What stuck out the most for you?

Chapter Three - God's Will

As mentioned before, I scoured all the talks given by apostles and prophets during Utah's Territorial years from 1849 to 1889, and found over hundreds of quotes where the Brethren were talking about building or establishing Zion. In this chapter, we review some quotes from the category of "It's God's will that we build Zion".

In my search, I found 6 apostles and 4 prophets who made it very clear in 60 separate statements that God <u>intends</u> for Zion to be built, and, that doing so is part of His work. Not only that, the early church leaders in Utah said we are actually *called* by God to build Zion, in fact, they even go so far as to say we are required and **commanded** by God to build Zion (so, it's gonna be tough to get out of this!).

God Intends Zion to be Built

The Lord <u>intends</u> that we shall unite ourselves together, and in building up the Zion of God, if we cannot attain to all that is required of us today, we will do what we can, and progress as fast as we can, that the way may be prepared for the fulfillment of the words of the Lord. - Wilford Woodruff, April 1873 General Conference

*Before the organization of the Church of Jesus Christ of Latter-day Saints, Joseph Smith received revelations which he said were revelations from God. They are now embodied in this book, which we call the Book of Doctrine and Covenants and among the earliest of these revelations is found a statement given by the Lord Jesus Christ, through Joseph Smith, to the effect that he **intended** to bring forth and establish Zion . . .* - George Q. Cannon, October 20, 1881

For God has set his hand to gather Israel, according to the Prophets; <u>God has set his hand to establish his Zion</u>; God has set his hand to build his kingdom in the earth, according to the prediction of the holy prophets. - Erastus Snow, October 1882 General Conference

*The Lord **intends** to build up His Zion through us His weak and feeble creatures. He intends to make Zion strong and powerful in the earth.* - Wilford Woodruff, January 27, 1883

Building Zion is Part of God's Work

In a talk entitled, "The Work of God", given May 6, 1870, Wilford Woodruff mentions "Zion" twenty-two times, suggesting he saw a relationship between the two terms. This first quote shows his resolute stance about the topic:

Now this Zion of God has been before his face from before the foundation of the world, and it is no more going to fail in the latter days than any of the purposes of God are going to fail, hence I look upon this work as the work of God, and it makes no difference to the Lord Almighty, nor to his Saints, what the world may think or do about it, or what course they may pursue with regard to it; they cannot stop its progress, because it is the work of God. If it were the work of man it would not exist as it does today. If God had no hand in this work, we should not have seen this assembly here today in this Tabernacle, nor this Territory filled with cities and towns.

Then he ends his talk this way, leaving no doubt as to his belief that God's work includes the building of Zion:

*Let us lay hold and build up Zion. Let us realize that we are the children of God, that he is at work with us and that we are at work with him . . . He has got a great many good men on the earth, and **he is gathering them together to build up Zion, to carry out his work and to do his will**. He will also control the course of human events so as to forward his purposes. He holds the destinies of the nations in his hands. He holds Zion in his hands and he will carry out his work and do all he has promised.*

Following are other quotes mentioning that Zion is part of God's work. Notice how several of them bring light to God's purposes for building Zion.

<u>This is the work of God</u>, and the servants of God that are called to preside over us are the messengers of the Most High, and they have the light and the power . . . From the very hour that the light began to shine and it will blaze and burn, and it will go forth and will consume out of our midst all those that work iniquity; and <u>Zion will be established</u> in its purity, no more to be thrown down. - George A. Smith, January 3, 1858

God has commenced a work in these last days to elevate mankind, to save them, to increase them, to place them on a footing of independence; to cause them to love one another and to lay a foundation for peace and harmony, that bloodshed and war, contention and devastation shall cease; that the power of the oppressor shall be broken and that the honest in heart may have the privilege of dwelling together and building up Zion in all the earth . . . - George A. Smith, April 1872 General Conference

God had revealed himself to the human family and had restored the everlasting Gospel . . . What for? For the building up of a something that is called Zion or the pure in heart. - President John Taylor, December 1, 1878

The above two quotes, along with the next one, suggest that one of God's purposes for restoring the Gospel was so that Zion could be built in the last days, presumably to receive His son.

On August 26, 1883, President George Q. Cannon compares the Lord's attempt to build Zion among the Saints with His efforts to make a peculiar people out of the ancient Israelites, newly freed from bondage in Egypt.

Now, there are many points upon which we need correction. We are guilty of many things that are not in accordance with the mind and will of God. **There is a certain policy connected with the building up of Zion, a policy which God has sought to enforce upon us from the beginning until the present time.** *It is to a great extent the same policy that He urged upon and endeavored to enforce in the midst of Israel, when He led Israel out of Egypt. When He inspired Moses to take the steps that He* *did towards the emancipation of the children of Israel from the thralldom of the Egyptians, He had a definite purpose in view, and that was to make them a nation of His own, a people who should acknowledge Him as their God, and He wished to make a distinct race of them. For forty years He led them through the wilderness teaching them, counseling them, pleading with them, training them, in order to relieve them as far as possible from the old traditions with which they were burdened . . .*

Now, God in like manner has designed in these days in laying the foundation of Zion to establish a new order of things on the earth; to gather us out from the nations of the earth; to make us a peculiar people; to make us a holy and a pure people upon whom He could place His name and through whom He can accomplish His great designs and purposes on the earth; to make us a distinct people from every other people that lives upon the face of the earth, and through us to establish and perpetuate a new order of things on the earth which shall be preparatory to the ushering in of the full reign of righteousness through our Lord Jesus Christ. It is for this that the heavens have been opened.

I find the ideas in that last quote uncommonly interesting, and prophetic. The comparison of us modern Saints to ancient Israel is particularly poignant in that, in my personal opinion, we are nearly as much in bondage in modern Egypt (Babylon, actually), as were the ancient Israelites, it's just a more comfortable form of bondage, like that of the people of King Noah, right before the Lamanites enslaved them even further.

President Cannon's words in that last paragraph apply directly to the Latter-Day Saints in their first four decades in the Utah Territory. Think of the Mormon pioneers as you re-read this part: *"For forty years [1847-1887] He led them through the wilderness teaching them, counseling them, pleading with them, training them, in order to relieve them as far as possible from the old traditions with which they were burdened . . ."* In chapter 9 we'll see that these traditions he mentions are those we blindly follow from "Babylon".

God Has Declared Zion, So It <u>Must</u> Rise

Perhaps the best example of this concept is given in a January 12th, 1873 talk by Wilford Woodruff. He states:

The Lord has had Zion before his face from before the foundation of the world, and he is going to build it up. 'Who am I,' saith the Lord, 'that I promise and do not fulfill?' The Lord never made a promise to the sons of men which he has not fulfilled, therefore Latter-day Saints, you have all the encouragement in the world to sustain you in the faith that the Zion of God will remain on the earth. The work is in our hands to perform, the God of heaven requires it of us and if we fail to build it up we shall be under condemnation, and the Lord would remove us out of the way and he would raise up another people who would do it. Why? <u>Because the Almighty has decreed that this work shall be performed on the earth, and no power on earth or in hell can hinder it</u>.

But of course, Elder Woodruff wasn't alone in sharing this idea. Here are two additional quotes by men who were, or would become, the prophet of the Church:

What has already become of those who, during our short existence as a Church, have come out against us, politically, judicially, or otherwise, those who have raised their puny arms to destroy the kingdom of God from the earth? They have become powerless, like the dew before the rising sun; they have vanished away, their names are almost forgotten; and if this is not the case with all, it will be. For <u>Zion must be established on the earth, and God, in his power and might, will accomplish it, and none can stay His purposes</u>. - Brigham Young, September 17, 1876

They won't believe us any more than they would believe Joseph Smith in his day, or Brigham Young in his day. But **what these inspired men said is coming to pass. Every word that they uttered in relation to the building up of Zion, and to the progress of the kingdom of God upon the earth will be fulfilled**, *and not one jot or tittle will fail. You and I as individuals may fail, but <u>the work of God cannot fail. It is His work. He hath decreed its consummation, and no power on earth or in hell can alter the decree</u>. The work is marching forward, and if we do not keep pace with it, we must eventually be left behind.* - Joseph F. Smith, August 19, 1883

Then 11 years after first mentioning this idea, Wilford Woodruff revisited it on June 29, 1884, as President of the Quorum of the Twelve Apostles, when he said:

We have come to this earth in this time upon a mission. We have been born on purpose in this generation to take part in this work. The Lord required an element to labor with. <u>He will build up Zion</u>. And I bear my testimony here to all men, and would to all the world if I had the power, that the work in which this people are engaged, small and insignificant as it may appear, is the work of God. It will roll forth. It will become a mountain. It will fill the whole earth. It will break in pieces all other kingdoms, and it will stand forever; <u>for God Almighty has decreed it</u>. Write it down. - Wilford Woodruff, June 29, 1884

Just before becoming the prophet himself, on February 24, 1889, Woodruff said:

We have a great future before us. Zion will arise and shine, and the glory of God will rest upon her. Israel will be gathered, Jerusalem will be rebuilt, <u>Zion be established and thrown down no more forever</u>. These things are in the record of divine truth. **Not one of them will ever fail of fulfillment**. <u>They were given by revelation</u>. *No matter what the feelings of our enemies may be.*

Then as newly-ordained President of the Church, Woodruff stated, on July 29, 1889:

I do not pretend to know how many tribulations or how much suffering we shall yet have to endure before Zion is established in her beauty and glory; but I do know that Zion is not going to be moved out of her place. The Lord, however, will chastise us until we become purified before Him. He will plead with His strong ones, and <u>what He has said concerning Zion will come to pass</u>. I hope that we may exercise wisdom in all things, that we may escape these afflictions.

You may have noticed that a few of the above quotes mention, but do not share a common idea on, what the consequences will be for the Saints if they do *not* build Zion. In his first quote of this section, Elder Woodruff said that if we failed to build Zion God "would raise up another people who would do it". Joseph F. Smith's statement above that ". . . if we do not keep pace with it, we must eventually be left behind" seems to agree. However, as prophet, Wilford Woodruff later shares a different outcome for the Saints mentioning in that last quote above, "tribulations", "suffering", chastisement, and "afflictions". He's not saying the task will be given to some other group, he's saying the

Lord will run the Saints through the wringer of adversity *until* they obey and build Zion.

I say, "Why wait? Why not avoid the afflictions and start now? What holds us back except our own blind allegiance to Babylon's values and our avarice for her goods?"

The Lord is Working through His Church to Build Zion

Five different apostles, one of whom later became prophet, over a span of 31 years, mentioned seven times that the Lord is building Zion through His church. Here are three of those statements in chronological order:

*As a people <u>if we will do the will of God we have the power to build up Zion</u> in beauty, power and glory, as the Lord has revealed it through the mouth of the Prophet. It rests with us, **the Lord working with us**. We are called upon to work with the Lord just as fast as we are prepared to receive the things of his kingdom.* - Wilford Woodruff, April Conference 1862

[W]e are a chosen people, a royal Priesthood, selected by the God of Israel for the accomplishment of His purposes, for the organization and purification of His Church, for the establishment of His Kingdom, and <u>for the building up of His Zion</u> on the earth. - President John Taylor, June 24, 1883

If our enemies conspire against us, let us be true to our God, true to Zion, true to the methods that God has revealed unto us for the building up of His Kingdom, and take the course that will be right and pleasing in the sight of God . . . <u>God has established His Zion, and He is building it up in the way He has revealed and that He communicates to His servants</u> [in the Church] <u>from time to time</u>. - Elder George Q. Cannon, First Counselor in the First Presidency, September 2, 1889.

We are *Called* by God to Build Zion

*[W]<u>e shall have</u> all the skill, and all the power, and all the wisdom, and all the treasures, and <u>all the means necessary to build up Zion</u> and do all things necessary to accomplish the purposes of God **whereunto we are called**."* - Elder Parley P. Pratt, April 1856 General Conference.

God has called us to turn away from the folly of sustaining and building up Babylon—the worshippers of mammon—those who have no interest in common with us in establishing Zion and building up the Kingdom of our God upon the earth." - Erastus Snow, April 1868 General Conference

The Lord wants to build up His Zion, and He wants to build it up through you and me. **We are the ones He has called upon.** *Will we consent to do this?* - Brigham Young, April 17, 1870

For as I have said, we are not here to build up ourselves, but to build up Zion and establish the principles of righteousness upon the earth. That is our calling . . . - John Taylor, October 21, 1877

God has called us to build up Zion. *He has called us from the world for this purpose. He has not called us to be like other people, but to become a peculiar people unto Himself a people upon whom he can pour out His Holy Spirit to enable us to accomplish His designs.* - Elder George Q. Cannon, First Counselor in the First Presidency, October 31, 1881

At this point, assuming the reader is persuaded by the above authoritative quotes, one may begin to question, "If it's true that the Church was called by the Lord to build up Zion, why is there no Zion-building program in the Church today?" A more orthodox answer would be, "But there is! What do you think 'Perfect the Saints' means? The Church is preparing the Saints to be spiritually able to build the future Zion." This is likely true. However, there is a large pattern to be discovered in Last Days events and prophesies that may provide an even better answer. We'll outline that in Chapter 13.

Two Prophets & One Apostle Declare It's God's Will that We Build Zion

Over a 14-year span, **President Brigham Young** declared at least five times that the Lord wants His Saints to build Zion. Here are his first and last quotes (rest in Appendix A):

8/31/1862: *It is his will that we should* prepare ourselves to build up his kingdom, gather the house of Israel, redeem and **build up Zion** . . . revolutionize the world, and bring back that which has been lost through the fall.

10/8/1876: *The Lord has declared it to be his will that his people enter into covenant, even as Enoch and his people did,* which of necessity must be before we shall have the privilege of building the Center Stake of Zion, for the power and glory of God will be there, and none but the pure in heart will be able to live and enjoy it.

The first statement to follow was made by **John Taylor** as he served as President of the Quorum of the Twelve Apostles. It doesn't explicitly *say* it's God's will that we build Zion, but it is easily inferred by the context. However, his second statement below, made once he became Prophet, is very clear on this point.

4/8/1879: *It is not with us a question of what we shall eat, or what we shall drink, or what kind of houses we shall live in; it is not a matter of so much importance as it is to be* **doing the will of God** *to have our hearts engaged in his service, to feel that we are* <u>building up the Zion of the Lord of Hosts</u> . . .

6/15/1884: *We are here to accomplish the purposes of God, to build up His Zion, and to establish His Kingdom upon the earth, and* **He expects us to do it**.

Then there's Wilford Woodruff. In his 34th year as an Apostle, in both General Conferences held in 1873, he makes it clear that building Zion is something we must do and that God is behind the work:

4/7/1873: <u>*The Lord intends that we shall unite ourselves together, and in building up the Zion of God*</u>*, if we cannot attain to all that is required of us today, we will do what we can, and progress as fast as we can, that the way may be prepared for the fulfillment of the words of the Lord.*

10/8/1873: **The Lord has raised up a set of men and women, and he will inspire and move upon them to carry out this great work, and we have got it to do. Zion is going to rise and shine**, *and to put on her beautiful garments; she will be clothed with the glory of God . . . All these revelations touching the last days have got to be fulfilled. President Young is moved upon to call upon Zion to do her duty. Why is he thus moved upon? Because the power of revelation surrounds him and crowds upon him to magnify his calling and do his duty among the sons of men.* <u>*The power of God rests upon him, and he will never hold his peace until Zion is built up and perfected*</u>*, the house of Israel gathered and the work of God performed under his administration as long as he dwells in the flesh.*

We are Required/Commanded to Build Zion

The next ten quotes span 21 years and correspond closely to the Church leaders' efforts to unify the Saints economically. Once the Church was forced to stop that effort, the mentions of God requiring us to build Zion faded away. Below are snippets from seven of the ten quotes; the full quotes are all in Appendix A.

1. Brigham Young, 9/2/1860: *The <u>commandment</u> has gone forth for the Saints to gather and build up Zion.*

2. Wilford Woodruff, 6/12/1863: *The Lord **requires** of us to build up Zion . . .*

3. Brigham Young, 2/10/1867: *. . . <u>the commandment of God</u> to us is to build up Zion and her cities.*

4. George Q. Cannon, 7/21/1867: *We are **required** to build up Zion on the earth . . .*

5. Brigham Young, 2/16/1868: *. . . we have been <u>commanded</u> to . . . build up the Zion of our God . . .*

6. Brigham Young, 4/17/1870: *. . . we are called to build up Zion . . . The <u>command</u> has been given . . .*

7. Orson Pratt, 7/25/1875: *. . . we are **required** to build up a Zion . . .*

After the Church was forced to stop "building Zion" *temporally*, the number of affirmations faded about the doctrine that it is God's will that we build Zion. Here are the only three cases I could find that were given since the 1880s where the Brethren have mentioned this command:

Abraham O. Woodruff, 1899 General Conference: *We ought to desire to build up the <u>material</u> Zion; and while we may not be commanded in these things, <u>we should</u>, as the revelation which I have read says, <u>be willing to do many things of our own free will and choice</u>.*

George Teasdale, 1901 General Conference: *. . . as members of the Church in good standing **we are required** to keep the commandments and **to seek to establish the Zion of God** upon the earth.*

Elder Bruce R. McConkie, April 1977 General Conference: <u>*We have been commanded to lay the foundations of Zion*</u> *and to get all things ready for the return of Him who shall again crown the Holy City with his presence and glory.*

In Elder McConkie's 1977 talk, he focuses on the "pure in heart" definition of Zion, which is valid, of course. You can't build a Zion society when the people are greedy and self-serving. In later chapters we'll see that the Brethren taught that our motives must be for the welfare of all. This is rightly the focus of the Church's preparations for Zion-building—try to get the hearts of the people prepared.

Afterthoughts

The Church members today appear to be operating under the general belief that we can't build Zion physically now, "So why even think about it?" Here's why: **What makes us think God will ask us to participate in a physical Zion society to which we've never given any thought or made any preparations?** It makes more sense that if we at least *start* exploring in thought and deed how such a material Zion might be established, we would be far better prepared than if we gave it no thought at all.

"Practice Makes Perfect" right? And, as Abraham Woodruff suggests above, if we of our "own free will" start practicing some of the temporal principles of Zion, then we would again be far better prepared than if we just kept floating along to wherever the River Babylon takes us.

As our leaders taught above, God is determined that Zion be built, and, He has commanded us to build it. Yes, we had a serious setback in the late 1880's, and yes, the Church is doing all it can to encourage us to prepare spiritually. However, while reading the following words of the Lord, it's difficult for me not to believe there's more we as Saints can do ourselves, and working together, to prepare temporally for Zion:

D&C 58:26—For behold, it is not meet that I should command in all things; for he that is compelled in all things, the same is a slothful and not a wise servant; wherefore he receiveth no reward. [Are we waiting to be commanded in all things Zion?]

27. Verily I say, men should be anxiously engaged in a good cause, and do many things of their own free will, and bring to pass much righteousness; [Would getting anxiously engaged in preparing to live in a Zion society qualify as a "good cause"?]

28. For the power is in them, wherein they are agents unto themselves. And inasmuch as men do good they shall in nowise lose their reward.

29. But he that doeth not anything until he is commanded, and receiveth a commandment with doubtful heart, and keepeth it with slothfulness, the same is damned. [We know God wants Zion to be built . . . why wait until we are commanded?]

With a track record of such teachings from these Champions for Zion, how can we members continue to justify dragging our feet? Are we waiting to be commanded in all things Zion? Or, are we acting in that regard as "agents unto [our]selves"?

In Summary

The early LDS leaders during Utah's territorial years plainly taught:

- God intends Zion to be built.
- Building Zion is part of His work.
- God has declared Zion will be built, so it _must_ rise.
- The Lord is working through His church to build Zion.
- We are called by God to build Zion.
- He has required and commanded us to build Zion.

Chapter Four – Prophecies about Zion

Of all the quotes where the Brethren were talking about building or establishing Zion, roughly seven percent of them were about prophecy. Not only did the early LDS leaders teach the members that ancient prophets had foretold about Zion in the last days, but they taught four specific additional ideas about those prophesies:

- First, that they would be fulfilled before Christ returns in his glory.

- Second, that those prophesies were to be fulfilled in "our day".

- Third, that Isaiah prophesied that Zion was going to be built "in the mountains of Israel".

- Fourth, that the Latter-Day Saints were working to fulfill all of these prophesies by establishing Zion in the Rocky Mountains.

Let's look at each of these four teachings separately.

Prophets Foretold of a Latter-Day Zion

This should be no surprise to anyone who has read Isaiah, Jeremiah, or Ezekiel. They all prophesy of Zion in the latter-days. However, our point here is to review what early LDS apostles and prophets actually taught concerning the establishment of Zion.

Wilford Woodruff is the earliest we found to teach this idea. In this first example he quotes Robert Mason, who used to visit Woodruff's boyhood home, long before he joined the LDS Church. Mason went about teaching the families in his community about the Bible and that its prophecies would find literal fulfillment in the last days. Woodruff quoted Mason's teachings in the October 1856 General Conference, saying:

*"When you read the Bible do you ever think that what you read there is going to be fulfilled? The teachers of the day spiritualize the Bible, but when you read in the Bible about the dreams, visions, revelations and predictions of Ezekiel, Isaiah, Jeremiah, or any other of the Prophets or Apostles, relative to the gathering of Israel and **the building up of Zion**, where they say that Israel shall be gathered upon litters, swift beasts and dromedaries, you may understand that it means just what it says, and that it will be fulfilled upon the earth in the last days."*

Early the next year, Elder Woodruff mentioned again that Jeremiah taught about Zion being established in the last days:

The Prophet Jeremiah saw this kingdom established, and saw that Ephraim was the firstborn, and in gathering the children of Jacob and establishing Zion in the last days, their nobles should be of themselves, and their governor should proceed from the midst of them.

Wilford Woodruff was the apostle who mentioned this doctrine the most over the next quarter century, bringing it up at least a dozen more times, along with several others who taught it as well, as seen in the following quotes, with many more in Appendix A:

[W]e actually have that surer word of prophecy delivered to us through the Prophet Joseph, that in the last days the Lord would gather Israel, <u>build up Zion</u>, and establish His kingdom upon the earth. - Brigham Young, June 23, 1867

He has set His hand to establish Zion—the great Zion of God—about which the prophets have said so much. *No prophet has spoken more pointedly on this subject than Isaiah. Our drivings from Missouri, our persecutions, our travels along the Platte River, the manner of our coming to the mountains of Israel, our return again to the land of Zion and the building of the Temple in Jackson County have all been spoken of by Isaiah as well as by all the prophets who have spoken concerning the Zion of the latter days.* - Wilford Woodruff, December 12, 1869

We will now read something more about this Zion. Isaiah, as I have already quoted in the second chapter, has told us about the house of the Lord, and the great peace that should come, the beating of swords into ploughshares, etc., and then he goes on to portray **the blessings that are to come upon Zion**. *He says, "... In that day shall the branch of the Lord be beautiful and glorious, and the fruit of the earth shall be excellent and comely." Thus we see that Zion is to become glorious. The branch of the Lord, the branch of his own planting, established by his own power, the building up of a people and city by his own instructions and administration by the inspiration of his servants, the establishing of Zion no more to be thrown down.* - Orson Pratt, March 10, 1872

<u>Zion will be built up</u>; *Zion will be redeemed, and she will arise and shine and put on her beautiful garments; she will break from off her neck her yoke, and she will be clothed with the glory of our God. Zion has been sold for naught; she will be redeemed without money; she will arise in her beauty and glory,* <u>as the Prophets of God have seen her</u>; *she will extend her borders and strengthen her stakes, and the God of heaven will comfort her, inasmuch as we will unite together to carry out his purposes.* - Wilford Woodruff, April General Conference, 1878.

And then the Lord understood another principle, namely, that the time would come when the power of Satan, and the power of the wicked would be overthrown; **when the Zion of God would be established**; *when a reign of righteousness would be introduced; when there would be a communion between the Priesthood on the earth and the Priesthood in the heavens, and when correct principles would be introduced, and the rule and government of God would be established in the earth, and continue until the kingdoms of this world would become the kingdoms of our God and His Christ, and He would reign with universal empire over the nations of the earth.* **This is a thing that has been spoken of by all the Prophets**, *and it is the time of the restitution of all things since the world was.* - President John Taylor, December 9, 1883

Zion is to be Built Before Christ Returns

The first of the four sub-doctrines taught by the Brethren in regards to Zion being prophesied, is that it is to be built before the Savior's coming in glory. The most obvious of the quotes is this one by Wilford Woodruff, given January 1, 1871:

Now if Mr. Miller had been acquainted with the prophecies contained in the Bible, and with the Spirit by which the Scriptures were written, <u>he would have known very clearly that Christ would not come</u> until certain events had taken place. He would have been aware that the Messiah would not make his appearance until an angel of God had delivered the everlasting Gospel from the heavens to be preached to the nations of the earth; until the honest and meek of the earth are gathered out from every sect, party and denomination under the whole heavens; <u>until the Zion of God had gone up into the mountains of Israel and there established Zion</u>, and lifted up a standard to the people.

President Brigham Young's quote from June 7, 1857 was the earliest mention of this idea during the Utah territorial period:

*It now remains with us to bear off this kingdom, **build up Zion**, and establish the law thereof, **until** Christ shall reign King of nations . . .*

From 1872 to 1875, Elder Orson Pratt mentioned the doctrine five times, here are two:

*What? Immortal beings sitting upon thrones, having a table set for them and eating and drinking at the table of Jesus in Jerusalem? Yes, this is what is promised, and what we are looking for; <u>this is the order of things that will come when Zion is fully established on the earth</u> **preparatory** <u>to that order of things</u>. No wonder that nations will no longer lift up sword against nation! No wonder that kings will no longer fight against kings, and emperors against emperors! No wonder that they will beat their swords into ploughshares, and their spears into pruninghooks, for it will be a day of peace and rest, of which our present Sabbath is typical.* - March 10, 1872

Jeremiah tells us where [the ten tribes] will go; he tells us <u>there is to be a place called Zion before these tribes come out of the north countries</u>, and when they come with a great company, the blind and the lame with them, and the Lord God leads them with supplication and with tears and with prayers, bringing them forth from those dreary, desolate, cold arctic regions: <u>when that day shall come there shall be a Zion prepared to receive these ten tribes</u>, before they finally go back to Palestine. Is there anything in the Scriptures about this? Yes. In the same chapter of Jeremiah we read that "they shall come and sing in the height of Zion." <u>Zion, then, will have to be built up before they come</u>; Zion will have to be reared somewhere and prepared to receive them; and it will be a holy place, and it will be a holy people who will build up Zion, so much so that the Lord will bring these ten tribes in to the height of Zion, into the midst of it. (Jer. 31:6-8) - April 1875 General Conference

That this last quote belongs in this section can be discerned from the chapter headings of Revelation chapters 7 and 8. Chapter 7's heading says, "John also sees in the **sixth** seal the Restoration of the gospel, the sealing of the 144,000, and the hosts of the exalted from all nations" and chapter 8's heading says, "John sees fire and desolation poured out during the **seventh** seal and <u>preceding</u> the Second Coming." It shouldn't be too much of a stretch to assume that events prophesied in the sixth seal precede those in the seventh which themselves precede His return. So, we can safely assume that the gathering of the Twelve Tribes to Zion comes prior to the Second Coming, thus allowing us to place that last Orson Pratt quote firmly in this category.

The last three quotes suggesting Zion is to be built before Christ returns come from Elder, and then President, Wilford Woodruff, two of which were given in General Conferences:

Somebody or other has got to build up Zion . . . But <u>before Christ comes</u>, a people have got to be prepared by being sanctified before the Lord. Temples have got to be built; <u>Zion has got to be built up</u>; there must be a place of safety for the people of God while his judgments are abroad in the earth . . . - April 1876 General Conference

We live, in fact, in the dispensation of the fullness of times, the last dispensation in which the Lord will reveal his mind and will to the inhabitants of the earth, the last time in which the Lord will prune his vineyard, the last time in which he will set up his kingdom upon the earth, establish His Church, and **build up His Zion, to <u>prepare</u> for the coming of the Son of Man**. – December 10, 1882

The kingdom of God is here, and the Lord will sustain it. But I can bear record as my brethren have, that this kingdom will stand; and that <u>the Zion of God will remain upon the earth</u> **until** *<u>Jesus shall come to receive us unto himself.</u>* - October 1889 General Conference, as prophet.

Prophecies about Zion are to be Fulfilled in Our Day

This subcategory has six quotes spanning fifteen years, from 1860 to 1875. Here are three of them:

[T]his is the time the Lord has fixed for building up his Zion—that this is the time spoken of by the Prophets in which the Saints are commanded to gather out from the wicked. - Brigham Young, June 7, 1860

It has certainly been very interesting to the Latter-day Saints to watch the history and progress of this Church and kingdom during the last forty-two years. **This is one of the most important generations that men, or God, or angels have ever seen on the earth**: *it is a dispensation and generation when the whole flood of prophecy and revelation and vision given through inspired men for the last six thousand years is to have its fulfillment, and* **especially in relation to the establishment of** *the great kingdom and* **Zion of God** *on the earth.* - Wilford Woodruff, April 1872 General Conference

Thus you see that **the people who organize Zion** *through the everlasting Gospel which the angel brings, have good tidings to declare to all the inhabitants of the earth. But these people* **are required, according to this prophecy, to get up into the high mountains. You Latter-day Saints are four thousand three hundred feet above the level of the ocean**, *scattered over four hundred miles of Territory, north and south, and you are extending your settlements continually, and are building up some two hundred towns, cities and villages in the mountains of the great American desert,* **fulfilling the prophecies of the holy Prophets**. - Orson Pratt March 9, 1873

Isaiah Prophesied Zion to be Built in the Mountains of Israel

Some of the previously-mentioned quotes have hinted at this idea. There are seven quotes, spanning 26 years; four are given here, the rest in Appendix A. Most of these point directly to the subject at hand, especially the last two quotes. All of them are from two of our champions of Zion, Orson Pratt and Wilford Woodruff.

You here see the beginning of the fulfillment of this ancient prophecy. Isaiah in his 40th chapter also says, "<u>Zion shall go up into the high mountains</u>." Zion in the high mountains! <u>Zion in the midst of the great</u>

<u>American desert is beginning to redeem it and make it blossom as the rose</u>, making it like the garden of Eden, that joy and thanksgiving and songs of praise and prayer and gladness may ascend up from all her habitations and settlements throughout the length and breadth of this desert, <u>and thus the prophecies will be fulfilled</u>. Amen. - Orson Pratt, November 27, 1870

These are some of the grand events spoken of in this Bible; **these are events that the Latter-day Saints believe in, and that so far as it lies in their power, they are trying to fulfill**. If we are not Jews we are not required to go to old Jerusalem, but **we are required to build up a Zion**; that is spoken of as well as the building of Jerusalem. Zion is to be built up in the mountains in the last days, not at Jerusalem. - Orson Pratt, June 25, 1875

God has set his hand a second time to build up that kingdom which Daniel was permitted to see in vision, and to establish that Zion <u>in the mountains which Isaiah saw</u>. - Wilford Woodruff, June 30, 1878.

Was that Prophet inspired by the Spirit and power of God? I say in the name of Israel's God he was, and so was Isaiah when he spoke of **the gathering of the people unto the mountains of Israel to establish the Zion of God** . . . - Wilford Woodruff, January 6, 1884

Early Utah Saints were Working to Fulfill the Prophecies about Zion

The fourth sub-doctrine regarding the prophecies about Zion in the Last Days was spoken of by three other apostles, in addition to Wilford Woodruff and Orson Pratt. There are at least nine quotes by five different apostles spanning twenty-nine years. Here's a sampling:

If I feel at our approaching Conference as I now do, I shall ask to move that our home missions be not diminished, but increased, if possible; and all set to raising wheat, and <u>make Zion a house and city of refuge for the Saints</u> and for the sons of strangers, that they may come and build up our walls, <u>even as the old Prophet hath spoken</u>. - Orson Hyde, March 18, 1855

The Lord has put into **our hands** *the power to build up this great Zion, which all the ancient prophets rejoiced in and prophesied about.* - Wilford Woodruff, May 6, 1870

This is what has brought this people together in the valleys of the mountains; and <u>they are laboring now to bring forth and establish the Zion of God upon the earth, according to the words of his Holy Prophets</u>, whose prophecies have been and are being fulfilled in the history of this people. - Daniel H. Wells, June 8, 1872

The calling and mission of the Latter-day Saints are to fulfill what is here promised in these Scriptures—to bring about the restoration of scattered Israel, **the establishment of Zion**, the preparing a people for the coming of Christ . . . - Erastus Snow, May 6, 1882

Summary

Looking back over the quotes in this chapter, we see that not only did early LDS apostles teach that the ancient prophets foretold of a latter-day Zion, but they also taught again and again that the ancient prophets had prophesied that:

1. Zion is to be built before Christ returns,

2. The prophecies about Zion are to be fulfilled in this dispensation,

3. Isaiah prophesied that Zion would be built in the mountains, and that

4. The Territorial Utah Saints were working to fulfill the prophecies about Zion.

Chapter Five – Our Obligations Regarding Zion

As in the last chapter, around 50 of the 700+ quotes by early LDS leaders about building or establishing Zion are covered in this chapter. Our Champions for Zion specifically spoke about our obligations as members of the Church to build Zion. Their quotes fell neatly into 6 subcategories:

1. Building Zion is the work we've been given to do.

2. It is our duty & responsibility to build up Zion.

3. Building Zion is one of our callings from God.

4. We are obligated to build Zion.

5. The Priesthood obligates us to build Zion.

6. Building Zion is the whole point of receiving the Priesthood.

Those last two subcategories were a complete and total surprise! In fact, later we'll see some evidence that building Zion is perhaps also the whole point of the temple endowment. But first, let's read all the apostolic quotes, spanning from 1857 to 1884, about how it's our obligation as Latter-day Saints to build Zion.

Building Zion is the Work We've been Given to Do

A less elegant, but briefer way to describe this subcategory is, "We *have to* build Zion". That building Zion was a "have to" can clearly be discerned from the following quotes by two apostles, George A. Smith and Wilford Woodruff, and by two prophets, Brigham Young and John Taylor. Again, these quotes span from 1857 to 1884, nearly half of them were given in General Conference, all this suggesting that our having to build Zion was not a flash-in-the-pan doctrine but was one taught by those in the center of things.

*Let us know that we **have to** build up Zion until the Spirit of peace shall overrule our country.* - Brigham Young, July 5, 1857

Incorrect traditions, though long followed, have to be surrendered, and we have to build up Zion. - George A. Smith, April 1856 General Conference

We have to build up Zion, a temporal work here upon the face of the earth, and we have got to establish righteousness and truth. - Elder Wilford Woodruff, April 1867 General Conference

*We **have to** build up Zion, and make it the praise of the whole earth.* - John Taylor, January 9th, 1881

It should be pointed out here that President John Taylor ceased to preach about building Zion only because he was forced to go into hiding to avoid prosecution under the Edmunds Act, which declared polygamy to be a felony. Taylor died three years to the month of his last quote (found in Appendix A for this subcategory). Due to the large number of quotes by John Taylor (as mentioned elsewhere, he spoke about Zion in all but two of the 80 sermons he gave), and his extensive efforts to prepare the Saints to re-enter the United Order (which we'll get a taste for in later chapters), it is obvious that, along with several others, he was truly a Champion for Zion.

It is Part of Our Duty & Responsibility to Build up Zion

Thirteen times, over a 26-year span, five LDS apostles and two prophets used the words "duty" or "responsibility" in regards to the establishment of Zion. Here are five of those thirteen:

*[T]here is another commandment binding upon them, which is a part of the law of the Lord; and if they are required to contribute to feed the poor, clothe the naked, and assist this people in the great work of the gathering, and donate for **the building up of the Zion of our God, this is a part of their duty**, and it is included in the commandments of the Lord to them as heirs of celestial glory.* - Erastus Snow, August 26, 1860

5 - Our Obligations Regarding Zion

*We have to build up Zion, if we do our **duty**.* - Brigham Young, May 24, 1863

Every person who has obeyed the Gospel has a share of <u>responsibility</u> to bring forth and establish this work upon the earth. None can shirk this responsibility, but it is shared by all according to their spheres and positions. Those engaged in raising families are doing their part <u>to establish the Zion of God</u>, just as much as in the performance of any other labor. - Daniel H. Wells, June 8, 1872

*As an individual, I will say that **I feel a great responsibility resting upon me, and it also rests upon you**. Joseph Smith and Brigham Young alone have not been called to build up in the latter day that great and mighty kingdom of God which Daniel foretold, and which he said should be thrown down no more forever. I say, they were not called to be the only ones **to labor in building up that great and glorious Zion**, which was to become terrible to all nations; nor their counselors; nor the Twelve Apostles; but **this responsibility rests upon every one of the Lord's anointed upon the face of the earth, I do not care who they are, whether male or female, and the Lord will require this at the hands of all the Latter-day Saints**.* - Wilford Woodruff, January 12, 1873

<u>Every man is in duty bound to</u> do all he reasonably can to roll on the work of God, to maintain himself and family and <u>assist to build up Zion</u>. - Joseph F. Smith, April 1879 General Conference

We have gathered to these valleys of the mountains. What <u>duties</u> now devolve upon us? <u>To build up a Zion unto our God</u>. - President John Taylor, February 11, 1883

President John Taylor's answer to his own question in that last quote is very revealing, is it not? Of all the answers he *could* have given, he chose to say "To build up a Zion unto our God." He could have said, "preach the Gospel", "redeem the dead", or "build temples", but no! He said, "build up a Zion unto God". This seems to suggest, as do dozens of quotes in this book, that building Zion was what they saw themselves doing in the Mountain West.

Building Zion is One of Our Callings from God

1. **We are called to build up Zion,** and we cannot build it up unless we are united; and in that union we have got to carry out the commandments of God unto us, and we have got to obey those who are set to lead and guide the affairs of the Kingdom of God. - Wilford Woodruff, April 1867 General Conference

2. I do not mean that we shall cease feeding the hungry, no matter whether he is Saint or sinner; but cease to feed and build up the wicked who will not labor with us to develop the resources of the country and help to build up Zion. **God has called us to turn away from the folly of sustaining and building up Babylon**—the worshippers of mammon—those who have no interest in common with us in establishing Zion and building up the Kingdom of our God upon the earth. - Erastus Snow, April 1868 General Conference

3. I realize that we are called and ordained of God to labor with him and the heavenly hosts, in the accomplishment of his purposes, <u>the bringing forth and establishing of his Zion</u> and Kingdom in the earth, and all that has been designed to be consummated in this the dispensation of the fullness of times. - Wilford Woodruff, April 1878 General Conference

4. <u>The calling and mission of the Latter-day Saints are to fulfill what is here promised in these Scriptures</u>—to bring about the restoration of scattered Israel, <u>the establishment of Zion</u>, the preparing a people for the coming of Christ . . . . - Erastus Snow, May 6, 1882

5. **We, as Latter-day Saints, are called upon to build up Zion.** - Wilford Woodruff, January 6, 1884

These quotes leave no question that, at least during the mid- to late-1800s, the Latter Day Saints were called by God to build Zion. There is some evidence that that calling is on hold. However, since God has shown prophets like Isaiah, Jeremiah, and Ezekiel that Zion would *eventually* be built in the Last Days, and since Moses 7 suggests at least one Zion society will be built before Christ returns, if we Saints show the Lord by our actions and desire that we are determined to be prepared to take up that calling again, no doubt He will re-issue the call when the time is right. It is up to us to be ready.

We are Obligated to Build Zion

This subcategory has only three quotes. If it weren't for the support that the next two subcategories give to this one, this topic would probably have been left out of this book.

1. But so long as they remain upon the earth in the flesh, they remain under the same <u>obligation</u> to serve the Lord today as much as yesterday, . . . to gather up their substance, come to the gathering place, <u>and assist in building up the Zion of our God</u>, and to assist in establishing his kingdom in the tops of the mountains. - Erastus Snow, August 26, 1860

2. **Are we not all under obligation to be Saints**, to build up the kingdom of God, to bring forth righteousness and deliverance to the honest-in-heart, to gather up the lost sheep of the house of Israel, to send the Gospel to the uttermost parts of the earth, giving all a privilege to hear and believe it and **to build up the Zion of our God upon the earth?** Is not this obligatory upon every member of this Church and kingdom, upon one as well as upon another in their calling and capacity? - Brigham Young, June 7, 1863

3. <u>We are under obligations to establish the Zion of our God upon the earth</u>, and establish and maintain its laws, so that the law of the priesthood of the Son of God may govern . . . the people. - Brigham Young, December 8, 1867

The Priesthood Obligates us to Build Zion

This topic was also a surprise to me as I gathered quotes on establishing Zion. There can be little doubt that it's true given the authoritative comments on it, and especially after reading the quotes in the subcategory that follows this one.

<u>Every man that has received the Priesthood</u>, whether an Apostle, Prophet, High Priest, Elder, Bishop, Priest, or Teacher—all <u>should live as one man—be of one heart and one mind</u>. - Heber C. Kimball, July 1, 1860

Read the revelations in the Book of Doctrines and Covenants given through Joseph, and you will find that **the burden of** the gathering of the House of Israel, **the building up of Zion**, and the sanctifying of the *people, and the preparing for the coming of the Son of Man **is upon the elders of this church***. - President Brigham Young, July 23, 1867

We ought not to treat lightly the holy priesthood, or attempt to use it for any other purpose under the whole heavens other than to build up the Zion of God. - Wilford Woodruff, July 3, 1880

<u>*Joseph said in the beginning that it was the duty of the Elders of this Church to labor constantly to build up Zion and not to build up that which is opposed to Zion*</u>. *That embodies in these few words the policy that we should observe.* - George Q. Cannon, August 26, 1883

The Whole Point of Receiving the Priesthood is to Build Zion

Again, discovering this theme among the hundreds of quotes by our Champions for Zion was a big surprise to me. Yet, the ten quotes by the Lord's own servants suggest it is so. Here are a representative four:

The Latter-day Saints cannot stand still; we cannot become stereotyped. God has decreed that his Zion must progress . . . It becomes us, as Latter-day Saints, to realize these things as they are, and also our position and calling before God. **We must build up the Zion and kingdom of God on the earth, or fail in the object of our calling and receiving the Priesthood of God in these latter days**. - Wilford Woodruff, April 1873 General Conference

As mortal and immortal beings, as men holding the holy Priesthood **that the Lord has conferred upon us for** *the establishment of his kingdom,* **the building up of his Zion**, *the redemption of the living and the dead, it is of the utmost importance that we stand forth, every one of us, and magnify our several callings; for with all our weakness, with all our infirmities, God has given unto us great treasures, which we hold in these earthen vessels.* - President John Taylor, October 1877 General Conference.

For as I have said, we are not here to build up ourselves, but to build up Zion and establish the principles of righteousness upon the earth. That is our calling, <u>*that is what the Priesthood is conferred upon us for*</u>, *and it behooves us to magnify it and honor our God.* - President John Taylor, October 21, 1877

<u>*What is this Priesthood given us for? That we may be enabled to build up the Zion of our God*</u>. - President John Taylor, January 9, 1881

Summary

Reviewing the quotes in this chapter, we see that not only did our early Champions for Zion teach that it is our God-given duty, responsibility, and calling to build Zion, and that holding the Priesthood obligates us to build Zion, but also that establishing Zion was a primary reason for God giving the Priesthood to us in the first place! A remarkable teaching indeed!

Chapter Six – The Saints were Actively Building a Zion in Utah

I suspect this chapter will be one of the most pivotal for any skeptical Saints reading this book. It contains 97 quotes by modern apostles and prophets, roughly a seventh of all the Zion quotes by such men. Together these quotes make it clear as day that the early LDS Church leaders were *determined* to build a Zion society here in Utah, and, that they were anxiously engaged in doing so.

From these quotes, we see that the Brethren taught that God wants a Zion society to be built **in Utah**; that establishing Zion in Utah was the whole point of coming here. And the leaders taught that we *can* build Zion, we <u>want</u> to, and we **will** build a Zion in Utah.

The last third of these 97 quotes gives evidence that the Saints were deeply engaged in building a real, live, brick-and-mortar, Enoch-style Zion society right here in Utah.

God Wants a Zion Built in Utah

When we first came here, the people were told, and many saw and believed it as much then as they can now, that <u>the Lord in his providence led the people into these mountains</u> to separate them from the Gentile world, <u>in order that he might</u> establish his kingdom—his laws, and <u>commence his Zion in the mountains</u>, where his people could have but little connection with the world. - Brigham Young, January 17, 1858

I would to God that the eyes of the Latter-day Saints were open far more than they are to those things that rest upon them! **The Lord is looking to them alone to build up his Zion <u>here</u> in the mountains of Israel**, *and to prepare the bride, the Lamb's wife, for the coming of the Great Bridegroom.* - Wilford Woodruff, January 12, 1873

6 - The Saints were Actively Building a Zion in Utah

<u>The Latter-day Saints have a work to do</u>, not only in proclaiming the Gospel and warning the people, but <u>to build up Zion right here</u> upon the earth. Not afar off in some far distant sphere, but <u>here, where the Lord has planted their feet, in the valleys of the mountains</u>. - Daniel H. Wells, October 1875 General Conference

Now, then, God has gathered us together for a purpose, and that purpose is to build up Zion and to establish His kingdom on the earth . . . **We are here, then, to build up Zion**. - President John Taylor, January 9, 1881

God Almighty has set His hand to establish His Church and Kingdom on the earth. <u>He has set His hand to gather His people to the mountains of Israel to build up a Zion. That Zion is here</u>. We have made a beginning. We came here, on the 24th of July, 1847, a little handful of pioneers. - Wilford Woodruff, June 29, 1884

We Can, Want to, and WILL Build Zion Here in Utah

The following quotes show that not only did our Champions for Zion believe we *can* build Zion here in Utah, they said we <u>want to</u>, and expressed the determination that we **will** do so:

- *This is a work at which we* ***can*** *all labor; for it is by our united efforts that Zion will be produced in our own bosoms, <u>in this city, in our Territory</u>, or anywhere else. If we will do this, and be united as the heart of one man, we shall banish Satan from our presence, and eventually from this earth; and this we have to do.* - Daniel H. Wells, March 22, 1857

- *We* ***can*** *make a Zion of God on earth at our pleasure . . . by the judicious management and arrangement of this ever-existing material a Zion of God can always be built on the earth.* - Brigham Young, February 23, 1862

- *[W]e* ***can*** *build up Zion and be of one heart and of one mind . . .* - Brigham Young, April 1867 General Conference

- *Then I might say, O ye wicked nations of the earth, why do you quarrel with us all the time for doing you good? We* ***want to*** *build up Zion and bring up your fathers and mothers to enjoy a*

- *glory, and you are trying to prevent us. They are contending against their own lives—quarrelling against their own salvation and being.* - Brigham Young, July 31, 1859

- *[L]et us try to build up Zion. Zion is the pure in heart. Zion cannot be built up except on the principles of union required by the celestial law. It is high time for us to enter into these things. It is more pleasant and agreeable for the Latter-day Saints to enter into this work and build up Zion, than to build up ourselves and have this great competition which is destroying us.* - Lorenzo Snow, April 21, 1878

- *We are **seeking to** build up the Zion of our God. And shall we accomplish it? With the help of the Lord we will.* - John Taylor, December 11, 1881

- *I desire [Congress] to let us alone . . . Let them attend to their own business, and we **will** build up Zion while they go to hell.* - Brigham Young, August 31, 1856
  [Personal note: This quote made me chuckle when I found it, so much so that I had it made into a t-shirt with a nice photo of Brigham looking all stern.]

- *But in spite of the follies that some among us delight in, we are **going to** build up Zion. We are going to fill <u>these mountains</u> with the cities and people of God. The weapons formed against Zion will be broken, and the nations of the Gentiles will visit her and their kings will, come to the brightness of her rising.* - Wilford Woodruff, October 1873 General Conference

- *[A]ll heaven is interested in the work in which we are engaged; and whatever other men may think about these things, we know what we are doing, and **we shall try, in the name of the Lord**, and under His guidance and direction, to build up his Zion upon the earth . . . and [establish] **not only the Church of Christ, but His Zion** and the kingdom of God upon the earth.* - John Taylor, October 1881 General Conference

- *We are living in a great day. <u>These mountains</u> are filled with Latter-day Saints, in fulfillment of the revelations of God. The Lord has commenced this work, and He is not going to leave it. I* *warn all men of that. Zion is **going** to be built up. Zion is **going** to be established. Zion is going to be clothed with the glory of God.* - Wilford Woodruff, March 5, 1889

As you read the above quotes, did you feel the determination they had in their hearts for building Zion? Indeed, they were truly Champions for Zion, fueled with the fire in their souls to bring about God's will on the earth by establishing His Zion in these last days.

Then again, the reader may still be skeptical with the conclusion that the early LDS leaders differentiated between Zion and the Church. The idea is still strong today that "Zion" = LDS Church. If you still believe this, go back and re-read the last half-dozen quotes and ask yourself, "If Zion = LDS Church, then why do the Brethren keep saying, long after the Church is established, 'we are <u>going to</u> build Zion' if Zion already exists in the form of the Church?"

Building Zion was the Whole Point of Gathering to Utah

This is the third-most widely mentioned topic by early LDS leaders in regards to establishing Zion.

There is a handful of people in these valleys. <u>They have come to</u> erect his temple, <u>build the towers of Zion</u>, to attend to the ordinances of the Gospel, and prepare for the great things that await the earth. - Joseph Young, October 11, 1857

We came here inspired with a feeling to awaken in our breasts an unlimited desire to labor for the building up of Zion, *and this desire exists in a great many Elders.* - George A. Smith, October 20, 1861

<u>We are gathered together in the tops of these mountains for the express purpose of building up Zion</u>, *the Zion of the last days, the glory of which was seen by the prophets of the Almighty from the days of old.* - Brigham Young, January 2, 1868

We have no business here other than to build up and establish the Zion of God. - Brigham Young, April 1877 General Conference (his last).

[W]e have been wandering about from place to place, and the Lord has blessed us in a remarkable degree. <u>And we are gathered together</u>, as I

have said, <u>for the purpose of building up Zion</u> . . . . - President John Taylor, September 21, 1878

<u>*We have been gathering the people from Babylon through the power of God to build up a Zion here.*</u> *But see the results that attend our labors in this city and in this Territory. It seems as though all hell is endeavoring to defeat our object, and to defeat the cause of God in gathering the people out from the nations of the earth.* - George Q. Cannon, January 6, 1884

Persuaded yet? If not, there are 18 more such quotes in Appendix A. All but two of them are from President John Taylor, who as detailed in Chapter One, mentioned gathering to, or building, Zion 81.25% of the times he spoke. I would encourage the reader to review the quotes for this subcategory in Appendix A to better see and understand John Taylor's divine obsession with establishing Zion.

Building Zion to Fulfill Prophecy

Several of these quotes in this subcategory express the belief that the Saints not only came to Utah to build Zion, but that they were doing it in order to fulfill prophecy.

Still, we are here as Latter-day Saints; **we have assembled ourselves together to become one; to become the people of God, the children of Zion**, *the children of light.* <u>*We are here for the express purpose of separating ourselves from the world and establishing that order of government that we read of in the Holy Scriptures*</u>*; and we desire to see the glory of Zion upon the earth that has been spoken of by the Prophets of God.* - Brigham Young, May 17, 1868

<u>*Why have we gathered to Zion? To fulfill the revelations of God*</u>*.* *Isaiah and Jeremiah and* **nearly all the prophets since the world began have foretold the gathering of the people in the last days to establish Zion**, *from which the law of the Lord should go forth to rule the nations of the earth, while the word of the Lord should go forth from Jerusalem. We are here to do these things, and to receive teachings and instructions that we may be prepared for the coming of the Son of Man.* - Wilford Woodruff, July 19, 1868

6 - The Saints were Actively Building a Zion in Utah

We have been gathered here. What for? What did we come here for? Who knows? <u>We came here because God said he would build up his Zion in the latter days.</u> - John Taylor, May 26, 1872

Read the fortieth chapter of Isaiah, where he speaks of the glory of the Lord being revealed, and all flesh to see him when he comes the second time and how the mountains and hills should be lowered and the valleys be exalted; and in the same chapter the Prophet also says that, before that great and terrible day of the Lord, **Zion is required to get up into the high mountains.** *Isaiah predicts this. Says he, in his fortieth chapter—"Oh Zion, thou that bringest good tidings, get thee up into the high mountains." Thus you see that the people who organize Zion through the everlasting Gospel which the angel brings, have good tidings to declare to all the inhabitants of the earth. But these people are required, according to this prophecy, to get up into the high mountains. <u>You Latter-day Saints are four thousand three hundred feet above the level of the ocean, scattered over four hundred miles of Territory, north and south, and you are extending your settlements continually, and are building up some two hundred towns, cities and villages in the mountains of the great American desert, fulfilling the prophecies of the holy Prophets</u>.* - Orson Pratt, July 25, 1875

And what is the result of our preaching? Let facts speak for themselves. You can behold for yourselves, **a people gathered here from the different nations, all prompted by the same motives, namely, to build up and establish Zion on the earth**, *in fulfillment of the words of God, through the mouths of his Prophets. <u>We have gathered here for the express purpose of establishing Zion</u>, which,* **according to the Scriptures**, *must be before the Gospel can be sent to the Jews.* - Wilford Woodruff, August 13, 1876

They Called Utah "Zion" <u>Because</u> They were Building One Here

Not long since, I was talking with one of the brethren, who has crossed the Plains this season, in regard to the propriety of companies starting so late. He argued that it was far better for the Saints to be striving with all their might, doing all they could to serve the Lord and keep His commandments, and **traveling the road to Zion** *with intent to build it up and establish the kingdom of God on earth, even though they should lay* *down their lives by the way, than to stop among the Gentiles and apostates.* - Brigham Young, November 16, 1856

There must be a change in the way of the gathering, in order to save them from the calamities and the scourges that are coming upon the wicked nations of the earth. It would require more gold than all the Saints possess upon the earth, to gather the Saints <u>unto Zion</u> from all nations <u>in the way they have been gathering</u>, but now the handcart operation has been introduced to this people, it will bring five here to where one has been brought heretofore. - Wilford Woodruff, October 1856 General Conference

One part of the Gospel is that we should be gathered together to a land that should be called Zion. **Have we been doing this? Yes**. - John Taylor, April 1882 General Conference

<u>*We are gathered here to the place we denominate Zion. There have been Zions before. Enoch had a Zion*</u> *which was translated and which is reserved till the latter days. And we have a Zion to build up, which we shall do with the help of the Lord. We certainly shall accomplish these things no matter what the ideas and feelings of men may be in regard to it. Zion is onward and upward, and the Lord is directing and manipulating the affairs of His Church.* - John Taylor, August 20, 1882

Evidence the Saints were Anxiously Engaged in Building a Zion in Utah

As we modern Saints work in "Gentile" businesses with the hopes of enjoying our work and our lives and in preparation for retirement, our LDS forefathers, in contrast, were apparently anxiously engaged in building an Enoch-style Zion society in Utah. So far, I've found 39 quotes that attest to this engagement, which appears to have crescendoed just before the polygamy raids began, forcing President Taylor into hiding. [The word "a" is bolded in these quotes to point out that they were building a Zion, not *the* Zion.] Here are some quotes, in reverse chronological order, that make this point glaringly obvious:

We are preparing ourselves to build up **a** *Zion of God . . .*
- President John Taylor, October 1884 General Conference

6 - The Saints were Actively Building a Zion in Utah

*<u>In addition to establishing His Church</u>, He has told us to build up **a** Zion to His name, and we are gathering the materials together for that purpose.* - President John Taylor, June 22, 1884

They strive to practice what they preach, and <u>the Saints in the South</u> are no exception to this rule. <u>They are seeking</u> to live their religion, to serve God, to perfect themselves in the knowledge of the truth, and <u>to build up a Zion here in this Territory</u>. - Brigham Young, Jr., April 1884 General Conference

It is upon President Taylor night and day, I know. <u>Every thought and desire of his heart is</u> for the salvation of this people, and <u>to establish and build up the Zion of our God</u>. - George Q. Cannon, October 29, 1882

This next quote, by President John Taylor, clearly shows that he was determined to build City-of-Enoch style communities in Utah.

*Then again, <u>did Enoch build up a Zion? So we are doing</u>. What is it? The Zion of God. What does it mean? The pure in heart in the first place. In the second place those who are governed by the law of God—the pure in heart who are governed by the law of God. <u>Shall we build up a Zion? We shall</u>; but we shall not, every one of us, have our own way about it. We shall feel that we need the will of God; and we shall feel that we require the Priesthood, under His direction, to guide and direct us, **not men who are seeking to aggrandize themselves; but men who are seeking to build up the Church and Kingdom of God upon the earth**; men of clean hands and pure hearts, every one honoring his Priesthood and magnifying it . . . Now, <u>this is what we are building up, and they built up a similar thing before the flood;</u> and the Elders went forth in those days as they now go forth; and they baptized people and laid hands upon them, and gathered them to Zion; and after a while that Zion was caught up from the earth. <u>And we will build up a Zion: that is what we are aiming at</u>. And that Zion also, when the time comes, will ascend to meet the Zion from above, which will descend, and both, we are told, will fall on each other's necks and kiss each other. These are some of the things we are after. And we are traveling about to teach the people. Why? Because <u>we want all to have the spirit of Zion</u>. We sing sometimes and talk about Zion, that she shall arise, and the glory of God shall rest upon her. We want to lift up Zion.* - President John Taylor, October 20, 1881

Note in the bolded text above how he contrasts those who seek to benefit themselves with those who seek to build the Church and Kingdom of God. It gives us the insight that perhaps "pure in heart" does not mean something close to perfection, as we may imagine, but rather God-centered motives for our day-to-day labors.

And then on the previous day:

We are endeavoring to build up the Zion of our God, *that we may fill the measure of our creation upon the earth, and fulfil the various duties which devolve upon us, and also teach others to do the same. It is for this reason that we travel around among the people; and there are a great many people to see now. In a short time hence we shall have traveled all through the Territory, visiting almost all the settlements.* <u>We are building up Zion</u>, *and Zion is not confined to our prominent cities, but includes all the cities of the Saints.* - President John Taylor, October 19, 1881

This next quote shows us that apparently it wasn't just the apostles and prophets who were diligently working to bring about a Zion society.

And **when I see our Bishops engaged in** *doing the will of God, and exerting themselves to promote the welfare of His people over whom they preside, and seeking counsel from God and other sources, and* **doing all they can to build up Zion unselfishly**, *with pure hearts and clean hands, I say, God bless you and may the spirit and power of your office rest upon you, that you may magnify it and honor your God.* - President John Taylor, January 9, 1881

Now, I won't bore the reader with all thirty one of the other quotes in this subcategory. The following few are representative of the concept that the Saints were anxiously engaged in the good cause of building a real live, brick-and-mortar Zion society:

And what is the result of our preaching? Let facts speak for themselves. You can behold for yourselves, a people gathered here from the different nations, <u>all prompted by the same motives, namely, to build up and establish Zion on the earth</u>, *in fulfillment of the words of God, through the mouths of his Prophets . . . Had not this been the case, Utah would be today, what it was on the 24th of July, 1847, when the pioneers first set foot on its soil—a barren, desolate land, unfit for the habitation of man. The results of our preaching bespoke the fulfillment of prophecy. Zion has arisen, and some of the prophecies concerning her, recorded in the Old and New Testament, are having their fulfillment.* - Wilford Woodruff, August 13, 1876

This is what has brought this people together in the valleys of the mountains; and **they are laboring now to bring forth and establish the Zion of God upon the earth***, according to the words of his Holy Prophets, whose prophecies have been and are being fulfilled in the history of this people.* - Daniel H. Wells, June 8, 1872

<u>*We have labored, in the midst of persecution, for forty years past in trying to establish Zion among the Gentiles.*</u> *-* Orson Pratt, May 26, 1871

Again, note the comparison of the Saints' efforts to Enoch building his Zion:

[Enoch spent t]hree hundred and sixty-five years teaching and instructing the people, and setting examples before them, and forming a city that should be a model city of Zion. . . .when we consider the time that it took Enoch to accomplish this work, we have every reason to rejoice at the progress of Zion at the present time. Most of the efforts we have made to advance the cause of Zion we have been able to carry through successfully. - George A. Smith, May 6, 1870

These four quotes, along with some from Chapter One, not only illustrate that they were engaged in building Zion, but also show the struggle the LDS leaders encountered early on when converts had no interest in sharing in the primary focus of building Zion:

[I]f all the numbers that have been baptized into this Church since its first organization were added together I do not suppose that there would be less than a million, and but few of these have remained to the present time, the rest have built up cities for the Gentiles, and have populated such towns as St. Louis, San Francisco, and in fact almost all of the cities of California and the Western States. <u>*The rest are still laboring to build up Zion,*</u> *to spread abroad the fulness of the everlasting Gospel and to save all who will give heed to its teachings and the dictates of the Holy Spirit, while those who cannot "bear the sieve of vanity" are occasionally leaving the Church and going again to wallow in the wickedness of the world.* - George A. Smith, May 11, 1862

But only a portion of those who have embraced the Gospel under the auspices of those successful Elders, have had faith and energy enough to gather with the Saints <u>to take part in helping to build up Zion</u>. - George A. Smith, October 20, 1861

If they then begin to say in their hearts, "I have served the Lord for a little season; I have been baptized; I have received the Holy Ghost and have become some great one; I have received the gift of tongues, and have prophesied; I have received the power of healing the sick, and other manifestations of the power and mercies of the Almighty; I think I can remain where I am and do well in disregarding the counsels of the Almighty respecting gathering together and dividing my substance for the gathering of the poor and building up of Zion." It will be said to them who speak and act thus, as it was said to Nebuchadnezzar of old. If they cling to that which is given, and set their hearts upon the things of this world, and love them more than they do the kingdom of our God, those blessings will be withdrawn, the Holy Ghost will be taken from them, and that light received through obedience to the first principles of the Gospel will flee away; that love which they possessed will leave them, and they will become weak as before and darker than ever, unless they speedily repent and turn unto the Lord with all their hearts. - Erastus Snow, August 26, 1860

[H]ow long will it take us to build up Zion, [when we] emigrate people from the far off corners of the earth, and they apostatize and run away when they get here? - Amasa M. Lyman, December 2, 1855

This next quote was saved for last. It shows Elder Wilford Woodruff's positive outlook at the Saints' efforts to build Zion, in spite of setbacks caused by traditions from within and opposition from without:

I rejoice in this work because it is true, because it is the plan of salvation, the eternal law of God that has been revealed to us, and <u>the building up of Zion is what we are called to perform</u>. I think we have done very well considering our traditions and all the difficulties which we have had to encounter; and I look forward, by faith, if I live a few years, to the time when this people will accomplish that which the Lord expects them to do. If we do not, our children will. <u>Zion has got to be built up</u>, the Kingdom of God has got to be established, and the principles revealed to us have to be enjoyed by the Latter-day Saints. - Wilford Woodruff, May 19, 1867

What traditions within and without the Church distract us from shouldering our duty to build Zion in preparation for Christ's return?

Summary

In review, we've seen numerous quotes from our early LDS apostles and prophets showing there is abundant evidence that the LDS Church leaders and members were anxiously engaged in building a real, live, brick-and-mortar Zion society in Utah. Remarkable, eh? Again, they show:

1. God wanted a Zion built in Utah,
2. Our leaders were determined that we can, want to, and *will* build Zion here in Utah,
3. Building Zion was the whole point of gathering to Utah in the first place, and
4. LDS apostles and prophets believed they were building a Zion society in Utah in order to fulfill ancient prophecies about the Last Days,

Afterthoughts

Today, locals sometimes refer to Utah as "Zion". They even name their Babylon-style businesses after Zion! Given the assumptions behind all the quotes covered in this chapter, it's not a stretch to conclude that Utahns today refer to their state as "Zion" because their forefathers were actually building one here! It wasn't just a nickname—it was their anxiously-pursued goal.

Chapter Seven – What is Required of Us to Establish Zion?

If it's God's will that Zion be built prior to the glorious return of His Son, then we might ask ourselves, "What does building Zion require of us?" While classifying the 700+ quotes by early LDS leaders about establishing Zion, well over 100 of them fell into this category.

Due to the wide-ranging variety of teachings by our early apostles and prophets as to what is required of us, it was a challenge to find some underlying order in all the quotes in this category. During the process of seeking patterns among the quotes, no less than 16 subcategories were identified. Here they are:

Unity

Gather

Sacrifice

Consecration

Faith & works

Pure in heart

Live the Gospel

We must desire it

7 - What is Required of Us to Establish Zion?

So this list suggests there are a great deal of "shoulds" required of us in order to build Zion—we should forsake Babylon's values, we should live the Gospel, we should become united, etc., etc. But, something tells me that there *has* to be an underlying order in there somewhere (remember how God said, "for my house is a house of order"?). I believe I may have found it.

After studying it out in my mind and experiencing at least two epiphanies, it appears that all sixteen of these requirements fit rather neatly under three headings: **Heart, Gospel, and Temple**. It is evident these three topics reflect the three primary relationships—to oneself, to one's fellowman, and to God.

Let's quickly look at Heart first. In order to achieve the status of "Pure in heart" (one scriptural definition of Zion), it appears that the teachings of early LDS leaders suggest we must 1) get Zion into our hearts, 2) we must *desire* it, 3) our eye must be single to building Zion (and not Babylon), and 4) we must demonstrate to God through our actions that we earnestly seek to build Zion. We'll review the quotes for these subcategories below.

Under the heading of Gospel, one might organize some of the related subcategories according to their relationship to the first principles and ordinances of the restored Gospel:

- Faith: **Faith & good works**
- Repentance: **Forsake Babylon's values**, and, **Sanctify ourselves**
- Baptism: **Gather** and **Unify** with our fellowmen (as in join the Church with a covenant that we are "willing to bear one another's burdens, that they may be light" - Mosiah 18:8).
- Gift of the Holy Ghost: **Inspiration/Revelation**

Now to Temple. As I am acutely aware of the *cultural* tradition of not discussing anything that goes on in the Lord's house, the reader will be left to draw the connections themselves among the rest of the subcategories of what the early Brethren said was required of us to establish Zion, and, what goes on in our temples:

A. Obedience to God's will
B. Sacrifice
C. Live the Law of the Gospel
D. The Law of Consecration

Some will notice that the Law of Chastity is missing from this list. Not a single quote was found that linked that principle to the building of Zion. However, isn't it obvious that we could not possibly build a Zion society if that principle were not strictly obeyed by all the community's inhabitants? Disobeying that law would sow distrust and strife, both being destructive to a peaceful, united society. Perhaps that is exactly why the Lord insists on that law being kept.

Let's first look at the quotes under the heading of <u>Heart</u>.

1. Zion in our hearts

What is required of us to build Zion? The early Brethren taught that we must get Zion in our hearts.

<u>We must begin and make Zion in our own hearts</u>, and then extend it to our neighborhoods, and so continue until the Lord shall reign upon the earth. - Brigham Young, July 4, 1853

[I]t is for those who have the principles of the kingdom <u>in their hearts</u> to seek to permanently establish the Zion of God upon the earth, whether they will be able to maintain the kingdom or not is the Lord's business. - Daniel H. Wells, September 29, 1861

When we [decide] to make a Zion we will make it, and this work commences in the heart of each person. When the father of a family wishes to make a Zion in his own house, he must take the lead in this good work, which it is impossible for him to do unless he himself **possesses the Spirit of Zion** . . . Visit them when you will, and you find them dwelling in peace; a heavenly influence constantly broods over them and over everything they possess. But are they perfect? No. - Brigham Young, February 23, 1862

<u>To build up Zion should be the thought of every heart</u>—to labor to establish the cause of God in the earth, to be a [covenant] people. - George Q. Cannon, August 26, 1883

(More in Appendix A)

We must desire it

To build Zion, we must truly want it, with "firm determination". It must be a "cherished desire".

There is not one thing wanting in all the works of God's hands to make a Zion upon the earth <u>when the people conclude</u> [ie. decide] <u>to make it</u>. - Brigham Young, February 23, 1862

Consequently our teachings during Conference will be to instruct the people how to . . . accomplish the work devolving upon them in building up Zion on the earth. To accomplish this will require steady faith and **firm determination***, and we come together in this capacity that our faith and determination may be increased and strengthened.* - Brigham Young, Oct. 1870 General Conference

When shall we establish the principles of Zion? You can say, "I do not know." If we had power to do it, we should do it; but we are just in the position and condition, and upon precisely the same ground that God our Father is—He cannot force his children to do this, that or the other against their will . . . The consent of the creature must be had in these things, and <u>until you and I do consent in our feelings and understand</u>

that it is a necessity that we establish Zion, *we shall have Babylon mixed with us.* - Brigham Young, August 18, 1872

If we are to adopt the order of Zion now, it should become in our hearts **a cherished desire**, *an earnest and determined purpose that, in all our actions, we will seek to love our neighbor as ourselves, that we will labor for the good of Zion, and put away selfishness, corruption and false principles.* - George A. Smith, May 9, 1874

Eye Single to Building Zion and Not Babylon

Here are four quotes of twelve in which the Brethren explain that our eyes need to be single to building Zion. Several in Appendix A for this section show even more clearly that they did not want the Saints to labor for their own selfish motives, but for the good of all—perhaps that is what "pure in heart" actually means, not some kind of perfection, but unselfish motives.

Let your whole soul—affections, actions, wishes, desires, every effort and motive, and every hour's labor you perform be <u>*with a single eye to the building up the Zion of God*</u> *on the earth. If you will pursue this course, you will learn every day and make advancements every hour. But when you so love your property as to quarrel and contend about this, that, or the other trifling affair, as though all your affections were placed upon the changing, fading things of earth, it is impossible to increase in the knowledge of truth.* - Brigham Young, October 1859 General Conference

[D]o you want to be useful? If you do, take a course to be so, for this will bring us to the point where we can build up Zion and be of one heart and of one mind, and it will lead us to do all that we do in the name, in the love, and in the fear of our God. By so doing, if the fear of God is upon us, and we work **with an eye single to the building up of Zion**, *our labors will be blessed.* - Brigham Young, February 10, 1867

[T]he man who is faithful to his calling and to this holy Priesthood, never goes hunting for gold or silver unless he is sent. Such men are found following their legitimate pursuits, working in their fields, in their workshops and gardens, making beautiful their habitations; in other words, engaged building up and assisting to establish the Zion of God on the earth, **with their minds centered on the true riches and not upon the things of this world**. - Brigham Young, June 17, 1877, two months before his passing.

We will send out the Gospel to them, and continue to advocate the principles of truth, and to organize ourselves according to the order of God, and seek to be one—for if we are not one we are not the Lord's and never can be, worlds without end. Hear it, you Latter-day Saints! And do not be figuring for yourselves and for your own aggrandizement; but <u>feel to say in your hearts, "What can I do to help to build up Zion? I am here, and everything that I have got is upon the altar, and I am prepared to do the will of God no matter what it may be</u>, or where it sends me, to the ends of the earth or not." - President John Taylor, March 22, 1880

Prove to God we are Earnest about Building Zion

This subcategory is one that barely made the cut. Apostle Daniel H. Wells taught this concept three times within two years and, apparently, never again (there may be other occasions, but I didn't find them). Only because Elder Wilford Woodruff brought it up again twelve years later, do we include this topic now.

We need everything else that is necessary to build up any other kingdom, and we have to produce it from the elements with which we are surrounded. We have been brought far from the wicked world, to give us <u>an opportunity to show that we will do it</u>, or that we will not do it—<u>to prove our integrity to the cause of righteousness and to God</u>—to prove to him that we will struggle to obtain the knowledge and the ability to create the means of our own subsistence—that we will struggle to subdue the elements, to sanctify the earth, chase unholiness *from it, and beautify it by building up beautiful places, ornamenting our grounds, cultivating fruits of every variety that will flourish in our country, and thus bless ourselves with the blessings the Almighty has placed within our reach, and <u>prove to him that we are willing to abide his high behest</u>, acknowledging that he throws in our way all these advantages, <u>and by our works show that we are willing to make all our efforts point to the building up of the kingdom of God</u> . . .* - Daniel H. Wells, September 10, 1861

While we are professing to be righteous, **let us take a course to prove to God, angels, and men that we are in earnest, and will live and produce those things that are needed for our own sustenance, and build up cities and make Zion the joy of the whole earth.** *It is not a mere theory that we have to do with, but it is the building up of the kingdom of God, and it is for those who have the principles of the kingdom in their hearts to seek to permanently establish the Zion of God upon the earth, whether they will be able to maintain the kingdom or not is the Lord's business.* - Daniel H. Wells, September 29, 1861

Then let us step forward and take hold, <u>prove to God and angels</u> that we will strive to overcome this spirit of contention that is in the world, and each and all magnify our callings, get together and consult for the interests of the kingdom and for each other's welfare, <u>that we may act in unison in all things that there may be union throughout the house of Israel, and in all the branches and settlements of Zion</u>. - Daniel H. Wells, April 1862 General Conference

From the commencement of this work to the present day, the labor has been harder with the servants of God to get the people prepared in their hearts **to let the Lord govern and control them in their temporal labor and means** *than in regard to matters pertaining to their eternal salvation . . . This Gospel has been preached in every Christian nation under heaven where the laws would permit, and people from these various nations have overcome their traditions so far as to obey it; but, as I remarked before, it has been hard work for the Latter-day Saints to* bring themselves to such a state of mind as **to be willing for the Lord to govern them in their temporal labors**. There is something strange about this, but I think, probably, it is in consequence of the position that we occupy. There is a veil between man and eternal things; if that veil was taken away and we were able to see eternal things as they are before the Lord, no man would be tried with regard to gold, silver or this world's goods, and no man, on their account, would be unwilling to let the Lord control him. But here we have an agency, and we are in a probation, and there is a veil between us and eternal things, between us and our heavenly Father and the spirit world; and this for a wise and proper purpose in the Lord our God, **to prove whether the children of men will abide in his law or not in the situation in which they are placed here** . . . we certainly ought to be as ready to permit the Lord to govern and control us in all our temporal labors as we are in our spiritual labors. - Wilford Woodruff, May 8, 1874

You may have to go back and read that last quote slowly. What Elder Woodruff appears to be saying is that part of the test of life on this side of the veil is to see whether we will let the Lord govern us in *economic* as well as spiritual matters. It's hard to imagine that we can land in the celestial kingdom happy to be governed spiritually by God, but then we buy and sell as we please there without God's direction or organization. It should be obvious that we can't govern ourselves economically within the celestial kingdom down on a telestial or terrestrial level, we will have to happily conform to God's economic plan in order to be comfortable there.

That God would prefer we conform to his economic plan here in mortality is clear from D&C 105:1-9. Remember verse 5? "And Zion cannot be built up unless it is by the principles of the law of the celestial kingdom; otherwise I cannot receive her unto myself."

Verses 3 and 4 of that same section make it clear that the Lord is delaying the "redemption of Zion" (i.e. the taking back of full control of the lands for the future New Jerusalem) until his Saints are ready.

9 Therefore, in consequence of the transgressions of my people, it is expedient in me that mine elders should wait for a little season for the redemption of Zion—

*10 That they themselves may be prepared, and <u>that my people may be taught more perfectly,</u> **and have experience**, and know more perfectly concerning their duty, and the things which I require at their hands.*

"Have experience" with what? Babylon? No, with living on a Celestial level economically, as indicated in verse 4: "And are not united according to the union required by the law of the celestial kingdom". It's likely the Lord is talking here about the United Order of Enoch – an economic organization of God's people.

How can we "have experience" and become "prepared" to live a higher law, if we never attempt to do so? Can we gain experience in living on a Celestial level if all we do every day is to work our eight hours in Babylon for Babylon? The old adage "Practice makes perfect" suggests we have to actually *practice* living the higher law in order to get good at it! *When* should we start getting experience with it? After we die? . . . or now?

I believe that if Zion is in our hearts, we will work to show God that we are determined to build His Zion, and that He will open the way.

2. Zion in the Gospel

Again, the idea here is that many of the assertions by early LDS leaders concerning what is required of us to build Zion neatly fall under the heading of **Gospel**. It appears that they were suggesting by their comments that living the first principles and ordinances of the Gospel is required of those who "seek to bring forth my Zion at that day". This makes perfect sense in light of 1 Nephi 13:37 which promises "And blessed are they who shall seek to bring forth my Zion at that day, for they shall have the gift and the power of the Holy Ghost". Reception of the Holy Ghost, of course, is the promise to those who exercise faith, repent, and are baptized.

Let's look at quotes about Faith and Good Works

We all know that we have to live our religion here as well as in England; and I sometimes think it takes more faith to live in Zion than in another place . . . . - Ezra T. Benson, January 24, 1858

[F]aith is required on the part of the Saints to *live their religion, do their duty, walk uprightly before the Lord and* ***build up his Zion*** *on the earth. Then it requires works to correspond with our faith.* - Wilford Woodruff, October 1874 General Conference

And if we are faithful, *God will stand by Israel; he will preserve his elect; he will listen to our prayers: and we will go to work by his help to build up Zion and establish the Kingdom of God upon the earth.* - John Taylor, January 2, 1881

And now Repentance, with quotes from **Forsake Babylon's Values**, and, **Sanctify Ourselves**

Much patience and forbearance will need to be exercised before the Saints will get completely rid of their old traditions, Gentile notions, and whims *about property, so as to come to that perfect law required of them in the revelations of Jesus Christ. But the day will come when there will be no poor in Zion, but the Lord will make them equal in earthly things, that they may be equal in heavenly things; that is, according to His notions of equality, and not according to our narrow, contracted views of the same.* - Orson Pratt, April 1855 General Conference

I do not wish you to carry away a wrong impression of our true situation before the heavens relative to perfection. For you to be perfect, in one

*sense of the word, is to be prepared to inherit eternal glory in the presence of the Father and the Son. Should any mortal attain to this state of perfection, he could not longer remain among his fellow mortals. I do not want you so very perfect, but I am anxious that we should commence the growth of Zion in ourselves, and when we do this, we shall **cease to willingly hold fellowship with that which is evil**. But so long as we willingly hold fellowship with that which tends to death and destruction, we cannot progress as we should in the work of perfection in ourselves, nor in building up and beautifying Zion.* - Brigham Young, February 23, 1862

When Zion existed upon the earth it took 365 years to prepare the people thereof to be translated. But the Lord in these last days will cut His work short in righteousness. Therefore let us do right. . . . <u>do not be partakers of the practices of the wicked</u>. Do not mix up with the corrupt and evil. If they are hungry, feed them; if they are naked clothe them; if they are sick, administer to them; but <u>do not associate with them in their abominations and their corruptions</u>. <u>Come out from the world and be ye separate</u>, ye that bear the vessels of the Lord, and let "Holiness to the Lord" be written in every heart; and let us all feel that we are for Zion and for God and His Kingdom, and for those principles that will elevate us in time and throughout the eternities that are to come. - John Taylor, November 30, 1884

There are four more quotes about forsaking Babylon's values in Appendix A.

More on Repentance from the subcategory **Sanctify Ourselves**

We are all sinners, and it is our duty to cast sin from us when we learn what it is. If we are a little good, become a little better; if we have a little light, get a little more; if we have a little faith, add to it; and by-and-by we shall be prepared to build up and beautify Zion, and to be exalted to reign in immortality and be crowned with the Gods. - Brigham Young, July 22, 1860

7 - What is Required of Us to Establish Zion?

Let us look at our neighbors as they are, and not as we want them to be; let us learn enough to know what we are ourselves and what our brethren and sisters are, and learn the true designs of their hearts, and then judge them as God judges them and not according to outward appearance; then every contention will cease, every heart will beat high to build up Zion, and the follies and weaknesses of our neighbors we shall not think of. - Brigham Young, May 24, 1863

If the people in the world could sanctify themselves and prepare themselves to build up Zion they might remain scattered, but they cannot, they must be gathered together to be taught, that they may sanctify themselves before the Lord and become of one heart and of one mind. - Brigham Young, April 14, 1867

[Selfishness] produces disunion and is inconsistent with the profession of a Saint of God. We should labor, each and every one of us to <u>put such feelings from our hearts</u>, and then we, in our family organizations, should strive to promote the general interest of the members thereof; but the interest of Zion and the kingdom of God should be first with us all the time, for we are all members of that kingdom and its welfare is ours. - Wilford Woodruff, May 6, 1870

That last quote reminds me of what President Gordon B. Hinckley said 121 years later in the October 1991 General Conference. He stated, *"If we are to build that Zion of which the prophets have spoken and of which the Lord has given mighty promise, we must set aside our consuming selfishness. We must rise above our love for comfort and ease, and in the very process of effort and struggle, even in our extremity, we shall become better acquainted with our God."*

How's that coming?

After Faith and Repentance comes **Baptism**.

The quotes by early LDS leaders about what is required of us to build Zion under the subcategories of **Gather** and **Unify** seem to fit best here. Baptism, as mentioned above, is a covenant with God which includes an affirmation that we are "willing to bear one another's burdens, that they may be light" (Mosiah 18:8). The Church is the organization given humankind by God to unitedly govern ourselves in spiritual matters. This *unity* through mutual care and service can only be enjoyed if we *gather* together with other Saints after baptism. And, as many already know, the early LDS converts were encouraged to gather to Utah, as we today are encouraged to gather to the various "the Stakes of Zion" in our respective countries.

Here are a few of the dozen quotes showing the connection between gathering and building Zion, the rest are found in Appendix A:

[T]he Lord has set his hand to accomplish his designs in these last days; he has opened the heavens and revealed his purposes to his servants the Prophets, and has called his people from the ends of the earth to gather together, that he might establish his Zion upon the earth, and bring to pass these things which have been spoken of by all the holy Prophets since the world was. - John Taylor, January 10, 1858

*Go and preach the gospel, and help the honest-in-heart to **gather, that they may aid in building up Zion**, for that was the design of the Lord when He said, through the Revelator John, "Come out of her my people that ye be not partakers of her sins and that ye receive not of her plagues."* - Brigham Young, April 14, 1867

[The Lord] has got a great many good men on the earth, and he is gathering them together to build up Zion, to carry out his work and to do his will. - Wilford Woodruff, May 6, 1870

7 - What is Required of Us to Establish Zion?

*[T]he time had come, in the councils of heaven, that it was necessary to start the latter-day work, and to prepare a people, **gathering them together to build up Zion** and establish the kingdom of God upon the earth, that His will might be done upon the earth as it is done in heaven.*
- John Taylor, March 2, 1879

As baptized members, we are told by our early leaders in the quotes below that we cannot establish Zion without sharing a **unity** of purpose and becoming "like a single family". They taught that we cannot build Zion if we all are seeking our own interests (including our own economic interests), separate from each other.

Here are some of the early LDS leaders' teachings about how crucial unity is to building Zion:

This body of people, or church, has got to build up the Zion of God in the last days, and this work cannot be accomplished upon any other principle than that of our being united together as the heart of one man.
- Wilford Woodruff, April 1867 General Conference

We have come here to build up Zion. How shall we do it? I could tell you how if I had time. I have told you a great many times. There is one thing I will say in regard to it. We have got to be united in our efforts. We should go to work with a united faith like the heart of one man . . . -
Brigham Young, November 14, 1869

And I will tell you another thing, God will not be with us unless we are one. Says Jesus, "That they all may be one, as thou, Father, art in me, and I in thee, that they also may be one in us." "I in them, and thou in me, that they may be made perfect in one." And the oneness will not consist in each one of us seeking his own interest, his own emolument, and to extend his own ideas and influence; but in his seeking the interest and welfare of [each other], the establishment of Zion, that the welfare of all may be cared for and reached. - John Taylor, November 5, 1876

Saving the best for last:

We cannot build up a Zion unless we are in possession of the spirit of Zion, and of the light and intelligence that flow from God, and under the direction of the Priesthood, the living oracles of God, to lead us in the paths of life. We do not know them without, and we need all these helps to lead us along, <u>that by and by we may come to such a unity in our temporal and in our spiritual affairs</u> . . . that we may be prepared to enter a Zion here upon the earth . . . and so operate and cooperate with the Gods in the eternal worlds, and with the Patriarchs, Prophets, Apostles, and men of God . . . **we want to be one with them, one with God, and one with each other, for Jesus said—"Except you are one you are not mine."** - John Taylor, August 31, 1875

See additional quotes under Unity in Appendix A.

Perhaps unless we unite together "as the heart of one man", we may be guilty of what the Lord warned against in His preface to the Doctrine & Covenants:

They seek not the Lord to establish his righteousness, but <u>every man walketh in his own way,</u> and after the image of his own god, whose image is in the likeness of the world, and whose substance is that of an idol, which waxeth old and shall perish in Babylon, even Babylon the great, which shall fall. (D&C 1:16)

Gift of the Holy Ghost: **Inspiration/Revelation**

Here it is pretty obvious that the topic taught by our Champions for Zion regarding the need for inspiration and revelation in order to build Zion, fits neatly with the 4th of the Gospel's first principles & ordinances – The Gift of the Holy Ghost. Without it we would be greatly disadvantaged in any effort to accomplish God's will in regards to the establishment of Zion.

7 - What is Required of Us to Establish Zion?

The following, along with the other great quotes in Appendix A, show quite clearly the need for inspiration and revelation for Zion to be built.

The Lord is building up Zion, *and is emptying the earth of wickedness, gathering his people, bringing again Zion, redeeming his Israel, sending forth his work, withdrawing his Spirit from the wicked world, and commencing to build up his kingdom.* **Can this be done without revelation? No.** *You will not make a move, or do anything—plant corn, build a hall or a temple, make a farm, or go to the States—no, not a thing towards building up Zion, without the power of revelation.* - Brigham Young, July 28, 1861

Do you want to know the true policy of building up Zion, *and what is required of us as a people? I can give it to you . . . if we live every day of our lives so as to possess the Spirit of the Lord, and are dictated in all our business transactions and in every move we make by the spirit of revelation, we should merit, and justly and righteously obtain greater blessings than we now possess.* - Brigham Young, April 1867 General Conference

In all these various dispensations God has directly spoken from the heavens; he has communicated his will to the human family. He has raised up revelators and inspired them, he has filled his servants with the spirit of prophecy, that they should foretell the future. He has inspired them to write revelations, and hence in all these different dispensations the God of heaven has thus authorized the children of men to build up his Zion on the earth, and without these no such thing as Zion can be built up among the children of men. - Orson Pratt, March 10, 1872

Our position, as Latter-day Saints, is such that **unless we have the guidance of the Lord our God**, *we are very likely to become involved in a series of difficulties and troubles. This work cannot be built up by man. Man's power, man's wisdom, man's skill, are all insufficient to establish and to carry on the work of our God in the earth connected with the building up of Zion. It is a glorious reflection that from the time this work* *was founded in these, the last days, up to present time, there has never been a moment when this people have been destitute of the guidance of the Lord, and of the revelations and counsel necessary to enable them to carry out the mind and will of the Lord. At no time have we been left to ourselves. At no time have the Latter-day Saints been at a loss to learn and to find out the mind and will and counsel of God concerning them, either as individuals or as a people.* - George Q. Cannon, October 29, 1882

In one of my dreams while in Arizona, I had the same admonition from President Young. I thought he was attending one of our conferences. I said to him: "Can you speak to us?" "No," he replied, ". . . But I want you to teach the Latter-day Saints to labor to obtain the Holy Spirit. It is one of the most important gifts that the Saints of the living God can possess. <u>You all need this</u>," he said, "<u>in order to build up Zion</u>. If you have not this Spirit—the Spirit of the Holy Ghost, the testimony of Jesus, the testimony of the Father and Son—you cannot get along. But if you are in possession of this Spirit, your minds will be open to comprehend the things of God." This is true. There is not a man in this Church and kingdom today, who, if he is in possession of this spirit, will set his heart upon the things of this world. Any man that loves the world, the love of the Father is not in him. We have received something better than the love of gold, silver, houses and lands; we have received the promise of eternal life. - Wilford Woodruff, December 10, 1882

*We are building up the Zion of God, and He is to be our instructor. We are building up the kingdom of God, and He is to be our guide. We are building up the Church of God, and **unless we are under the guidance and influence of the Spirit of God**, we neither belong to the Church of God, the Zion of God, nor the kingdom of God. And hence it is necessary that we should comprehend the position we occupy.* - President John Taylor, February 11, 1883

7 - What is Required of Us to Establish Zion?

3. Zion in the Temple

The third grand heading under which all the requirements for building Zion appear to fall is that of the Temple. As mentioned above, we LDS have developed a cultural aversion to speaking of anything that goes on in our temples. So, I will just share the quotes below and assume the temple-attending Saints will see how they relate.

Obedience

<u>What does this obedience lead people to</u>? It leads them to go where they are required to go, and to stay where they may be required to stay; in fine, it leads them to perform every labor that is required at their hands in the building up of the kingdom of God, and <u>the establishing of Zion</u>, or the cause of truth on the earth. - Amasa M. Lyman, December 2, 1855

Now I ask the Latter-day Saints, have you anything to fear? Yes, you have. Have I anything to fear? Yes. What is it? I fear lest I may slacken in my faith and <u>obedience</u> in living as the Spirit of the Lord Almighty has required me to live, and is urging this people to live, <u>so that we may be worthy to build up Zion</u>. - Brigham Young, April 17, 1870

We, the Latter-day Saints, have this great almighty work laid upon us, and our hearts should not be set upon the things of the world, for if they are we shall forget God and lose sight of his kingdom. The counsels, exhortations and instructions which we receive from the servants of God are just and true. As a people **if we will do the will of God we have the power to build up Zion** in beauty, power and glory, as the Lord has revealed it through the mouth of the Prophet. It rests with us, the Lord working with us. - Wilford Woodruff, April 1873 General Conference

If we were united . . . we could become rich, if riches were the desire of our hearts, there is nothing to prevent us; <u>if we will be guided by the counsel of God's servants</u>, we can have all the riches that heart can desire. But our miserable, shortsighted selfishness, that miserable, contracted, narrow policy that is not of God, blinds our eyes and darkens our understandings, and prevents us from seeing the true policy of building up the Zion of God on the earth, and preserving the liberty which God has given unto us. - George Q. Cannon, October 1875 General Conference

It is for us all to take a course that we may secure the favor and approbation of the Almighty, that we individually may be led by him, having his spirit always with us. Then if the Presidency be under the guidance of the Almighty, and God direct the Priesthood through them in all its ramifications, **carrying out his will in the building up of Zion** on the earth, then we shall be one with them and one with God. This is what we are after, and may God help us to carry out his purposes and designs. - John Taylor, November 5, 1876

Sacrifice

How was this miracle of Enoch's city accomplished? Not by an empty and vain profession of righteousness; not by men seeking themselves, and their own honor and glory; not by heaping up gold and silver and precious stones; not by making a golden calf and bowing down and worshiping it; not by the rich grinding under heel the poor; not by the proud despising the humble; not by the poor hating and envying the rich. It was not done by loving the things of this world. But it was <u>by the practice of the grand principle of self-denial, the principle of sacrifice</u>— the foundation stone of the great fabric of human salvation. - Orson F. Whitney, September 22, 1889

[A]ll that the Latter-day Saints have to do is to live within the confines of God's holy law and up to their privileges. Are we doing so? Are we walking in accordance with these principles? Let us ask ourselves these questions, and if any of us are remiss, let us immediately commence to reform, humble ourselves before God, and **be ready to sacrifice ourselves and all we have, if necessary, for the building up and**

redemption of Zion *and for our salvation.* - George A. Smith, May 5, 1870

We hold ourselves ready to go at a moment's warning to the uttermost parts of the earth to subserve the principles of our holy religion, by making them known to others, to save Israel and bring out those the Lord has scattered, to aid in building up Zion, and in building temples of the Most High, wherein we may go and receive the blessings of eternity. <u>We hold our property—our possessions—on the altar, ready at a moment's notice to be handed over to subserve the cause of Zion</u>. - Daniel H. Wells, February 22, 1857

[I]n 1833, the Saints commenced to build a Temple in Kirtland, the cost of which was not less than one hundred thousand dollars. A mere handful of Saints commenced that work, but they were full of faith and energy, **and willing, as they supposed, to sacrifice everything for the building up of Zion**. - George A. Smith, March 18, 1855

<u>Live the Gospel</u>

We have a great deal to do to destroy wickedness and establish righteousness upon the earth, and to prepare ourselves for the establishment of Zion, that she may become the head upon the earth. Will we bear correction and proper tutorage? Will we bear chastisement and throw aside our own faults and frivolous actions? <u>Will we live our religion</u>, or will we give way to every foolish thing that comes in our path . . . ? - Daniel H. Wells, September 30, 1860

Let us be just, merciful, faithful and true, and **let us live our religion, and we shall be taught all things pertaining to the building up of Zion**. Let us train our minds until we delight in that which is good, lovely and holy, seeking continually after that intelligence which will enable us effectually to build up Zion . . . . - Brigham Young, May 24, 1863

We talk about being a good people. Well, we are when compared with the rest of the world; but we ought to be twenty times better than we are today. And if we, as Latter-day Saints, were to <u>strictly observe the Sabbath day, and pay our tithes and offerings, and meet our engagements, and be less worldly minded</u> . . . Zion would arise and shine, and the glory of God would rest upon her. - John Taylor, July 7, 1878

<u>Law of Consecration</u>

Now I believe that before the redemption of Zion, there will be a voluntary feeling to carry out the celestial law. I found my belief on the prophecies that are given in the Book of Doctrine and Covenants. The Lord has said . . . that it is needful that Zion should be built up according to the law of the celestial kingdom, or I cannot receive her unto myself. He cannot receive her only as she is built up according to <u>the full law of consecration</u>. All the Zions that have ever been redeemed, from all the creations that God has made, have been redeemed upon that principle . . . Therefore <u>if the latter-day Zion would be counted worthy to mingle with the ancient Zion of Enoch</u>, caught up before the flood, if they would be counted worthy, when the Zion of Enoch comes, to be caught up to meet them, and to fall upon their necks and they to fall upon the necks of the Latter-day Saints, <u>and if they would enjoy the same glory, the same exaltation with ancient Zion, they must comply with the same law.</u> "I cannot receive Zion to myself," saith the Lord, "unless built up by this law." - Orson Pratt, August 16, 1873

Hence we learn that the Saints in Jackson County and other localities, refused to comply with the order of consecration, consequently they were allowed to be driven from their inheritances; and should not return until they were better prepared to keep the law of God, by being more perfectly taught in reference to their duties, and learn through experience the necessity of obedience. And I think **we are not justified in anticipating the privilege of returning to build up the Center Stake of Zion, until we shall have shown obedience to the law of consecration.**

One thing, however, is certain, we shall not be permitted to enter the land from whence we were expelled, till our hearts are prepared to honor this law, and we become sanctified through the practice of the truth. - Lorenzo Snow, October 1873 General Conference

If ever we build up a Zion here on this continent, and in case Zion ever comes down to us, and we expect it will, or that ours will go up to meet it, <u>we have got to be governed by the same principles that they are governed by, or we cannot be one</u>. - John Taylor, October 1874 General Conference

The Lord, in Kirtland, established a United Order. He called certain individuals, and united them by revelation, and told them how to proceed . . . He told those people and the Church afar off, to listen and hearken to what he required of men in this Order, and of every man who belonged to the Church of the living God—that all that they received above what was necessary for the support of their families, was to be put in the Lord's storehouse, for the benefit of the whole Church. This is what is required of every man in his stewardship. And this is a law that is required to be observed by every man who belongs to the Church of the living God. Now, this is one of the main features of the United Order. We are not going to stop here, in these valleys of the mountains. **Many of us expect to go forth and build up the Center Stake of Zion; but before we are called, we must understand these things, and conform to them more practically than many of us do at the present time***.* - Lorenzo Snow, April 21, 1878

Summary

I personally find it remarkable that all the teachings of the early LDS leaders about what is required of us to establish Zion appear to fit neatly under the three headings mentioned: Heart, Gospel, and Temple.

Under Heart:

We must 1) get Zion into our hearts, 2) we must truly desire it, 3) our eye must be single to building Zion, and 4) we must demonstrate to God through our actions that we earnestly seek to build Zion.

Under Gospel:

We must 1) exercise Faith and Good Works, 2) Sanctify ourselves and Forsake Babylon's values, 3) Gather with the Saints and develop Unity, and 4) Operate by Inspiration and Revelation.

Under Temple:

We must be governed by the principles of Obedience, Sacrifice, the Law of the Gospel, and the Law of Consecration.

Afterthoughts

It's almost as if the Gospel were restored and temples built in order that a people would be prepared by its doctrines and covenants to establish Zion, in order to prepare a people to receive the Savior upon His return. It's almost as if establishing Zion was the whole point of the Restoration—to raise the world up to the level where Celestial beings would be comfortable coming here.

Chapter Eight – Building Zion Is Spiritual AND Temporal!

One of the many remarkable things garnered from the numerous quotes about building Zion was that there was much more to it than the spiritual effort to become "pure in heart". From the quotes below, we will see that to the early LDS leaders, Zion-building was as much a "temporal" labor as a spiritual one.

It is a False Christian Tradition that God's Kingdom and Zion are Only Spiritual

The following three quotes show us clearly that early LDS leaders believed that God has as much right to direct our lives in temporal matters as He does in spiritual matters. They taught that religion encompasses the temporal as much as the spiritual, that prophets' directions in temporal matters are just as binding on us as the spiritual directives they give.

*You know the old theory is that the kingdom of God, and all pertaining to it, is spiritual and not temporal; <u>that is the traditional notion of our brother Christians</u>. But a person may merely think until he goes down to the grave, and he will never be the means of saving one soul, not even his own, unless he adds **physical labor** to his thinking. He must think, and pray, and preach, and <u>toil and labor with mind and body, in order to build up Zion in the last days</u>. - Brigham Young, October 1855 General Conference*

*Do we believe fully that God our Father has appointed men whom he influences day by day to lead forth his people, and direct them in all their spiritual <u>and</u> temporal labors? And do we so order our course as to correspond with the instructions given us? Or do we suppose we can entirely take our own way in temporal matters, **according to the traditions of our fathers** and the dictations of the spirit of the world, and at the same time please high Heaven, and do our duty faithfully in the building up of the kingdom of God? We think in spiritual "Mormonism," we need direction and constant instruction by the authorized servants of God; but we think we know as much about temporal affairs as anybody. We rejoice in the knowledge that has been revealed from the heavens to us; we rejoice in the word of the Lord that has gone forth; we rejoice that God has spoken in these last days, and that we have received these most valuable instructions—that we have received the knowledge that leads to life and salvation, and to exaltation in his kingdom. But do we realize that <u>God's kingdom in the latter days is to all intents and purposes a temporal kingdom</u>? . . . When [Christ] comes, he is going to reign over a temporal kingdom, composed of men and women who do his will on the earth. Everything that pertains to us in our life is temporal, and over us and all we possess our Heavenly Father and his Son Jesus Christ will reign, as well as over all the kingdoms of the world when they become the kingdoms of our God and his Christ.* - Daniel H. Wells, September 10, 1861

There is that terrible tradition, *that has such strong hold of all our minds,* **that the Priesthood of God and the religion of Jesus Christ have nothing to do particularly with temporal matters.** *It is a tradition almost as old as Christianity. It has come down to us for generations and centuries, and is fully interwoven in the hearts, minds and feelings of the children of men, and it is an exceedingly difficult thing to get them to comprehend that <u>temporal things and spiritual things are alike in the sight of God</u>; that there is no line of demarcation between the two; that the religion of Jesus Christ applies to one as much as another, and comprehends within its scope, temporal equally with spiritual matters.* - George Q. Cannon, November 13, 1870

8 - Building Zion Is Spiritual AND Temporal!

Building Zion has a Strong Temporal Element

To build up Zion is a <u>temporal</u> labor; it does not consist simply in teaching: teaching is to instruct us how to properly <u>apply</u> our labor . . . Bone and sinew is required to build up the kingdom of God in the last days. - Daniel H. Wells, September 10, 1861

The work of building up Zion is in every sense a practical work; it is not a mere theory. *A theoretical religion amounts to very little real good or advantage to any person. To possess an inheritance in Zion . . . —only in imagination—would be the same as having no inheritance at all. -- Then let us not rest contented with a mere theoretical religion, but let it be practical, self-purifying, and self-sustaining . . .* - Brigham Young, February 23, 1862

We have to build up Zion, <u>a temporal work</u> here upon the face of the earth . . . When I say a temporal work, I speak of temporal things. The Zion of our God cannot be built up in the hearts of men alone . . . - Wilford Woodruff, April 1867 General Conference

Strangers may think this a very strange subject to present in a religious meeting, but we are building up the literal kingdom of God on the earth, and we have temporal duties to perform. We inhabit temporal bodies, we eat temporal food, we build temporal houses, we raise temporal cattle and temporal wheat; we contend with temporal weeds, and with temporal enemies in our soil, and these things naturally give rise to the necessity of attending to and performing many duties of a temporal and arduous nature, and they, of course, are embraced in our religion. **In building up the Zion and kingdom of God in these latter days, our agricultural and manufacturing interests are of the most vital importance**; *in fact manufacturing and agricultural pursuits are of vital importance to any nation under heaven.* - Wilford Woodruff, April 1872 General Conference

We have it to do, we can't build up Zion sitting on a hemlock slab singing ourselves away to everlasting bliss; we have to cultivate the earth, to take the rocks and elements out of the mountains and rear Temples to the Most High God; and <u>this temporal work is demanded at our hands by the God of heaven</u> . . . This is the great dispensation in which the Zion of God must be built up, and we as Latter-day Saints have it to build. People think it strange because so much is said with regard to this . . . [W]e never shall perform the work that God Almighty has decreed we shall perform unless we enter into these temporal things. We are obliged to build cities, towns and villages, and we are obliged to gather the people from every nation under heaven to the Zion of God, that they may be taught in the ways of the Lord. - Wilford Woodruff, October 1873 General Conference

Building Zion Requires Actual Physical Labor

...for if we are to build up the kingdom of God, or establish Zion upon the earth, we have to labor with our hands, plan with our minds, and devise ways and means to accomplish that object. - Brigham Young, July 13, 1855

If we talk to you and you sit and hear, that involves labor, and everything connected with building up Zion requires actual, severe labor. It is nonsense to talk about building up any kingdom except by labor; it requires the labor of every part of our organization, whether it be mental, physical, or spiritual, and that is the only way to build up the kingdom of God. - Brigham Young, October 1855 General Conference

As members of the body of Christ we are called upon to labor and to do our part towards building up his kingdom, and should all have equal interest in that kingdom. We manifest our attachment to the principles of progress and improvement, both of which are intimately connected with the building up of Zion, when we plant orchards and vineyards, and when we make good gardens, good farms, and when we build good houses; in doing all of which we get a liberal reward as we go along.

8 - Building Zion Is Spiritual AND Temporal!

Then let us stretch forth our hands and build up the towns and cities of Zion. - Heber C. Kimball, September 2, 1863

And it looks like this idea has carried over to more recent years:

The Prophet had a design to build a community of Saints. He had three major objectives: first, economic; second, educational; and third, spiritual . . . The second basic principle is that of work. Work is just as important to the success of the Lord's economic plan as the commandment to love our neighbor. - L. Tom Perry, April 2001 General Conference

We Must be Ready to Physically Build the New Jerusalem

Let every [tradesman] *and every scientific man of all classes and occupations, and every woman, improve to the best of their ability, faithfully living their religion, and we shall be none too well qualified to build up Zion when that time arrives. I never saw a stonemason who thoroughly understood his trade. We have not a quarryman who fully understands getting out rock for the Temple walls. Then <u>how, amid such ignorance, are you going to properly lay the foundation of the New Jerusalem—the Zion of our God</u>?* - Brigham Young, June 3, 1860

I know how to build a meetinghouse—how to place the first and last stone and piece of board, and how to put on the first and last touch of paint. I know how to build a mill and put the machinery in it, and I intend to keep improving as long as I live. There are mechanical branches that I do not understand, but I am constantly trying to learn. **Should I live—** *and I would not then be a very old man—***to hear the command, "Return and build the Center Stake of Zion," I intend to know how to build it***. - Brigham Young, June 12, 1860

Here we learn the arts of cultivation and of building; we learn to irrigate the land; we also, in many respects, prepare ourselves for a day when we shall go to the place that has been appointed for the building up of

the city of Zion and for the building of the house which shall be a great and glorious temple, on which the glory of the Lord shall rest—a temple that will excel all others in magnificence that have ever been built upon the earth. Who is there that is prepared for this movement back to the Center Stake of Zion, <u>and where are the architects amongst us that are qualified to erect this temple and the city that will surround it</u>? We have to learn a great many things, in my opinion, before we are prepared to return to that holy land; we have to learn to practice the principles that we have been taught; we have to study to fill up every hour of our time in industrial pursuits and the acquisition of knowledge, and by economy and patience <u>prepare ourselves as good and skillful workmen, as builders</u> in the great building which our Father has prepared. - George A. Smith, May 10, 1861

Building Zion requires our full-time labor

President Young tried to get the early Utah Saints to labor every day, "hour to hour" for the building up of the Kingdom and the establishment of Zion. These quotes all have in common the idea that we can labor for Zion all day, every day.

No man is going to inherit a celestial glory, who trifles with the principles thereof. <u>The man who does not labor from day to day and from hour to hour for building up this Kingdom</u> and bringing forth the fulness of the Kingdom of God on the earth, <u>and the establishment of Zion</u>, will sooner or later, fall and go out of the Church. - Brigham Young, June 29, 1864

*Let us be thankful for what we have in possession, and use it exclusively for building up the kingdom of God, the establishment of Zion, and the triumph of righteousness and truth. Let every penny, every dollar, every sum of money, large or small, be devoted to this all-absorbing interest, as also **every moment of time**.* - Brigham Young, January 26, 1862

Then I say let the blacksmith attend to his blacksmithing and let him charge a reasonable price for his labor, and not, as has been the custom, charge three or four prices. Let the joiner do likewise, <u>working constantly at that which will most conduce to the building up of Zion</u>, and let the farmer raise the grain. Where you find a man who has plenty of grain to serve him from three to five years . . . tell him to go to work and build for his family a comfortable dwelling house, and point out to him that he is in this way finding employment for the mechanics, making his family comfortable and building up Zion. - Orson Hyde, October 1862 General Conference

And our mechanics [i.e. tradesmen], <u>do they labor for the express purpose of building up Zion and the kingdom of God</u>? I am sorry to say that I think there are but very few into whose hearts it has entered, or whose thoughts are occupied in the least with such a principle; but it is, "How much can I make?" If our mechanics would work upon the principle of establishing the Kingdom of God upon the earth, and building up Zion, they would, as the prophet Joseph said, in the year 1833, never do another day's work but with that end in view. - Brigham Young, February 3, 1867

Here is Brother Woodruff, President of the Twelve Apostles. Is there any man in Israel who has **worked harder to support himself and family** than he? He is known for his persistent industry. He has set the people a great example in that respect. He has not been a burden to anyone. He has labored from morning till night for this people and for their salvation. He has not fattened upon your earnings, he has sustained himself by the blessing of God. And so have the rest of the Twelve. <u>They have labored continually for this people</u>. They have traveled thousands of miles, gone to the ends of the earth, to build up Zion, and not counted anything too great a labor. <u>That is the example the Twelve have set this people</u>. - George Q. Cannon, October 1881 General Conference

Building Zion apparently was not a nights-and-weekends activity, but to be done all day, every day. It appears from this that our motive for our daily work should be to build Zion.

We Can't Think, Talk, or Sing Zion into Existence

We can get up in our meeting and sing—"The cities of Zion soon shall rise." but how are they going to rise? <u>We are going to build them</u>, so that they will rise far above the clouds; and to accomplish this we are going to build them on the high mountains. **We are not only going to sing about building them, but we are going to do the labor requisite to carry out our designs***. - George A. Smith, October 20, 1861*

We talk and read about Zion, we contemplate upon it, and in our imaginations we reach forth to grasp something that is transcendent in heavenly beauty, excellency, and glory. But while contemplating the future greatness of Zion, do we realize that we are the pioneers of that future greatness and glory? <u>Do we realize that if we enjoy a Zion in time or in eternity, we must make it for ourselves</u>? That all who have a Zion in the eternities of the gods organized, framed, consolidated, and perfected it themselves, and consequently are entitled to enjoy it. - Brigham Young, February 23, 1862

We are not called to build up Zion by preaching, singing and praying alone; we have to perform hard labor, labor of bone and sinew, *in building towns, cities, villages; and we have to continue to do this; but while we are so engaged, we should not sin. We have no right to sin, whether we are in the canyon drawing wood, or performing any other hard labor, and we should have the Spirit of God to direct us then as much as when preaching, praying, singing and attending to the ordinances of the house of God. If we do this as a people we shall grow in the favor and power of God. We should be united together, it is our duty to be so. - Wilford Woodruff, January 12, 1873*

And another of this author's all-time favorite quotes about Zion:

We have it to do, **we can't build up Zion sitting on a hemlock slab singing ourselves away to everlasting bliss**; *we have to cultivate the earth, to take the rocks and elements out of the mountains and rear*

8 - Building Zion Is Spiritual AND Temporal!

Temples to the Most High God; and this temporal work is demanded at our hands by the God of heaven . . . This is the great dispensation in which the Zion of God must be built up, and we as Latter-day Saints have it to build. - Wilford Woodruff, October 1873 General Conference

Summary

From the quotes covered in this chapter we see the early Brethren were teaching these remarkable ideas:

1. Building Zion has a strong temporal element.
2. Building Zion requires actual physical labor.
3. We must be ready to physically build the New Jerusalem Zion society.
4. Building Zion requires our full-time labor; it's not a nights-and-weekends project.
5. We can't think, talk, or sing Zion into existence; we have to physically build it.

Afterthoughts

You may have noticed reading many of the quotes above that the Brethren mentioned certain activities as "temporal" where we today would use the term "economic" to describe productive labors in agriculture, manufacturing, and construction. Interestingly, the term "economic" is not used at all (as we use it today) in any recorded talk given by a general authority until the year 1906. We use the term today to refer to the production and distribution of goods and services. Apparently, in the early days of the Church, the word "temporal" referred to those things we call economic; and, as we have seen above, they made abundant use of that term in regards to building Zion.

If the above apostolic statements are accepted as true, and the term "temporal" was indeed used then to mean what "economic" means to us today, then it seems clear that building Zion is substantially (if not mostly) an *economic* activity. Today, most of us Saints work in businesses, schools, and government agencies that often are saturated with values opposite of Zion's. Just think! What if we could spend our full-time labor, Monday through Friday, 8 to 5, working in Zion-style organizations instead?! Now that too is a remarkable idea, isn't it?

Chapter Nine – Babylon, Zion's Opposite

In order to better understand the next few chapters, we pause here and review what the early LDS leaders taught about Babylon. Why Babylon? Because we can learn a great deal about something by studying its opposite.

In the October 2008 General Conference, in his talk entitled, "Come to Zion", Elder D. Todd Christofferson made a simple, yet profound statement about the relationship between Zion and Babylon. He said, "The antithesis and antagonist of Zion is Babylon." In simpler terms, Zion and Babylon are opposites, not like some consider men and women to be opposites (though they can work well together), Babylon and Zion are two incompatible, irreconcilable social systems. Or, as Elder Stephen L. Richards put it in the October 1951 General Conference, "Their underlying concepts, philosophies, and purposes are at complete variance one with the other."

By learning about an attribute of Babylon, we can then ask, "What is the opposite of that trait?" And it is quite likely that the opposite is an attribute of Zion, and vice versa.

What is Babylon?

The early Brethren taught about Babylon in both generalities and specifics. Let's start with the generalities. Note how often Zion is described as being the alternative to Babylon:

Describing his travels out in "Babylon", Elder John Taylor, in 1852, gave this description:

I feel as though I am among the honorable of the earth when I am here; and when I get mixed up with the people abroad, and mingle with the great people in the world, I feel otherwise. I have seen and deplored the weakness of men—their folly, selfishness, and corruption. I do not know how they feel, but I have witnessed a great deal of ignorance and folly, I think there is a great deal of great littleness about them. There is very little power among them, their institutions are shattered, cracked, and laid open to the foundation. It is no matter what principle you refer to—if to their religion, it is a pack of nonsense; if to their philosophy and politics, they are a mass of dark confusion; their governments, churches, philosophy, and religion, are all darkness, misery, corruption, and folly. <u>I see nothing but Babylon wherever I go—but darkness and confusion, with not a ray of light to cheer the sinking spirits of the nations of the earth, nor any hope that they will be delivered in this world, or in the world to come.</u>

Similarly, Brigham referred to Babylon as a confused, corrupt and wicked society:

And one of the last writers we have here in this book—John the Revelator—looking at the Church in the latter days, says: "Come out of her, my people"—out of Babylon, out of this <u>confusion and wickedness</u>, which they call "civilization." Civilization! It is <u>corruption and wickedness of the deepest dye. It is no society for you</u>, my people, come out of her. Gather out . . . and begin to build up Zion. Now, "come out of her, my people," for this purpose, "and partake not of her sins, lest ye receive of her plagues." - Brigham Young, February 3, 1867

Apostle Erastus Snow referred to Babylon as "the worshippers of mammon":

*[C]ease to feed and build up the wicked who will not labor with us to develop the resources of the country and help to build up Zion. God has called us to turn away from the folly of sustaining and building up Babylon—**the worshippers of mammon—those who have no interest in common with us in establishing Zion** and building up the Kingdom of our God upon the earth.* - Erastus Snow, April 1868 General Conference

In the April 1873 General Conference, six years after his definition of Babylon given above, President Young defined the term again when he said, ". . . Babylon—I use this term, because it is well understood that Babylon means confusion, discord, strife, folly and all the vanities the world possesses."

From these quotes we can construct a general definition of Babylon to be a civilization or society made up of the selfish worshippers of mammon along with all its resulting confusion, conflict, vanities, and hopelessness.

A False Organization of Human Society

This concept of Babylon being a false organization of society spans the teachings of the early Brethren from 1854 all the way through 1883. Here are three additional quotes illustrating this idea:

The world is more or less controlled all the time by influences that Lucifer evidently is not opposed to; he has little objection to the present organization of human society, from the fact that everything passes along in the wake that agrees with his religion, and rather tends to forward his purposes. - Jedediah M. Grant, February 19, 1854

Now then, in regard to our temporal affairs, these are the things which seem to perplex us more or less. **We have been brought up in Babylon, and have inherited Babylonish ideas and systems of business**; *we have introduced, too, among us, all kinds of chicanery, deception and fraud. It is time that these things were stopped, and that matters assumed another shape; it is time that we commenced to place ourselves under the guidance and direction of the Almighty.* - John Taylor, August 31, 1875

The evils under which mankind groan today are attributable to <u>the false organization of society</u>. The evils under which we groan as a people and from which we suffer are not due to any lack of knowledge as the method or the means that will correct these evils, but they are due to the fact that we ourselves fail to conform to the organization which God has prescribed, which God has revealed [i.e. Zion]. - George Q. Cannon, May 6, 1883

Since Babylon and Zion are opposites, it may be safe to conclude that where Babylon is the false organization of society, Zion then would be the true organization of society, the one God wishes for his children to enjoy, if they will.

Every Man for Himself

On a more personal level, according to our early LDS leaders, in contrast to Zion, Babylon is characterized by individual families working for their own personal interests, putting their faith in riches, without much thought for the interests of others. We'll also underline here the hints that Babylon's domain included economic elements.

Are we going to be prepared for the coming of the Son of Man? Are we going to be prepared to enter into the fullness of the glory of the Father and the Son? Not so long as we live according to the principles of Babylon. Now we are every man for himself. One says: "This is my <u>property</u>, and I am for increasing it." Another says; "This is mine,"

Another: *"I will do as I please; I will go where I please and when I please; I will do this, that, or the other; and if I have a mind to raise <u>grain</u> here and take it to <u>market</u> and give it away, it is none of your business." It will be said to all such persons, who profess to be Latter-day Saints—"I never knew you; you never were Saints."* - Brigham Young, April 18, 1874

For the last dozen years many of this people have been going on in the way that our fathers and the world generally walk in; and **instead of building up Zion, have been after their personal and individual interests**. - Erastus Snow, May 8, 1874

But will they return after the old order of things that exists among the Gentiles—every man for himself, this individualism <u>in regard to property</u>? No, never, never while the world stands. - Orson Pratt, June 14, 1874

Now, so long as the Latter-day Saints are content to obey the commandments of God, to appreciate the privileges and blessings which they enjoy in the Church, and will use their time, their talents, their substance, in honor to the name of God, to build up Zion . . . but the moment a community begin to be wrapt up in themselves, become selfish, become engrossed in the temporalities of life, and put their faith in <u>riches</u>, that moment the power of God begins to withdraw from them, and if they repent not the Holy Spirit will depart from them entirely, and they will be left to themselves. - Joseph F. Smith, April 1883 General Conference

Babylon is self-focus mixed with avarice

In the Gentile world, where the Gospel first reached us, our manner of training, our habits and our education, all went to influence our minds to look after self, and never to let our contemplations or meditations go beyond that which pertained to ourselves. In making any exertion that would in any way tend <u>to benefit ourselves, to exalt ourselves, and assist us in amassing riches</u>, or in gathering information that would confirm or

aid in the bringing about this object, we considered we were doing first-rate, for that was the object of life with us . . . This is what our parents taught us to a great extent, and it mattered, with us, but very little, how or what course was pursued if we could gain those things we desired, if we could secure to ourselves those things which were necessary for our own comfort, and for our own individual temporal convenience. -
Lorenzo Snow, March 1, 1857

It is well understood that the human race have been traditioned to the utmost extreme that tradition could possibly be impressed in the human breast, **in the practice of covetousness, the worship of money, the love of earthly goods, the desire to possess property, to control wealth, has been planted in the breast, soul, and heart of almost every man in the world from generation to generation.** *It has been the great ruling Deity, and the object worshipped by the whole Christian world. It has found its way into the pulpit, into the monastery, into the cloister, and into every department of life. No man seems to desire an office, or is called upon to fulfil an office for the public good, but the first thing to be considered is, What will it pay? How much can we make? "Is there money in it?" The god of this world has dominion over the souls of men to an unlimited extent." -* George A. Smith, October 20, 1861

Babylon is in the hearts of the people, that is to say, there is too much of it. What did you come here for? "Why," says one, "I understood they were getting rich in Utah, and I thought I would gather up with the Latter-day Saints and get rich also." Without making many remarks on this subject, I want to say to every one of those who come up here, their minds filled with Babylon, and <u>*longing for the fashions and wealth of the world*</u>*, you may heap up gold and silver, but it will leave you, or you will leave it, you cannot take it with you, and you will go down to hell. -*
Brigham Young, April 1873 General Conference

This last quote by Orson F. Whitney, in a talk given September 22, 1889, paints a very clear picture of what Zion is not, and by contrast, what Babylon is actually:

How was this miracle of Enoch's city accomplished? Not by an empty and vain profession of righteousness; not by men seeking themselves, and their own honor and glory; not by heaping up gold and silver and precious stones . . . not by the rich grinding under heel the poor; not by the proud despising the humble; not by the poor hating and envying the rich. It was not done by loving the things of this world. But it was by the practice of the grand principle of self-denial, the principle of sacrifice—the foundation stone of the great fabric of human salvation.

The Saints Left Babylon for Utah

Within a 13 month period beginning in September of 1871, four of our apostolic Champions for Zion made mention of the fact that the Latter-day Saints left Babylon to come build Zion in Utah. Here are three quotes where they express their hope that the values of Babylon could be left behind by the Saints coming to Utah:

We are living in that eventful time, and the Lord has set his hand to gather his people. He has called them forth out of Babylon. His voice is calling aloud to the inhabitants of the earth to come out of Babylon that they receive not of her plagues and that they partake not of her sins. We do not want to bring Babylon here—the gathering place appointed by the Lord for his people; but we want to take every precaution and to adopt every preventive measure in our power to stay the inroads of the evils which characterize Babylon, which are so condemned in the laws of God, and which are so repugnant to the spirit of the gospel. - Joseph F. Smith, September 3, 1871

Now mark another prophecy. "I heard a great voice," says John, "from heaven, saying, 'Come out of her, O my people!'" Out of where? "Mystery Babylon, the Great"—out of this great confusion that exists throughout all the nations and multitudes of Christendom. "Come out of her, O my people, that ye partake not of her sins, that ye receive not of her plagues; for her sins have reached to the heavens, and God hath remembered her iniquities!" Is this being fulfilled? Do you see any indications of the people of God coming out from "Mystery Babylon the Great?" Yes, for forty-two years, and upwards, God has commanded his people . . . by a voice from heaven which has been published and printed, requiring all who receive the everlasting Gospel to come out from the midst of great Babylon. One hundred thousand Latter-day Saints, approximately speaking, now inherit these mountain regions. They are here because of this prediction of John, because of its being fulfilled, because of the voice that has come from heaven—the proclamation of the Almighty for his people to flee from amongst the nations of the earth. I need not say any more in regard to this prophecy; it is in the Bible, and is being fulfilled before the eyes of all people. - Orson Pratt, April 1872 General Conference

While I am on this subject let me say a few words with regard to dress, though I have not as much reason to do so here as I have in Salt Lake City and Ogden. You know that we are creatures subject to all the vanities of the world, and very subject to admiring its fashions. We have left Babylon, and instead of introducing it here we want it to stay yonder, and just as much as we can, no, that is the wrong word—just as much as we will . . . - Brigham Young, August 18, 1872

Clinging to Babylon

It didn't take long for the Brethren to see that though the Saints fled Babylon to Utah to build Zion, they unfortunately brought Babylon's values with them and were "clinging" to them.

<u>Some of the daughters of Zion do not seem willing to forsake the fashions of Babylon.</u> I to such would say hasten it, and let the woe that is threatened [in Isaiah 3:16] *on this account come, that we may get through with it, then we can go on and build up the Zion of God on the earth.* - Wilford Woodruff, October 1873 General Conference

Have we separated ourselves from the nations? Yes. And what else have we done? Ask ourselves the question, Have we not brought Babylon with

us? Are we not promoting Babylon here in our midst? Are we not fostering the spirit of Babylon that is now abroad on the face of the whole earth? I ask myself this question, and I answer, Yes, yes, to some extent and there is not a Latter-day Saint but what feels that we have too much of Babylon in our midst. **The spirit of Babylon is too prevalent here.** What is it? Confusion, discord, strife, animosity, vexation, pride, arrogance, self will and the spirit of the world. **Are these things in the midst of those called Latter-day Saints? Yes, and we feel this.** - Brigham Young, April 18, 1874

One thing is certain, that if God accomplishes with the Latter-day Saints what the prophets have foretold, and establishes his Zion, and he makes them a holy nation, a kingdom of priests, a peculiar people to himself, as he has promised, it will not be by our <u>clinging to Babylon</u> and to her foolish ways . . . - Erastus Snow, June 3, 1877

We must overcome the traditions of Babylon to build Zion

Incorrect traditions, though long followed, have to be surrendered, and we have to build up Zion. The plan of Zion contemplates that the earth, the gardens, and fields of Zion, be beautiful and cultivated in the best possible manner. <u>Our traditions have got to yield to that plan</u>, circumstances will bring us to that point, and eventually we shall be under the necessity of learning and adopting the plan of beautifying and cultivating every foot of the soil of Zion in the best possible manner. - George A. Smith, April 1856 General Conference

I will now ask a question of the Latter-day Saints . . . How long will it take us to establish Zion, the way we are going on now? You can answer this question . . . I suppose, and say, "If forty years has brought a large percentage of Babylon into the midst of this people, **how long will it take to get Babylon out and actually to establish Zion**?" . . . I can inform you on that subject—Until the father, the mother, the son and the daughter take the counsel that is given them by those who lead and direct them in building up the kingdom of God, they will never establish

Zion, no never, worlds without end. When they learn to do this, I do not think there will be much complaining or grumbling, or much of what we have heard about today—improper language to man or beast. I do not think there will be much pilfering, purloining, bad dealing, covetousness or anything of the kind; not much of this unruly spirit that wants everybody to sustain its possessor and let him get rich, whether anybody else does or not. - Brigham Young, August 18, 1872

Now the Latter-day Saints are gathering from all nations and tongues, with divers customs and habits and traditions, and we have brought them with us, unfortunately we could not leave ourselves behind, while we gathered to Zion. <u>Having brought ourselves along we have the labor of separating the follies of Babylon, the traditions of the fathers and every foolish way, learning something better as fast as we can</u>; and this is the duty that is upon us. Many sermons would be necessary to teach us this lesson; we shall need the lesson often repeated before we can learn these principles and practice them thoroughly; we shall need a great deal of self-control, and a great deal of effort on the part of the brethren to help us, and by mutually assembling together, by doing business together, by learning correct principles and then living them. - Erastus Snow, June 3, 1877

Babylon *Will* Fall

Our Champions for Zion also taught that Babylon will eventually fall, so the Saints must prepare for that eventuality or go down with her. They saw the fall of Babylon in economic terms, as does John the Revelator when he describes it in Revelation 18:

2 And he cried mightily with a strong voice, saying, Babylon the great is fallen, is fallen, and is become the habitation of devils, and the hold of every foul spirit, and a cage of every unclean and hateful bird.

3 For all nations have drunk of the wine of the wrath of her fornication, and the kings of the earth have committed fornication with her, and the

merchants of the earth are waxed rich through the abundance of her delicacies.

11 And the **merchants** of the earth shall weep and mourn over her; <u>for no man buyeth their merchandise any more</u>:

12 The **merchandise** of gold, and silver, and precious stones, and of pearls, and fine linen, and purple, and silk, and scarlet, and all thyine wood, and all manner vessels of ivory, and all manner vessels of most precious wood, and of brass, and iron, and marble,

13 And cinnamon, and odours, and ointments, and frankincense, and wine, and oil, and fine flour, and wheat, and beasts, and sheep, and horses, and chariots, and slaves, and souls of men.

14 And the fruits that thy soul lusted after are departed from thee, and all things which were dainty and goodly are departed from thee, and thou shalt find them no more at all.

15 The **merchants of these things, which were made rich by her,** shall stand afar off for the fear of her torment, weeping and wailing,

16 And saying, Alas, alas, that great city, that was **clothed in fine linen, and purple, and scarlet, and decked with gold, and precious stones, and pearls**!

17 For in one hour so great riches is come to nought. And every shipmaster, and all the company in ships, and sailors, and as many as **trade** by sea, stood afar off,

19 . . .Alas, alas, that great city, wherein were **made rich** all that had ships in the sea by reason of her costliness! for in one hour is she made desolate.

22 . . .and no **craftsman**, of whatsoever craft he be, shall be found any more in thee; and the sound of a millstone shall be heard no more at all in thee;

23 . . .for thy **merchants** were the great men of the earth . . .

Here are three quotes showing the awareness the Brethren had of Babylon's prophesied fall, and hints to their strategy for surviving that fall, which we will review in greater depth in the next chapter:

The day is not far distant when **we shall have to take care of ourselves**. *Great Babylon is going to fall, judgment is coming on the wicked, the Lord is about to pour upon the nations of the earth the great calamities which He has spoken of by the mouths of His prophets; and no power can stay these things. It is wisdom that we should lay the foundation to provide for ourselves.* - Wilford Woodruff, May 19, 1867

Let us sustain ourselves, for by and by Babylon will fall. *What will be the result? The merchants will stand and look at one another worse than they do in this city. No man will buy their merchandise; and they will look here and there for a customer; but there will be no one to buy their merchandise, and the cry will be, "Babylon is fallen, is fallen!" Is this day coming? Yes; just as sure as we are now living. We are hastening it with all possible speed, as fast as time and circumstances will admit, when it will be said, "Babylon is fallen, is fallen!"* **Are you going to prepare for it?** *We say we are the people of God and are building up the kingdom of God. We say we are gathered out of the nations to establish Zion. Let us prove it by our works . . .* - Brigham Young, January 2, 1870

It appears that we have gathered many to Zion who do not fully appreciate the great work of these days—namely, to place the people of God in a condition that they can sustain themselves, against the time that Babylon the Great shall fall. *Some will say that it is ridiculous to suppose that Babylon, the "Mother of Harlots," is going to fall. Ridiculous as it may seem, the time will come when no man will buy her merchandise, and when* **the Latter-day Saints will be under the necessity of providing for themselves**, *or going without.* - George A. Smith, May 6, 1870

Summary

In conclusion, we see through these quotes that the early LDS leaders in Territorial Utah saw "Babylon", Zion's opposite, as a false *economic* organization of society. That false organization with its foundation of the self-interested pursuit of wealth leads to "confusion, discord, strife, folly and all the vanities the world possesses". They also pointed out that Babylon's prophesied fall will lead to destruction and economic woe. To avoid going down with the ship Babylon, the Saints moved to Utah, but sadly, clung to Babylon's values. Our leaders pointed out that we can't build Zion unless we overcome the false traditions of Babylon.

Afterthoughts

If Babylon is a false economic organization bearing bad fruit, then Zion as its opposite, must be the *true* economic organization of God's people with all the temporal blessings God seeks for his children.

We see from the bolded comments in the last three quotes above that the early leaders saw the proper response to Babylon's prophesied fall was for the Saints to provide for themselves economically. They were to do this by producing the merchandise themselves that at some point they will be unable to buy from Babylon's merchants. Has God revoked the prophecies of Isaiah, Jeremiah, Daniel, and John the Revelator? Are they null and void? Or, will they come true? If so, shouldn't we prepare as well?

Our Champions for Zion saw the forthcoming collapse of Babylon as a problem. In the next chapter, we will learn that they saw economic independence from Babylon as the solution.

Chapter Ten – Building Zion Includes Economic Independence from Babylon

In this chapter we review the teachings of prominent LDS leaders during the mid-1800s about the concept that building Zion requires us to seek economic independence from the world. The remarkable teachings contained in this chapter fly in the face of the most widely-accepted principles of Economics today, forcing us to answer the question, "What is right? The teachings of God and his prophets, or man's wisdom?"

Economic dependence on the world invites trouble

The following three quotes, spanning ten years, show our Champions for Zion explaining that if a people are dependent on others for their sustenance, they open themselves to many troubles.

While we are dependent upon others, we are in a poor position to look at the condition of the United States at the present time. We are happily preserved from their commercial troubles. Our very isolation preserves us from broken banks and ruinous credit. Let us only use our judgment and proper care and industry, and <u>we shall be free from a thousand contingencies to which we are liable when we depend upon others</u>. - John Taylor, January 17, 1858

These are some of the benefits derived from obedience to the fulness of the Gospel, and it becomes us as Saints of the Most High to strive to *preserve ourselves pure and holy before him, to take hold of good and righteous principles like men and women of God, to labor to sustain our present existence, to sustain ourselves by drawing from the elements all those good things which he has placed within our reach, and thus become a really independent people, to be no longer dependent upon those who would gladly sell us for the cloth we have to wear. It becomes an experiment for us to sustain ourselves, though not exactly one that is liable to fail, but it is to see whether a righteous and holy people, coming out from the world, can draw from the elements that have been previously scattered around them for their own immediate sustenance and support, <u>or whether they will forever be dependent upon those who would destroy them</u>. - Daniel H. Wells, 1862*

*There are certain rules in life and certain principles to be observed by this people. They must cease trading with those who would destroy us. To be called out from the wicked, and then take a course to call the wicked to us, how inconsistent it is! If the Lord were to say, "I will let the wicked drive you again, and I will call you to another place, where there is no one to disturb you;" how long would it be until the course taken by many would call the wicked in among us again, to seek to destroy us? The Latter-day Saints must stop this course, or they will bring evil upon themselves, and we will have to leave. These are the things we have to learn. We have the privilege of choosing now. It is in our hands, it is within our power, whether **we will stay in these mountains and build up the Zion of our God, or make the wicked and ungodly fat by our labor and give them our possessions**. This many are doing, by running in debt to our enemies, and pursuing a course that is wrong. **If they do not cease it they will have cause to weep and mourn**. - Brigham Young, 1868*

Economic Dependence is Servitude

These quotes, spanning three decades, show our Champions for Zion explaining that being dependent on others for our sustenance makes us their servants and them our masters.

See how dependent we are, when we have got no bread, clothing, sugar, [etc.]; and <u>those who possess these articles hold us in servitude</u>. It is the duty of every man to go to work and raise or make what he needs for his own consumption. - Heber C. Kimball, May 12, 1861

When we produce our food and clothing in the country where we live, then are we so far independent of the speculating, moneymaking world outside, *whereas, if we were to [mine] gold, and make this our business, then should we become slaves to the producers of food and clothing, and make fortunes for speculators and freighters; and instead of working to build up Zion and its interests, we [would] be laboring to build up Gentile institutions and Gentile interests. When this people are prepared to properly use the riches of this world for the building up of the kingdom of God, He is ready and willing to bestow them upon us.* - Brigham Young, July 1, 1865

There are hundreds of Elders here who have traveled through England, Scotland, Wales, Germany, Switzerland, Norway and elsewhere, who know very well that the people were found in most of those lands in circumstances of slavery—bondage . . . There was nothing before the people but the prospect of starvation; and <u>they were subject to the will and caprice of their masters, and dependent upon them for their labor and daily bread</u>; and when work was dull, they had before them nothing but the prospect of being turned from their employment and to have their only source of obtaining food for themselves and families entirely cut off. They did not own a foot of land, a plough, an ox, a wagon, a cow, a mule, a horse, in fact, nothing they saw around them could they call their own. They were, in short, entirely dependent upon the will and disposition of their employers for what they wanted, and had to look to *them for their only means of gaining a living.* - Lorenzo Snow, October 1869 General Conference

There is no real wealth in metallic or paper currency, in drafts, letters of credit, or any other representative of value. At best they are only the representatives of wealth, though convenient in carrying on our trade. But the real wealth may be summed up in a few words, to be the comforts of life; that is to say what is needed for us and our families and those depending upon us. How are these obtained? We might say money, when we have the money to exchange for them, and when these commodities are to be bought. But where do they come from? They are not in the market unless somebody has produced them; if in the shape of food, some farmer has raised it; if clothing, some manufactory has produced it; if boots and shoes, somebody did the work. It is the labor of men's hands with the aid of machinery that produced these articles; if not by the labor of our community, by that of some other; and <u>if we are dependent upon other people then are we their servants and they our masters</u>. - Erastus Snow, 1877

Building Zion Zion Includes Manufacturing All our Consumer Goods

Here is yet another remarkable teaching of the early LDS leaders that has somehow escaped us today. Economics 101 teaches otherwise, but the Brethren taught in the mid-1800s that not only must Zion become economically independent from Babylon, but that we achieve that independence by manufacturing our own consumer goods! Note how three of these five quotes were given in General Conference.

I hope all that has been said by the brethren in reference to the culture of hemp, flax, indigo, and in fact <u>all that will tend to build up Zion will be attended to</u>, for let it be remembered that it is coming to this necessity of producing for ourselves or to go without, and the question resolves itself into the simple proposition, "Clothes or no clothes." We must make our own woolen, flax, hemp, and cotton goods or we must go naked. - George A. Smith, October 1862 General Conference

10 - Building Zion Includes Economic Independence from Babylon

*Man's wants are very numerous, but his necessities are really very few, and we should abridge our wants, and go to work and manufacture everything we can within ourselves; and what we cannot manufacture we can import, and save ourselves the 40, 120, 400, or 1,000 percent that we are now paying for our merchandise, and so stop building up those who are laying a foundation, openly and above board, for our destruction. And furthermore, cease to fellowship every man that will not **build up Zion**. Amen.* - George A. Smith, October 1868 General Conference

We want to get at a correct understanding respecting all these matters which so materially concern us. <u>What would be the first lesson necessary to teach the people, were we to commence to direct their labors to the great end of becoming of one heart and one mind in the Lord, of establishing Zion and being filled with the power of God?</u> It would be to stop expending and lavishing upon our dear selves all needless adornments and to stop purchasing the importations of Babylon. We can ourselves produce everything necessary for our consumption, our wear, our convenience and comfort, right here at home . . . We can improve on what has been done, and we want you to do so. Plant out the mulberry tree, and raise the silk, and let your dresses, your shawls, your bonnets and your ribbons, and everything you use to clothe and adorn your bodies, be the workmanship of your own hands. Let the brethren take hold and carry out in every department the same principle of home manufacture until we shall be able to produce the materials, and make up every article necessary to clothe and adorn the body, from the crown of the head to the soles of the feet. Then we shall become a self-sustaining and growing people, and we shall have to do it. All this is in the elements in which we live, and we need the skill to utilize the elements to our growth and wealth, and this is true financiering. - Brigham Young, April 1877 General Conference

*My young sisters, instead of sitting continually at the piano and getting the consumption, **take hold and build up Zion**. The first thing is to do*

something for yourselves, and learn to labor; and when one thing is done, take up another item, and <u>continue until we manufacture everything that we need here</u>. - Brigham Young, July 19, 1877

*But the ship of Zion is onward; the "little stone" is hewn out of the mountain without hands, and will roll until it fills the whole earth . . . But let us unite closer together, and harmonize our temporal interests, until we shall manufacture everything we need to make us **independent** of the world.* - President John Taylor, September 22, 1878

Independence through Local Manufacturing

Can any of you tell me how you are going to get your next year's clothing? No man can be independent who is dependent upon others; no nation can be independent that is dependent upon another nation for its sustenance . . . but <u>we cannot be independent until we can make our own shoes, dresses, shawls, bonnets, pantaloons, hats, and all such things as we need.</u> When we can do these things, raise our own food, manufacture everything we need among ourselves, then we shall be independent of other people. - John Taylor, January 17, 1858

***I would like to see the people take a course to make their own clothing, make their own machinery, their own knives and their own forks, and everything else we need**, for the day will come when we will be under the necessity of doing it, for trouble and perplexity, war and famine, bloodshed and fire, and thunder and lightning will roll upon the nations of the earth, insomuch that we cannot get to them, nor they to us. If you do not believe me I want you to believe the Prophets; read the revelations that came through brother Joseph Smith, and through Daniel and Moses, and through Jesus, and through all the ancient Prophets. They spoke of these things, and declare they shall come to pass in the latter days.* - Brigham Young, April 1873 General Conference

While we continue to be purchasers and importers only, we will remain dependent to, and at the mercy of manufacturers and exporters from

abroad; but when we can produce what we need by our own industry and skill, from the elements which so abundantly surround us, we cease to import, to be dependent upon Babylon, or the world, we approach independence, and begin to assume the position in the earth which God has designed we should, to lead and not be led, to teach and not be taught, to be the "head and not the tail." - Joseph F. Smith, April 1879 General Conference

Why is Economic Independence so Important?

Nine apostolic quotes spanning a quarter century teach us that achieving economic independence from the world is important to the effort to build Zion because, it is prophesied, the world's economy, ie. Babylon, will fall. In order to endure that fall, Zion and her people must be able to provide for their own needs. Here are three representative quotes:

We have to build up Zion independent of the wicked; we have got to become self-sustaining, and the Lord is inspiring His prophets to preach to us to lay the foundation for the accomplishment of this work. The day is not far distant when we shall have to take care of ourselves. <u>Great Babylon is going to fall</u>, judgment is coming on the wicked, the Lord is about to pour upon the nations of the earth the great calamities which He has spoken of by the mouths of His prophets; and no power can stay these things. <u>It is wisdom that we should lay the foundation to provide for ourselves</u>. - Wilford Woodruff, May 19, 1867

*It appears that we have gathered many to Zion who do not fully appreciate the great work of these days—namely, **to place the people of God in a condition that they can sustain themselves, against the time that Babylon the Great shall fall**. Some will say that it is ridiculous to suppose that Babylon, the "MOTHER OF HARLOTS," is going to fall. Ridiculous as it may seem, the time will come when no man will buy her merchandise, and when the Latter-day Saints will be under the necessity of providing for themselves, or going without. "This may be a wild idea,"* *but it is no more wild or wonderful than what has already transpired, and that before our eyes. When we are counseled to "provide for your wants within yourselves," we are only told to prepare for that day. When we are told, "Unite your interests and establish every variety of business that may be necessary to supply your wants," we are only told to lay a plan to enjoy liberty, peace and plenty.* - George A. Smith, May 6, 1870

How long do you think it would take if we were all producers, and converting the raw materials into useful articles, to become a self-sustaining people? And then if we heard of <u>Babylon's downfall</u>, we would not of necessity lift up our hands and cry, "O Lord spare her a little longer, we are not ready for her to go down, we should suffer from the want of boots and shoes, and for our clothing, and our machinery, and so forth." The United Order is designed to help us to be self-reliant and to teach us to understand what it costs to produce that which we consume. One of the chief obstacles in the way of our progress towards becoming a self-sustaining people is the lack of this understanding among the people. They cling to the habits and customs of Babylon that they have learned abroad. - Erastus Snow, June 3, 1877

Zion and Her Saints Must Become Self-Sustaining

We have a great deal to do to destroy wickedness and establish righteousness upon the earth, and <u>to prepare ourselves for the establishment of Zion</u>, that she may become the head upon the earth . . . Do we feel that we will do right and hold ourselves and all that we possess upon the altar of the kingdom of God? Do we feel that we should be diligent and economical, that we should seek unto the elements that we are surrounded with, <u>and take that course that will make us the most independent people upon the earth</u>? If we should bless the earth and ask God to bless it, that it may bring forth for our support and sustenance, and that we may have power to draw forth and combine the elements, and thus make us independent of every nation, kindred, tongue, and people. - Daniel H. Wells, September 30, 1860

10 - Building Zion Includes Economic Independence from Babylon

What has been the teachings to this people for years? **To be self-sustaining**. - John Taylor, April 1867 General Conference

We have been talking about the United Order, and getting up tanneries, shoe shops, &c., and [initial] steps have been taken in some of the settlements with these objects in view; but it takes time to carry out and successfully accomplish such projects. But <u>we can produce these things within ourselves, and it is our duty to do it</u>, and instead of manifesting a disposition to oppose anything of this kind, we should exert all the influence and energy we possess to bring it about, and to make ourselves self-sustaining . . . the work of making Zion self-sustaining must be regarded as part of the work of the Lord; for <u>it is an obligation devolving upon us to provide within ourselves labor and the [necessities] of life</u>. We must take hold of this matter, brethren and sisters, with all our hearts, <u>and never let ourselves rest until Zion is independent of her enemies and all the world</u>. - George A. Smith, October 1874 General Conference

We should establish branches of industry from which we could at least provide for our own necessities and as soon as possible be able to export our home productions, and thus give employment to every faithful Latter-day Saint who is gathered to Zion, that individuals may not only become self sustaining but contribute their proportion to the general good.

Our manufactories should be fostered, patronized and protected, and their staple wares sought after and preferred by the people, even though they were more costly at first. It needs no argument to prove to the sagacious and far seeing that this policy will pay the best in the end. While we continue to be purchasers and importers only, we will remain dependent to, and at the mercy of manufacturers and exporters from abroad; but when we can produce what we need by our own industry and skill, from the elements which so abundantly surround us, we cease to import, to be dependent upon Babylon, or the world, we approach independence, and begin to assume the position in the earth which God has designed we should, to lead and not be led, to teach and not be taught, to be the "head and not the tail." - Joseph F. Smith, April 1879 General Conference

Summary

1. Economic dependence on the wicked invites trouble and is servitude.
2. Building Zion includes manufacturing all our own consumer goods.
3. Economic Independence is to be achieved through the local manufacturing of goods.
4. Economic independence is important because Babylon will fall and we will have to provide for ourselves our everyday needs.
5. Zion and her Saints must become self-sustaining.

Afterthoughts

In April General Conference in 2001, Elder L. Tom Perry made an interesting comment where he spoke of the original goal of the Saints becoming economically self-sufficient. Note which prophet Elder Perry mentions started it all:

The Prophet had a design to build a community of Saints [i.e. Zion]. *He had three major objectives: first, economic; second, educational; and third, spiritual.*

The Prophet Joseph Smith's desire was that the Saints should become economically self-sufficient . . . A treasured remnant of our heritage of economic self-sufficiency is the Church Welfare Services program.

"A **treasured** *remnant*" - it's almost as if Elder Perry were mourning the Saints' abandonment of that goal as a people. Also note how Elder Perry mentions that the first objective of Joseph's Zion-building plans was economic; Joseph wanted the Saints to be economically independent of

Babylon. Do we want that for ourselves? Are we willing to receive the blessings God wants for his children, or, will we "cling to Babylon" because it is familiar?

Does this teaching square with what the Lord says in scripture?

The teachings of this chapter are so counter-intuitive to us today because we, and our parents and grandparents, grew up in a society that operates under the assumptions taught in every college Economics 101 class [see Economism, by James Kwak, PhD.]. The American culture has trained us to accept as unquestioned Gospel Truth that economic *dependence* is actually good for everyone. We are taught, and everyone assumes it to be true, that being economically dependent on each other encourages abundance due to the specialization of labor, mutually-beneficial trading, and leads to the best possible world for all involved.

Because of this, it is likely many readers will question the wisdom of these early apostolic and prophetic directives for the Saints to achieve economic independence from the world. Or, some will use the principles taught in Econ 101 to justify our dropping economic independence as a goal altogether. We can simply dismiss these teachings by saying, "Well, clearly they didn't understand basic economics." Thus relieving ourselves of the responsibility to seek and do God's will in regards to temporal matters.

Only one problem—God wants his Church to be economically independent. Not only do all the quotes above strongly suggest it (many were given in General Conference!), but the Lord himself has declared it. Doctrine and Covenants 78 is where the Lord directs the early Church to embrace economic unity and reveals his goal "that the church may stand independent above all other creatures beneath the celestial world" (verse 14). During the entire chapter up to that verse, the Lord is talking about economic as well as spiritual themes.

In verse 3 they are told "the time has come, and is now at hand; and behold, and lo, it must needs be that there be an organization of my people, in regulating and establishing the affairs of the storehouse for the poor of my people." It is easy to conclude that this "organization of my people" is not a religious organization because the Lord's spiritual organization of his people, his church, had been established two years earlier in 1830. The fact that this verse talks about setting up the Bishop's Storehouse "for the poor of my people" suggests that the organization the Lord had in mind was an <u>economic</u> one.

Verse 4 then makes it clear that the Lord intended this economic organization of his people to be "permanent and everlasting". The purpose for doing this is given in verses 5 and 6, which says:

5 That you may be equal in the bonds of heavenly things, yea, **and earthly things also***, for the obtaining of heavenly things.*
6 <u>For if ye are not equal in earthly things ye cannot be equal in obtaining heavenly things</u>;

God wants us to be "equal in earthly things" so that we can be "equal in obtaining heavenly things". If one family has to spend every waking moment trying to scrape together enough food to survive, they certainly can't be "equal in obtaining heavenly things" with those who have abundant surpluses of resources.

The next verse apparently explains what "heavenly things" the Lord meant: *7. For if you will that I give unto you a place in the celestial world, you must prepare yourselves by doing the things which I have commanded you and required of you.*

So, apparently, our participation in this economic organization of God's people is meant to prepare us for "a place in the celestial world". Which makes sense, of course. Would a people who are steeped in and comfortable with the tradition of every-man-for-himself, competitive market economics be comfortable in a celestial society? Likely not.

Then, just before verse 14 where the Lord declares his intention that the Church stand independent, he repeats the idea that this economic organization of his people is to prepare us and give us the means to accomplish his latter-day work. The verse says:

13 Behold, this is the preparation wherewith I prepare you, and the foundation, and the ensample which I give unto you, whereby you may accomplish the commandments which are given you;

14 That through my providence, notwithstanding the tribulation which shall descend upon you, that the church may stand independent above all other creatures beneath the celestial world;

Economic independence from the world's economy is not just some fanciful idea stuck in the minds of early LDS leaders. <u>The Lord himself</u> desires it for us to prepare us to live in a celestial society with him.

Will we also say of God, "He just doesn't understand Economics 101"? Or, will we humble ourselves before Him, deny the wisdom of the world, and embrace and work towards God's economic goals for his children?

Chapter Eleven – Zion Requires Economic Unity

We must be one temporally, too.

This is a tough topic for most people, LDS or not. The idea of being "one" temporally brings up fear-based thoughts of Communism, cult-like collectives, and the lazy living off the industrious. The reader will likely be surprised to discover in this chapter that their fears about the redistribution of wealth existing in a Zion society are unfounded. [Actually, it's not wealth that's redistributed, but something else.] Apostle Lorenzo Snow spoke to this situation on March 1, 1857:

If the people had confidence in the things which are taught, and if they would let their minds expand, and throw in their substance for the establishment of Zion and the extension of the kingdom of God, they would learn that it is the very principle upon which they would receive stores of those things which they are after. But there is a fearfulness in the minds of the people, they are afraid to trust their substance in the hands of the Lord . . .

He spoke again to it two decades later on October 19, 1879:

Now, perhaps I do not believe as some do in regard to the United Order—that everybody is to come together and throw all their substance into a heap, and then come and take of it as they please, or that one man who does not understand temporal affairs at all should be placed as a steward over extensive concerns. I believe that there is an order in these things—a pleasing and an agreeable order—and that these things are arranged by the Lord in such a way that <u>when people properly understand them they will be satisfied and admire them</u>. It is because we do not get to understand the requirements of God that we are dissatisfied. God fixes these matters up and arranges them in such a way as will tend to the exaltation of every Latter-day Saint who is disposed to honor them. **It is because of our ignorance that we are displeased with the requirements of the Lord.**

Considering the following quotes about temporal oneness, if these fears crop up for us, it may be that we have a faulty spin on the concept of economic unity. Our vision of it may be skewed by the twist the world has given it. These next quotes, with many others in Appendix A, strongly indicate that true economic unity is essential for a celestial-level existence. If that is true, then our understanding of temporal unity may need adjusting.

The matters which have been laid before you this afternoon are inseparably connected with our spiritual well-being. There is no man on this earth who can receive the Kingdom of God in his heart and be governed according to the laws of that Kingdom, <u>without being governed . . . in all temporal matters</u>. If you are not of one heart and mind in these things, never think of Jackson County, for you will not be wanted there. <u>No man is going to inherit a celestial glory, who trifles with the principles thereof</u>. - Brigham Young, June 29, 1864

*We are one of heart and mind, as it regards faith, repentance, baptism, or the first principles of the gospel of Jesus Christ; but **the same unity must** exist in our midst in all our temporal labors—in building temples, tabernacles, cities, towns, villages, canals, cultivating the earth, or any other labor, if we ever accomplish the object for which we have been raised up. **No people, unless they are united together, can ever build up Zion** and establish the Kingdom of God on the earth.* - Wilford Woodruff, April 1867 General Conference

<u>The Lord wants to build up His Zion</u>, *and He wants to build it up through you and me. We are the ones He has called upon. Will we consent to do this? I firmly believe that, before we make any very effectual progress in the accomplishment of that work, we must become more united and more fervent in our faith and practice than we have ever yet been at any time. We have to become more like a single family, and be one, that we may be the Lord's; and not every one have his own individual interest. This is destructive, this disconnects the feelings of the people one from another, and causes divisions and disunion.* **But when we make the general cause of Zion our individual cause it brings us closer together**. - Brigham Young, April 17, 1870

*[W]e are gathered here to serve God and keep his commandments, and to build up his Zion upon the earth. After praying for years that God would inspire his servant Brigham with the Spirit of revelation, that he might be able to lead forth Israel in the path in which they should go, he tells us to be one, as Jesus told his disciples; <u>he tells us to enter into a united order</u>, that God has revealed it, <u>that we are to be one in spiritual things,</u> **and** <u>one in temporal things</u>, to be united together in all principles, as the Saints of God have been wherever they have existed.* - John Taylor, October 1875 General Conference

The feeling that was manifested here yesterday, is most creditable to Israel, it is approved of by the Gods in the eternal worlds; and if we carry out in our practice and daily lives that union which we manifested in our [sustaining votes], the Lord God will continue to pour upon us his blessing **until we shall be united in all things, temporal** *and spiritual, which unity we have got to come to. When this is achieved, Zion will arise and shine . . .* - John Taylor, October 1877 General Conference

"Being One Temporally" Defined

Briefly, let's consider what temporal unity is not. Most Saints are aware that the United Order, in some form or another, was the mechanism used historically to unite their ancestors economically. On January 12, 1868, President Brigham Young gave a talk where he appears to define what "being one temporally" meant to him (in bold), and, what it did not mean (underlined). He said:

*I have looked upon the community of the Latter-day Saints in vision and beheld them **organized as one great family of heaven, each person performing his several duties in his line of industry, working for the good of the whole** more than <u>for individual aggrandizement</u>; and in this I have beheld the most beautiful order that the mind of man can contemplate, and the grandest results for the upbuilding of the kingdom of God and the spread of righteousness upon the earth. Will this people ever come to this order of things? Are they now prepared **to live according to that patriarchal order that will be organized among the true and faithful before God receives His own**? We all concede the point that when this mortality falls off; and with it its cares, anxieties, <u>love of self, love of wealth, and love of power, and all the conflicting interests which pertain to this flesh</u>, that then, when our spirits have returned to God who gave them, we will be **subject to every requirement that He may make of us, that we shall then live together as one great family; our interest will be a general, a common interest.***

He then asks the very question I am asking with this book, "Why can we not so live in this world?"

Brigham continues his definition:

*The voice of God has not called us together from the uttermost parts of the earth <u>to build up and enrich those who are diametrically opposed to His kingdom and its interests</u>. No, but **we are gathered together expressly to become of one heart and of one mind in all our operations and endeavors to establish Christ's spiritual and temporal kingdom upon the earth, to prepare for the coming of the Son of Man in power and great glory.***

Just over two years later, in April of 1870, President Young shared again his view of economic unity:

The Lord wants to build up His Zion, and He wants to build it up through you and me. We are the ones He has called upon. Will we consent to do this? I firmly believe that, before we make any very effectual progress in the accomplishment of that work, we must become more united and more fervent in our faith and practice than we have ever yet been at any time. **We have to become more like a single family, and be one**, *that we may be the Lord's; <u>and not every one have his own individual interest</u>. This is destructive, this disconnects the feelings of the people one from another, and causes divisions and disunion. But when we* **make the general cause of Zion our individual cause** *it brings us closer together.*

As President of the Quorum of the Twelve, John Taylor shared Brigham's vision of God's people united both temporally and spiritually. On August 31, 1875 he said:

We cannot build up a Zion unless we are in possession of the spirit of Zion, and of the light and intelligence that flow from God, and under the direction of the Priesthood, the living oracles of God, to lead us in the paths of life. We do not know them without, and we need all these helps to lead us along, <u>that by and by we may come to such a unity in our temporal and in our spiritual affairs</u>, and in everything that pertains to our interest and happiness in this world and in the world to come, that we may be prepared to enter a Zion here upon the earth, help to build Temples of the Lord and to administer in them, and so operate and cooperate with the Gods in the eternal worlds, and with the Patriarchs, Prophets, Apostles, and men of God . . . we want to be one with them, one with God, and one with each other, for Jesus said—"Except you are one you are not mine."

President George Q. Cannon, gave his explanation of what temporal unity meant in the April 1878 General Conference:

11 - Zion Requires Economic Unity

*I have endeavored to describe to you the influence we wield because of our union in spiritual matters. The same remark will apply exactly to our union in temporal matters. Let this people be united in temporal matters; let it be known that **we work together for one another's good, that we labor, as a people to benefit the whole and not the individual**, and that our influence is in this direction; and I tell you that the same influence, the same power, that wield now as a spiritual organization will be felt in our temporal affairs, in our financial affairs, in all the affairs in fact which attract our attention.*

On August 4, 1878, about a year after Brigham Young's death, President John Taylor expressed what appears to be his understanding of temporal unity, which aligned quite closely with President Cannon's view:

Brethren and sisters, God bless you. <u>Let us love one another; let us seek to promote one another's welfare</u>. And let the Bishops and the Relief Societies, and the Young Men's and Young Women's Associations, and our [tradesmen] and manufacturers, and also our merchants, and all hands, <u>operate in the interests of the whole for the welfare of Zion</u> and the building up of the Kingdom of God upon the earth; and the blessings of God will begin to rest upon us, Zion will begin to arise, and the glory of God will rest upon her. Amen.

Benefits of Economic Unity

In May of 1874, then Elder Wilford Woodruff commented, "There are very many advantages that will accrue to us if we unite our hearts, feelings, labors, interests, property, and everything that we are made stewards over." Among the Brethren's teachings about building Zion are three benefits of being united economically as God's people. They are that God will give us the riches we need to bring about His will in the world, that a classless society will arise, and that poverty will be eliminated.

- God will grant us riches needed to accomplish His will.

Speaking about the Zion of the last days, Isaiah says that **the Lord will bring for brass gold, for iron silver, for wood brass, and for stones iron to build up the Zion of God.** *When will that be done? When we are united, so that we shall not consume the wealth that God will give us upon our lusts, upon creating class distinctions, raising one class above another, one class living in luxury and another class groveling in poverty; but when we are so organized that there will be no rich and no poor, but all partaking alike of the bounties that God shall give unto us, then, and in my opinion,* <u>not till then, can he bestow upon us the wealth that he has promised</u>*. - George Q. Cannon, October 1874 General Conference*

[W]e must learn to combine our interests in such a manner that it will be to the advantage of the whole community to consume and wear that which is produced and manufactured at home. It will be by cooperative action that we shall be tied together in temporal matters as we are now bound together in spiritual things. **As a thoroughly united people we can the better hasten the work of God in the earth**; *such as building temples, establishing settlements, civilizing the Lamanites, carrying the Gospel to the Jews, and building up the Zion of God in these mountains. - Brigham Young, Jr., April 1884 General Conference*

God will bless us in our labors and efforts; and if we will cooperate together in our temporal affairs and conduct our business on correct principles, the world will be better for us, and we will be better off in the world. <u>We will have more means to build up the kingdom of God; we will have more to use for the gathering of the poor, for the building up of Zion</u> *. . . - Joseph F. Smith, July 18, 1884*

11 - Zion Requires Economic Unity

- Economic Unity results in a classless society

    Though the class-conscious may not see this as a benefit, the scriptures suggests the Lord sees it as the best way for everyone to enjoy spiritual benefits equally. In D&C 78:5-6 the Lord declares his people are to be organized economically so . . . "That you may be equal in the bonds of heavenly things, yea, and earthly things also, for the obtaining of heavenly things. For if ye are not equal in earthly things ye cannot be equal in obtaining heavenly things . . ."

    Besides the Lord desiring economic unity for his people, the early LDS apostles and prophets did as well.

    Let us prepare ourselves for the coming of Enoch's Zion, that we may have the same order of things among us that they had in the beginning. Then, again, it will be a glorious thing in many other respects. What is it that creates this great inequality that we naturally see in the world, in regard to the high and low? It is the difference of parentage in many respects. One man is so situated he can train up his children in all the learning of the day; he can take them into his carriage, and they can ride at their ease, and in their grandeur, while the poor and needy and destitute bow before them, or are trampled under their feet. There is no such thing as union there, because they were unequal to begin with. When the Saints have this [union] established in their midst, you will see them all alike, where none can say that "such a person is richer than I am, and I have no right to associate with him." Neither can the rich look upon those that are poor, and say, "My children shall not marry with the poor, and unite with them in their festivities, etc., because I have more property than they." All these things will be done away, and the principle of equality will be established, and all will be stewards of the Lord's property. That is what I wish to see—that when one family of children have the privilege of being educated, the rest should enjoy it; when one family are in possession of the good things of the earth, the rest should enjoy the same privileges also. - Orson Pratt, September 10, 1854

Nearly 19 years later, Elder Pratt repeated the idea that class distinctions and Zion do not mix. In the April 1873 General Conference he pointed out:

There are certainly existing now among us distinctions of classes which if not checked, may prove the overthrow of many. For instance the rich can educate their sons and daughters in the best schools, academies and universities; others cannot do this, because of their poverty. This makes the children of the rich feel themselves above the children of the poor . . . **With the feelings engendered by these distinctions of classes, there is not that fellowship that should exist among the Saints of the living God.** *If we wish, brethren and sisters, to go back and build up the waste places of Zion, and to see the New Jerusalem erected upon the consecrated spot, let us endeavor to approximate more nearly to the celestial law, that when we do get back there, and that law more fully comes in force, we may be able to enter into it . . . .* - Orson Pratt, April 1873 General Conference

Later, presidents John Taylor and George Q. Cannon chimed in on the same topic:

We ought to be governed by correct principles and act wisely and consistently, and treat all men alike. There are a great many who have the idea that there are certain classes that have rights which do not belong to others. I do not know of any such people. We are all the freeborn sons of Zion; we all partake of the holy priesthood, and we all have our rights and privileges with God. <u>We want to act according to correct principle, and be governed by the law of God, not one law for</u>

<u>one man and another for another man</u>. But operating together and maintaining one another's rights upon the pure principles of truth and equity, as they exist in the bosom of God . . . We want to be united in our hearts and feelings: united to each other; united to the holy priesthood, bound together by those indissoluble ties that will unite us in time and through eternity . . . - President John Taylor, August 31, 1879

That condition is upon us, the growth of wealth in the hands of a few individuals, threatening us with greater danger today, than anything that can be done by outsiders . . . I know that this is true. **God does not design that there shall be classes among us**, *one class lifted up above another, one class separated from the rest of the people, with diverse interests; interests that are not strictly in accord with those of the masses of the people. Because when this is the case, there is a lack of union . . .. God designs in the organization of his kingdom on the earth to prevent this. If it is not prevented, then the Zion of God is not established.* - George Q. Cannon, October 1882 General Conference

3. The elimination of poverty.

In God's own definition of Zion (Moses 7:18), there are "no poor among them". This is *not* because we kick out all the poor! It is because we nurture them along, helping them become as self-reliant and prosperous as we are. Is this not what someone would do if they loved their neighbor as themselves?

Our early LDS leaders believed and taught that, in building Zion, poverty would be eliminated. Here are three representative quotes from Utah's territorial years:

But the day will come when **there will be no poor in Zion**, *but the Lord will make them equal in earthly things, that they may be equal in heavenly things; that is, according to His notions of equality, and not according to our narrow, contracted views of the same.* - Orson Pratt, April 1855 General Conference.

The Latter-day Saints, in their conduct and acts with regard to financial matters, are like the rest of the world. The course pursued by men of business in the world has a tendency to make a few rich, and to sink the masses of the people in poverty and degradation. Too many of the Elders of Israel take this course . . . Instead of being <u>united in our feelings to build up all</u>, each one takes his own course; whereas, if we were united, we would get rich ten times faster than we do now. - Brigham Young, April 1867 General Conference

The time must come when the talent of men of business shall be used for the benefit of this whole people, just as the talent of . . . the Twelve Apostles, and that of the leading Elders of this Church; as their talent is used for the benefit of Zion, so must the talent of men who are gifted with business capacity be used in like manner—not for individual benefit alone, not for individual aggrandizement alone, but for the benefit of the whole people, **to uplift the masses, to rescue them from their poverty**. <u>*That is one of the objects in establishing Zion*</u>, *and anything short of that, as I have said, is not Zion, it is not the Zion that the Prophets have foreseen, it is not that which God has promised.* - George Q. Cannon, October 1882 General Conference

Poverty's elimination is even mentioned more recently. In the 2008 October General Conference, newly-ordained apostle, Elder D. Todd Christofferson, made this observation:

Zion is Zion because of the character, attributes, and faithfulness of her citizens. Remember, "the Lord called his people Zion, because they were of one heart and one mind, and dwelt in righteousness; and there was no poor among them" (Moses 7:18). If we would establish Zion in our homes, branches, wards, and stakes, we must rise to this standard. It will be necessary (1) to become unified in one heart and one mind; (2) to become, individually and collectively, a holy people; and (3) **to care for the poor and needy with such effectiveness that we eliminate poverty among us**. *We cannot wait until Zion comes for these things to happen—Zion will come only as they happen.*

11 - Zion Requires Economic Unity

"In that the rich are made low"

This scriptural phrase from D&C 104:16 probably sparks more discomfort in the hearts of prosperous Saints than any other. But to quote the fictional character Inigo Montoya, "I do not think it means what you think it means." We do not find a single statement among all the Zion-building quotes that even *hinted* that redistribution of wealth was ever contemplated among the early LDS leaders. What that phrase likely means is that the rich are humbled, not financially, but in that <u>their focus is redirected to God and accomplishing His will, instead of their own will and benefit</u>. The rich are thereby "humbled". [Are you relieved?]

What we *do* find are statements suggesting a re*direction* of wealth's power to the benefit of the poor. Specifically, we find the early LDS leaders imploring the successful Saints **not** to focus on expanding their wealth even further. The leaders encouraged them to re-focus their wealth-building skills and capital into productive projects that:

1. Provided honest work with fair wages for the under- and unemployed,
2. Manufactured products needed in Utah to help the Saints become self-sufficient and independent of the U.S. economy ("Babylon"), and
3. Served to foster economic unity among the Saints.

Here are five quotes suggesting this *redirection* of wealth:

*The intention is to use the skill of the businessman in <u>elevating those who are not businessmen</u>, to bring up the poor from their level to the broad upper level, **not to pull down the upper level to the plane of the lower**. That is not the design, but it is that we shall work for each other's good . . .* - President George Q. Cannon, October 1874 General Conference

One great object we should aim to reach, that we should aim to accomplish, is <u>to make ourselves independent in regard to manufactur[ing]</u>. We have had, the last week, considerable conversation with leading men from various parts of this Territory concerning this principle of cooperation . . . I have felt that it will be a most excellent thing for us to have a permanent organization of our best business men, and the most practical men, from all parts of our Territory, acting in the capacity of a board of trade, whose duty shall be to look after our manufacturing, mercantile and other interests; and should there at any time be anything wrong in our systems of doing business, tending in the least to prevent perfect union, that the necessary measures might be devised to remedy these things <u>and bring about a concert of action upon all hands</u>. - President George Q. Cannon, April 1878 General Conference

We are told in one of these revelations that it is necessary that we should be equal. If we are not equal in temporal things, we cannot be equal in spiritual things. Men on whom God has bestowed financiering ability are the men that are wanted at this time—that God wants, and whom he would wish to call to step forth in the accomplishment of this great union . . . In regard to the building up the kingdom of God here at home, persons who have the ability are the ones who should step forward in things that would lead the Latter-day Saints to this union. It would be of more value to them than all the things of earth. The blessings of God upon them in time and eternity would well repay them to step forth and labor for the Zion of God. **We are told that the priesthood is not called to work for money, but to establish Zion**. - Lorenzo Snow, April 22, 1878

The time must come when the talent of men of business shall be used for the benefit of this whole people, just as the talent of President Taylor . . . and that of the Twelve Apostles, and that of the leading Elders of this Church; as their talent is used for the benefit of Zion, so must the talent of men who are gifted with business capacity be used in like manner— <u>not for individual benefit alone</u>, not for individual aggrandizement alone, *but for the benefit of the whole people, to uplift the masses, to rescue them from their poverty.* **That is one of the objects in establishing Zion, and anything short of that, as I have said, is not Zion, it is not the Zion that the Prophets have foreseen, it is not that which God has promised**. - President George Q. Cannon, October 1882 General Conference

Supposing that the property of the whole community were divided today equally amongst all, what might we expect? Why a year from today we should need another division, for some would waste and squander it away, while others would add to their portion. The skill of building up and establishing the Zion of our God on the earth is to take the people and teach them how to take care of themselves and that which the Lord has entrusted to their care, and to use all that we command to glorify his holy name. This is the work of regenerating, of elevating mankind to the higher plane of the Gospel; in other words, of simply teaching them their duty. - Brigham Young, April 1877 General Conference

Interim Thoughts

In that last quote, Brother Brigham makes the point that the economic unity of a Zion society, where Consecration & Stewardship hold sway, is less "income-sharing" and more "wisdom-sharing" and "skill-sharing". The point is that out of love for our fellowman, we are to help others become as productive and prosperous as ourselves. This cooperative view of economics is the spirit of Zion—where the more successful "rich" help the less successful "poor" *through training, mentoring, and guidance.*

In contrast, Competition, where we leave our neighbor to sink or swim in the dog-eat-dog economy, is Babylon's way. Our keeping of the Second Great Commandment to love our neighbor as ourselves is given expression through our cooperative efforts. In Zion's economic plan, the goal is, as Brigham put it in that last quote, "elevating mankind to the higher plane of the Gospel". It is simply Love applied to the realm of economics.

Economics under God's Direction

The primary attribute of an economically-united Zion society, as taught by early LDS leaders, is that economic, as well as spiritual, activities would be carried out under the direction of God.

As I have said in days that are past, the time will come, (and how soon we know not,) but it will come, when this people will become of one heart and of one mind in temporal things, as well as in spiritual: they will as individuals be identified with the Church, and all they possess, whether it be gold, or silver, or jewelry, or cattle, or flocks, or herds, or lands, or houses, or wives, or children, it matters not what they possess, **it will all go as it shall please the Lord, according to His counsel, and His direction** *for the building up of this kingdom.* - Orson Pratt, April 1855 General Conference

But do we realize that God's kingdom in the latter days is to all intents and purposes a temporal kingdom? And do we realize that if we had stayed in the world [back East] we could have served him spiritually there as well as here? But what kind of a kingdom would that have been for the Savior to rule over when he comes? <u>When he comes, he is going to reign over a temporal kingdom, composed of men and women who do his will on the earth.</u> *Everything that pertains to us in our life is temporal, and over us and all we possess our Heavenly Father and his Son Jesus Christ will reign, as well as over all the kingdoms of the world when they become the kingdoms of our God and his Christ. To build up Zion is a temporal labor . . . .* - Daniel H. Wells, September 10, 1861

We ought to have a heaven upon earth—to be really the Zion of our God, the pure in heart, each one seeking another's welfare. "Thou shalt love the Lord thy God with all thy heart, with all thy might, with all thy soul, with all thy strength, and thy neighbor as thyself." We have hardly

11 - Zion Requires Economic Unity

got to that yet . . . But if we could feel we are the children of God, all animated by that same Holy Spirit, producing peace and joy, and all welded together in one common brotherhood, in the bonds of the everlasting Gospel, **all operating with God and the holy priesthood who have lived in other ages, to carry out his purposes upon the earth**, *and assisting to redeem the earth and establish his kingdom, never more to be thrown down. If we could feel like this, we should drop our individuality and self-esteem a little, we should seek to do not our own will, but the will of Him who sent us.* - John Taylor, December 1, 1878

We have been harassed from the beginning unto this day, and I fear will be, until we conform to this law [the United Order], *and <u>are willing that God shall rule in regard to these temporal matters</u>.* - Lorenzo Snow, October 19, 1879

Here, Apostles Wilford Woodruff and Charles C. Rich echo this idea that economic unity must be under God's direction, either through the Spirit or through the Lord's prophets:

Does any man or woman wonder that President Young leads out, and calls upon us to follow, in directing temporal affairs? What would become of us and Zion if there were no one to give counsel in temporal matters? We could not advance if such were the case; but we have been guided so far by the servants of God and the Spirit of God. - Wilford Woodruff, May 6, 1870

There is but one way to be united [in temporal matters], according to the will of God, and that is **by being dictated in our affairs by the Spirit of the Lord**. *When we were baptized we received the spirit of the Gospel, and by that spirit we obtained a knowledge of its truth. And the same spirit we then received, if it continues with us, will lead us into all truth and reveal to us things to come. We have need of revelation at every step after we are baptized, for when we take a step it ought to be a right step, and the only right step we can take will be one that is in accordance with the principles of truth, <u>as dictated by those authorized</u>*

to teach and instruct the Saints. This is the only principle on which we can be united, and when this principle fully is carried out, then perfect union will exist among the Saints. - Charles C. Rich on February 10, 1878

The following are quotes by early LDS leaders which reinforce the point that the Spirit's guidance is required for the Saints to unite economically:

When one goes into cooperation [i.e. economic unity] with proper spirit and proper views, to superintend or operate in any of its departments, **he has a lawful claim to the Spirit of inspiration, to aid him in his calling.** *We read that Jacob, through his honesty of purpose, fair-dealing, and freedom from selfishness, was assisted by an holy Angel with information how to increase and multiply his flocks. It is far better to build up the kingdom of God, in its temporal interests, by the Spirit of God and the wisdom of God, than by the spirit of man and the wisdom of man; on the latter principle we shall always fail, but on the former the results will always be successful.* - Lorenzo Snow, October 1873 General Conference

The object of this perfect organization is that we may be entitled to greater blessings therefrom; that we may be entitled to **a greater fullness of the Holy Spirit**; *that everything may be dictated according to the mind and will of God, not only in spiritual things, but also in regard to our temporal matters . . . .* - Orson Pratt, May 13, 1877

All these things concern every head of a family; therefore, **if he had the spirit of revelation, if he could go and inquire of the Lord, if he found it to be the whisperings of his spirit which course to pursue in temporal matters**, *what a great blessing it would be for him . . . Again, how great would be the benefit to a body of people—to say nothing of households and families—located for instance, in one region of the country, a people who were united together according to the law of God, desiring to advance each other's welfare and happiness, and each man was required to love his neighbor as himself; a people who knew how to so* *conduct their, temporal affairs that each man's neighbor might be benefited as well as himself; and each one looking not only for his own welfare or that of his own household, but for the welfare of the whole community, with whom he was associated, <u>producing at last that unity and oneness which the Lord requires in the numerous revelations which he has given</u>.* - Orson Pratt, August 25, 1878

There is but one way to be united, according to the will of God, and that is by being dictated in our affairs **by the Spirit of the Lord** *. . . This is the only principle on which we can be united, and when this principle fully is carried out, then perfect union will exist among the Saints.* - Charles C. Rich, February 10, 1878

Along with others in Appendix A, the following three quotes by early LDS leaders support the idea that God's direction in economic matters needs also to come through prophets to unite us. As a reminder, during the early Utah years they used the term "temporal" where we today use the term "economic".

Do we believe fully that God our Father has appointed men whom he influences day by day to lead forth his people, and direct them in all their spiritual <u>and temporal labors</u>? And do we so order our course as to correspond with the instructions given us? Or do we suppose we can entirely take our own way in temporal matters, according to the traditions of our fathers and the dictations of the spirit of the world, and at the same time please high Heaven, and do our duty faithfully in the building up of the kingdom of God? We think in spiritual "Mormonism," we need direction and constant instruction by the authorized servants of God; but we think we know as much about temporal affairs as anybody. . . .[W]e rejoice that God has spoken in these last days, and that we have received these most valuable instructions—that we have received the knowledge that leads to life and salvation, and to exaltation in his kingdom. But do we realize that God's kingdom in the latter days is to all intents and purposes a temporal kingdom? - Daniel H. Wells, September 10, 1861

This people, the Latter-day Saints, are of one heart and mind respecting the spiritual things of the Kingdom of God; in temporal things they have not yet become so well united. Brother George Q. Cannon this morning referred to affairs that took place in Kirtland. Some of the leading men in Kirtland were much opposed to Joseph the Prophet meddling with temporal affairs; they did not believe that he was capable of dictating to the people upon temporal matters, thinking that his duty embraced spiritual things alone, and that the people should be left to attend to their temporal affairs, without any interference whatever from Prophets or Apostles... In a public meeting of the Saints, I said, "Ye Elders of Israel, Father Smith is present, the Prophet is present, and here are his counselors, here are also High Priests and Elders of Israel, now, will some of you draw the line of demarcation, between the spiritual and the temporal in the Kingdom of God, so that I may understand it?" Not one of them could do it. - Brigham Young, November 6, 1864

So we see that almost the very first teachings the first Elders of this Church received were as to what to eat, what to drink, and how to order their natural lives, that they might be united temporally as well as spiritually. This is the great purpose which God has in view in sending to the world, by His servants, the gospel of life and salvation... We have met in these valleys of the mountains with an eye to the perfection of the Latter-day Saints as individuals or as a community, that instead of every man turning to his own way, all should be willing to be controlled by the God of heaven. - Brigham Young, February 8, 1868

Notice that in all three of the above quotes the Brethren were also saying that we can't please God and go our own separate ways in our economic labors (as we do today). For emphasis, let's repeat Elder Daniel H. Wells' question from above, "But do we realize that God's kingdom in the latter days is to all intents and purposes a *temporal* kingdom?"

What Economic Unity Looks Like

11 - Zion Requires Economic Unity

Twenty-one quotes have been found by this author where our early LDS leaders described what the economic unity looks like that God desires for our happiness. About three-fourths of those quotes describe some single element of economic unity that is only mentioned once. Since we are focusing this book around those points of doctrine taught by multiple leaders on multiple occasions, we'll look at the one element that qualifies. That single common element is that the Saints would perform their daily economic labors for each other's mutual benefit, instead of for their own benefit as we do today in "Babylon".

I have endeavored to describe to you the influence we wield because of our union in spiritual matters. The same remark will apply exactly to our union in temporal matters. Let this people be united in temporal matters; let it be known that <u>we work together for one another's good, that we labor, as a people to benefit the whole and not the individual,</u> and that our influence is in this direction; and I tell you that the same influence, the same power, that wield now as a spiritual organization will be felt in our temporal affairs, in our financial affairs, in all the affairs in fact which attract our attention. - George Q. Cannon, April 1878 General Conference

*Brethren and sisters, God bless you. Let us love one another; let us seek to promote one another's welfare. And let the Bishops and the Relief Societies, and the Young Men's and Young Women's Associations, and our [tradesmen] and manufacturers, and also our merchants, and all hands, **operate in the interests of the whole for the welfare of Zion** and the building up of the Kingdom of God upon the earth; and the blessings of God will begin to rest upon us, Zion will begin to arise, and the glory of God will rest upon her. Amen.* - President John Taylor, August 4, 1878

Again, how great would be the benefit to a body of people—to say nothing of households and families—located for instance, in one region of the country, a people who were united together according to the law of God, <u>desiring to advance each other's welfare and happiness</u>, and each man was required <u>to love his neighbor as himself</u>; a people who *knew how to so conduct their, temporal affairs **that each man's neighbor might be benefited as well as himself; and each one looking not only for his own welfare or that of his own household, but for the welfare of the whole community**, with whom he was associated, producing at last that unity and oneness which the Lord requires in the numerous revelations which he has given.* - Orson Pratt, August 25, 1878

What prevents economic unity?

Simple answer? Avarice – "greed for wealth or material gain". Back in Chapter 9, we read quotes showing that "Babylon is self-focus mixed with avarice". Here are three (rather long) quotes from early LDS leaders saying that economic unity is prevented by the avarice of the members. (Ouch):

Can you go to work and make a people of one heart and mind while they are possessed of the spirit of the world? You cannot . . . How can they devote their lives to the building up of the Kingdom of God when they do not delight in it, but <u>delight in building themselves up, in making gain, and in gathering around them the riches of the world</u>? The Latter-day Saints, in their conduct and acts with regard to financial matters, are like the rest of the world. The course pursued by men of business in the world has a tendency to make a few rich, and to sink the masses of the people in poverty and degradation. Too many of the Elders of Israel take this course. No matter what comes they are for gain—for <u>gathering around them riches</u>; and when they get rich how are those riches used? Spent on the lusts of the flesh, wasted as a thing of nought, and they who were once rich are left in poverty, as they are this day . . . Instead of being united in our feelings to build up all, each one takes his own course; whereas, if we were united, we would get rich ten times faster than we do now. - Brigham Young, April 1867 General Conference

We assembled in Missouri, at the place of gathering on the borders of the Lamanites, and there we bought our farms and built our houses; but could we stay there? Were we prepared then to enter into Zion, to build

up the Zion of God and possess it? We were not, we must suffer. "You Latter-day Saints, you, my children," says the Lord, "are not prepared to receive Zion." Why, we have heard detailed by Elder Carrington the conduct of Elders at the present time, dishonest **in the matter of a few shillings or dollars**. Dishonest, **covetous, selfish**, grasping for that which is not our own; **borrowing and not paying**; taking that which does not belong to us; dishonest in our deal; **oppressing each other**. Are we fit for Zion? . . . Do the people understand it? Scarcely! Scarcely! - Brigham Young, April 1872 General Conference

I think that our lives, our desires, our feelings and our acts ought to be to try to build up Zion and establish the kingdom of God upon the earth; that we should be united in our temporal as well as in our spiritual affairs, for God says: "If you are not one you are not mine." Do you believe it? You elders of Israel, do you believe that saying? And if we are not the Lord's then whose are we? We have our own plans, our own notions and our own theories; and as one of old expressed it, <u>we are seeking for gain, every one from his own quarter</u>. *And we are governed to a very great extent by selfishness, and too much by our own personal feelings, and allow these things to influence us instead of being governed by those high, noble, dignified and glorious principles that dwell in the bosom of God, which emanated from him, and which dwell also in the bosoms of those who in sincerity fear God and keep his commandments.* - John Taylor, September 21, 1878

Now as far as I could tell, only Lorenzo Snow identified *fear* as the barrier to economic unity, as seen in the following one-off quote:

Well, I was thinking of these things as brother Kimball was speaking this morning. If the people had confidence in the things which are taught, and if they would let their minds expand, and throw in their substance for the establishment of Zion and the extension of the kingdom of God, they would learn that it is the very principle upon which they would receive stores of those things which they are after.

*But there is a **fearfulness** in the minds of the people, they are **afraid** to trust their substance in the hands of the Lord . . .* - Lorenzo Snow, March 1, 1857

But isn't avarice rooted in fear? We fear losing the status and/or security temporal goods and wealth offer us. Seems likely that if we trust the Lord and gain a witness of our status before the Him, and thus overcome our fear of economic loss, perhaps avarice would disappear and economic unity would appeal to us.

Summary

- To become Zion, we must be one temporally too.
- "Being One Temporally" means we are "organized as one great family . . . each person performing his several duties in his line of industry, working for the good of the whole . . ."
- Economic Unity includes at least these three benefits: God will grant us riches needed to accomplish His will, it results in a classless society, and it eliminates poverty.
- In Zion, economic unity is not achieved through the redistribution of wealth, but through the *redirection* of wealth. Wealth's power is redirected into creating meaningful work for everyone and achieving local economic self-sufficiency.
- In a Zion society, economic activity is carried out under God's direction.
- Economic Unity looks like everyone laboring to benefit his neighbor as himself, to look out for the welfare of the whole community, and not just his own household.
- It's the avarice of the members that prevents economic unity.

Afterthoughts

It would be easy to conclude that if we are not working each day for each other's mutual benefit, then we are laboring in Babylon *for* Babylon, and not for Zion, as we have covenanted to do. And who is the king of Babylon? Let's be reminded of the teaching of our true King, Jesus Christ, that we cannot serve two masters. Perhaps we should re-commit to overcome our avarice and find a way to labor in the realm of economics for God and cease serving his enemy.

How is this done? Well, since we Saints aren't generally demonstrating by our actions that we are ready to enter Zion's economic United Orders, perhaps we can move in the right direction by participating in what several early Utah LDS leaders labeled, the "stepping stone to the United Order"—the topic of the next chapter.

Chapter Twelve – Cooperation is a Stepping Stone to Zion

As mentioned in earlier chapters, the early Utah-era LDS leaders saw that the Saints were quickly dividing into classes of rich and poor. They saw the values of Babylon were being brought into Utah by immigrating Saints. They were determined to establish Zion, but knew that the Saints had blown their opportunity under Joseph's tutelage to live the celestial-level law of economics. However, the LDS leaders found an intermediate step between Babylon's telestial-level economics and Zion's celestial-level United Order. That "stepping stone" was Cooperative Free Enterprise—pursuing mutual economic independence and self-sufficiency in a cooperative fashion in a free market. The Church leaders fully embraced the cooperative as a means to prepare the Saints for the higher economic law.

What are Cooperatives?

In case the reader is unfamiliar with cooperatives, one online dictionary defines a cooperative (also known as, a "co-operative" or "co-op") as "a farm, business, or other organization that is owned and run jointly by its members, who share the profits or benefits."

In some co-ops the owners are the individual people who work there. These are called worker-owned co-ops. In the United States, worker-owned co-ops can range from a handful of worker-owners, to thousands. An example of the former is a computer programming firm

12 - Cooperation is a Stepping Stone to Zion

in Madison, Wisconsin called Codeversant. Whereas, Cooperative Home Care Associates, in the Bronx, has over 2,000 on staff.

Marketing co-ops are usually owned by individual companies (often industrial farmers) and work together to sell their goods. Well-known examples of marketing co-operatives are Land O'Lakes, ACE Hardware, Ocean Spray Cranberries, and Sunkist Growers. All of America's top 25 largest marketing co-ops sell billions of dollars' worth of products to Americans every year.

Co-operatives in Utah History

Many Latter-day Saints may not be aware of the extent of co-operatives in Utah's history. LDS historian, Leonard J. Arrington, in his landmark book, "Great Basin Kingdom: An Economic History of the Latter-Day Saints, 1830-1900", reported about the most impressive example of Cooperative Free Enterprise among the Saints: Brigham City, Utah. Under the direction of Apostle Lorenzo Snow, Brigham City, over the span of 10 years, became a world-renown cooperative community. At their peak, all 2,000 inhabitants owned shares in and were employed in one of 40-odd manufacturing cooperatives in town. It was estimated that they produced 85% of all the consumer goods their community needed. In fact, during the world-wide banking panic of 1873, Brigham City had its best year ever.

Arrington noted that Lorenzo Snow began this economic miracle by establishing a single marketing co-op in Brigham City. The co-op bought goods produced locally and sold them locally. The profits were used to organize local producers into new cooperatives which manufactured consumer goods needed there in Brigham City. This process was repeated until everything produced in Brigham City was sold through the co-op. The town was so prosperous that they built homes for all the widows and would give food and work to passing indigents.

Cooperative Free Enterprise rolls out Church-wide

In <u>Great Basin Kingdom</u>, Brother Arrington also noted that the Church established a marketing co-op in every ward and settlement. They were patterned after Brigham City's initial marketing co-op. The goal was three-fold: to curb the drain of money out of Utah by non-member merchants, to help Utah become more self-sustaining, and to prevent the rise of a wealthy class in Utah.

Salt Lake City had 17 of the marketing co-ops. These stores were called "Zion's Co-operative Mercantile Institute". ZCMI sold locally-produced products as well as products imported from the Eastern United States. After five and a half years, ZCMI was reported by the First Presidency and the Twelve as a smashing success (See "An Encyclical Letter Upon Co-operation" in Appendix C).

Arrington described the degree to which co-operatives saturated the Utah territory:

As we have seen, for many years . . . the Mormons seem to have regarded cooperation as a distinctly Mormon way of doing business. Virtually every important enterprise organized by the Mormons after 1868 bore the name "cooperative". Mercantile cooperation [through ZCMI] was but the first step in a movement which saw the establishment of cooperative institutions in almost every realm of economic activity. Cooperative farming, cooperative herding, cooperative processing and manufacturing of grain, dairy products, leather, wool, cotton, and silk— cooperation in each activity and in each community was the dominant organizational pattern of Mormon economic life . . ."

So . . . Co-ops Help Us Build Zion?

They did, and they can. Some may be unaware that early LDS leaders taught that co-operatives were a means of uniting the Saints

12 - Cooperation is a Stepping Stone to Zion

economically and preparing them for their eventual return to build the New Jerusalem Zion.

A great quote showing this was given by Elder George A. Smith in the October 1873 General Conference:

We are looking forward to the day when we shall return to Jackson County . . . That will one day be the Center Stake of Zion, the center spot of the New Jerusalem which God is to build on this land. We can only be prepared for that work by being united . . . Can we not unite a little in erecting a [co-operative] factory, in establishing a store? Can we not learn, step by step, the principles of unity, which will enable us to be the people of God, like the Zion of Enoch, and prepare us for a dwelling with the blest? Every step we take of this kind is in the right direction. Sustain our Cooperative stores, and cease to sustain those who do not build up Zion.

One year after Brigham's death, President John Taylor made the point as well that economic cooperation was connected to building up Zion. He said:

And we are gathered together, as I have said, for the purpose of building up Zion, and we are supposed to be the servants of God having engaged to perform this work . . . We must carry out the word and will of God, for we cannot afford to ignore it nor any part of it. If faith, repentance and baptism and laying on of hands is right and true and demands our obedience, <u>so does cooperation</u> . . .

As early as June of 1856, Apostle Parley P. Pratt chimed in on this topic:

*[W]e are sure to progress in that oneness, and in that union nationally, religiously, politically and socially, and in every way to learn to **cooperate**, and to be more and more in the spirit, one in heart and in mind . . . We have much to do with each other in order to bring us into union more perfectly as families and communities . . .*

In May of 1874, Elder George A. Smith expressed the idea again that cooperation was entered into in preparation for eventually building the New Jerusalem. He said, "In order to make a step in the right direction, and to prepare the people to return to Jackson County, the principles of cooperation were taught and their practice entered into . . ."

So . . . How Do Co-ops Actually Help Prepare us to Build Zion?

<u>1. No poor among them.</u>

The Lord himself in Moses 7 says that one attribute of Zion is that "there were no poor among them"—not because they were all kicked out, but because those who were more gifted economically assisted those who weren't to prosper as well. Cooperation was implemented by early LDS leaders in order to make progress in the direction of achieving the "no poor among them" status of Zion.

Here are three of seven quotes which explain how cooperation brings about the elimination of poverty through a voluntary "spreading of the wealth":

I want to impress one thing on the minds of the people, which will be for their advantage if they will hear it. When you start your Cooperative Store in a ward, you will find the men of capital stepping forward, and one says, "I will put in ten thousand dollars;" another says, "I will put in five thousand." But I say to you, bishops, do not let these men take five thousand, or one thousand, but call on the brethren and sisters who are poor and tell them to put in their five dollars or their twenty-five, and let those who have capital stand back and give the poor the advantage of this quick trading. This is what I am after and have been all the time. - Brigham Young, 1869

We have had [cooperation] *established in our midst, and what are its effects? We witness a gradual diffusion of means throughout the community, greatly benefiting all its members. One of the effects of this which we witness is that wealth does not increase so rapidly in the hands of the few, and that the poor are not kept in poverty so much.* - George Q. Cannon, 1872

It is not his will that one should be lifted up and another put down, one be made rich and another poor. We have to keep this principle in view in our cooperative labors and be one, or we are not the Lord's. It is the purpose of the Lord to build up the poor, and these principles are revealed for its accomplishment. If twenty or thirty persons engage in business and we make them more wealthy, and others poor, what difference is there between us and the gentile world? If we do as is done in the world, wherein are we better than they? If we carry out the principle of cooperation with unselfishness of spirit and singleness of heart, it will build us up, and the poor also. - Charles C. Rich, 1877

The Church embraced cooperatives as a means of creating prosperity for all, and, at the same time, preventing the division of the people into unequal economic classes of rich and poor. In co-operatives, unlike the typical corporation today, the profits are distributed among the local population. Those who work in the co-op, and sometimes even the customers, receive a portion of the profits. The point of Cooperative Free Enterprise is to maximize well-being for the many, not exorbitant profits for the few.

2. "Of one heart and one mind"

As just mentioned, in an effort to unite the Saints economically, and prevent the rise of classes, the LDS Church leaders organized the Saints into numerous cooperatives. The goal was to attain that unity that God also mentions in Moses 7—"they were of one heart and one mind". That one heart was to be found in individuals working unitedly for their mutual benefit.

In the October 1873 General Conference, while pointing out the great financial benefits cooperation brought to Brigham City, Lorenzo Snow mentions the spiritual blessing of becoming one:

I notice the great interest which is now being taken by the Saints in the various settlements in establishing cooperative institutions. These embrace the great principles, in connection with the Order of Enoch, which are intended to join together our hearts, feelings and interests, and effectually build up the kingdom of God and redeem the earth. The people of Brigham City have been operating a number of years upon these principles, and are beginning to derive therefrom various financial advantages, as well as many spiritual blessings. **The hearts and feelings of the people are being considerably united through practicing this system of cooperating in our temporal interest.**

President George Q. Cannon in the April 1869 General Conference expressed it this way:

A great many of the Latter-day Saints scarcely understand the persistency with which the Presidency of the Church has labored to bring about the oneness of the people in temporal things; and this cooperative movement is an important step in this direction . . . It has already produced greater union, and <u>*it will produce still greater union than anything that has been witnessed among us*</u>*; and if we carry it out in the spirit in which it has been taught to us it will produce immense results.*

Then President John Taylor in December of 1878 said:

Well, the time is passing, but before closing, I wish to say a word or two in regard to this cooperation in temporal things . . . But for the time being it is expected that as honorable men and women, we will honestly and truly carry out our covenants in regard to these little temporal things; and **let us be one, for the Lord has plainly told us, if ye are not one, ye are not mine.**

Cooperatives are a Stepping Stone to Zion's United Orders

This remarkable teaching is another one that surprised me as I gathered all these quotes regarding the building of Zion. In fact, it was this connection tying co-ops to United Orders that prompted me to explore their teaching about co-ops even further.

The early brethren clearly saw and taught that cooperatives were a preparatory economic organization, preparing the people for Zion's economic order that the Lord had outlined through Joseph Smith. Here is how two prophets and two soon-to-be prophets expressed the relationship between cooperation and the United Order:

*This cooperative movement is only **a stepping stone to what is called the Order of Enoch**, but which is in reality the Order of Heaven.* - Brigham Young, April 1869 General Conference

I view cooperation, when properly understood and practiced, as being a steppingstone to the Order of Enoch, and will enable the Saints who receive it in a proper spirit, to gradually prepare themselves to enter, in due time, more fully into the practice of principles necessary to accomplish the building up of the kingdom of our God. - Lorenzo Snow, October 1873 General Conference

*We must give our earnest support to cooperation, for **it is a step in advance towards establishing the Order of Enoch and the building up of the Zion of God**.* - Wilford Woodruff, October 1873 conference.

What was the principle of cooperation intended for? Simply as a stepping stone for the United Order, that is all, that we might be united and operate together in the interest of building up Zion. - President John Taylor, December 1878

Other Early Teachings about Cooperation

Besides teaching that cooperation would prepare the people for Zion by uniting them economically and eliminating poverty, the early LDS leaders taught other things about it. These teachings included that cooperation was desirable for various additional but related reasons. They taught that cooperation would bring prosperity and that would lead to them becoming self-sustaining as a people. Presidents Brigham Young and John Taylor also taught that it was God's will that the Saints engage in cooperation. These two and other leaders also taught that our motives in taking up cooperation matter. They also repeatedly encouraged the Saints to "sustain co-operation" by patronizing the co-ops.

Generally, Cooperation is Awesome!

I spoke a little here yesterday and the day before; but I have not really said what I wish, and whether I shall be able to answer my own feelings with regard to our success in our cooperative system of merchandising I do not know. I want to say to the Latter-day Saints <u>we have wrought wonders</u>. - Brigham Young, April 1869 General Conference

Cooperation, it is well known to every Saint who has his eyes and ears open, **has brought much good to Israel** *. . . .* - Wilford Woodruff, May 1870

We have cooperative institutions established among us, and if they are conducted properly <u>they will be a blessing to us</u>. - Charles C. Rich, February 1878

There is another principle connected with [the United Orders] *that has been in force also upon our attention for many years past, namely, the system of cooperation in temporal matters.* **We have felt to a very great extent the importance of this**; *I believe the spirit of it has rested upon*

12 - Cooperation is a Stepping Stone to Zion

the Latter-day Saints. - George Q. Cannon, April 1878 General Conference

As for these other matters of a temporal nature before referred to, if we cannot cooperate together and do it honestly and in good faith, as <u>this is one of the very best things that can be required of us</u>, it is very little that we can do. - President John Taylor, December 1878

Cooperation Offers us Advantages

It is well for us to adhere to the principle of cooperation and everything else that is calculated to advance our interests as a people. - Orson Hyde, October 1869 General Conference

]C]o-operation and its necessity . . . has required days, weeks, and it may be said years of preaching to bring this principle home to the minds of the Latter-day Saints, so that they could see and understand its beauty and propriety, and the advantages which would result from its adoption in our midst. - George Q. Cannon, November 1870

Our Cooperative cattle herd, together with our sheep herd, and hogs kept at the dairy, supply our butcher shop, and partially our tannery with hides, and our woolen factory with the raw material. All these, together with other branches of industry, working in union, afford us important advantages in the present financial crisis, and supply, in a great measure, our real wants in a way that is easily [attainable] by the very poorest in the community. - Lorenzo Snow, October 1873 General Conference

Cooperation leads to prosperity

I will relate a little circumstance in relation to cooperation at Lehi. Five months after they had commenced their retail store on this cooperative system there, they struck a dividend to see what they had made; and they found that every man who had paid in twenty-five dollars—the *price of a share, had a few cents over twenty-eight dollars handed back or credited to him . . . It is ridiculous to think that they are making money so fast. Did they sell their goods cheaper than the people of Lehi could buy them before? Yes. Did they fetch the goods to them? O, yes, and yet they made money. A few weeks ago I was in the Wholesale Store in this city, and I was asking a brother from American Fork how cooperation worked there; and I learned that three months after commencing every man who had put in five dollars, or twenty-five dollars had that amount handed back to him and still had his capital stock in the Institution; and still they had sold their goods cheaper than anybody else had ever sold them there.* - Brigham Young, April 1869 General Conference. See Appendix B for the entire talk.

Do you not remember, before cooperation was started, how long and loud the President of this Church and his counselors, and other men, had to plead with the people to get them to see this plain matter of self-preserving policy? . . . If we were united, we could control things in this country to an extent you have no conception of, and **we could become rich, if riches were the desire of our hearts, there is nothing to prevent us**; *if we will be guided by the counsel of God's servants, we can have all the riches that heart can desire.* - George Q. Cannon, October 1875 General Conference

But I will promise the Latter-day Saints that if they will go into these [cooperative enterprises] allowing God to dictate in the interests of Israel and the building up of his Zion on the earth, and take themselves and their individual interests out of the question, feeling they are acting for him and his kingdom, **they will become the wealthiest of all people**, *and God will bless them and pour out wealth and intelligence and all the blessings that earth can afford; but if you will not, you will go downward, and keep going the downward road to disappointment and poverty in things spiritual as well as temporal. I dare prophesy that, in the name of the Lord.* - President John Taylor, March 1879

12 - Cooperation is a Stepping Stone to Zion

But the better way of all is—in a small community where every man knows his neighbor, and where all are on neighborly terms, to consult together, and to form into cooperative bodies for the purpose of transacting the business necessary to be transacted outside of their little community. By thus consulting together, and using the combined wisdom of the community as to the number of reapers, mowers, etc., they will need to do the work of the community, a great deal might be saved. One man need not own the machinery. They could all join together, each contributing a certain sum towards its purchase, which they could use to mutual advantage, and see that it is well housed and taken care of when out of use. **In this way a community could save thousands of dollars year after year**, *and I know the principle is a correct one for the people of Zion.* - Joseph F. Smith, July 1884

Cooperation Helps us Become Self-Sustaining

When we talk about cooperation, we have entered but very little into it, and it has been almost exclusively confined to the purchase of goods. There is not much in that. I wish we would learn how to produce them instead of purchasing them. I wish we could concentrate our energies, and organize all hands, old, middle-aged and young, male and female, and put them under proper directions, with proper materials <u>to manufacture everything we need to wear and use</u>. - John Taylor, May 1874

In order to make a step in the right direction, and to prepare the people to return to Jackson County, the principles of cooperation were taught and their practice entered into; and for the purpose of instructing and encouraging the minds of the people upon the benefits of united action, from the earliest settlement of this Territory to the present time, the presiding Elders of the Church have, every Conference, endeavored to impress upon their minds **the necessity of making themselves self-supporting**. - George A. Smith, May 1874

No one man, until quite recently, has had sufficient means to carry on any great undertaking; but by the masses of the people uniting under a cooperative plan, and putting their funds in the hands of those who are judicious and good business men, we can establish every kind of manufacture that is necessary in this country <u>to make us self-sustaining</u>.
- George Q. Cannon, April 1875 General Conference

I would like to have said something, too, about our co-operative associations. I am pleased to inform you that the Co-operative Institution of this city is doing remarkably well; it is on a solid foundation and everything is moving along pleasantly and agreeably . . . Then we expect to spread and grow in manufactures of all kinds, **that we may become a self-sustaining people***, a people who shall be independent, under God, of all other powers.* - President John Taylor, April 1879 General Conference

Cooperation is a Matter of Self-Preservation

I advise the Saints to form cooperative societies and associations all over the Territory, and to import everything they need that they cannot manufacture, and not to pay their money to men who use it to buy bayonets to slay them with, and to stir up the indignation of our fellow men against us. - George A. Smith, October 1868 General Conference

Do you not remember, before cooperation was started, how long and loud the President of this Church and his counselors, and other men, had to plead with the people to get them to see this plain matter of self-preserving policy? - George Q. Cannon, October 1875 General Conference

The Elders of Israel have traversed the earth and gathered you from distant nations, and you have come here to serve the Lord; but if you expend your energies and means in sustaining those who would destroy the Saints, you are only laying the foundation of your own degradation, for as the Lord God lives, the man who will not sustain Zion will be cut off. - George A. Smith, October 1873 General Conference

If we do not so cooperate, others may come in who have no interest in our prosperity, who will trade and traffic, and when they become wealthy would leave us and spend their means elsewhere. This has been our experience in years past with those who have come among us with their merchandise. We can prevent this in the future by our cooperative institutions. It is right and proper that we should combine for self-defense against this world, and so protect our general interests. - Charles C. Rich, November 1877

Cooperation is God's will for us

[C]ooperation was referred to by Brother Taylor. <u>The man or woman who is opposed to this is opposed to God</u> . . . We cannot do his will, nor be his disciples unless we are one. We must have the same faith and feelings for the building up of the kingdom of God, and for the salvation of ourselves and others, jointly, together, or we shall fail in our attempts to accomplish the work which the Lord has given us to do. - Brigham Young, June 1873

During the lifetime of President Young—several years ago, it seemed as though he was wrought upon to introduce cooperation and the United Order, to quite an extent. He told us at the time that **it was the word and the will of God to us**. *I believed it then; and I believe it now.* - President John Taylor, September 21, 1878

But let us sustain one another, and place things on a proper basis, and not be governed by the rules of the Gentiles . . . The first thing started in relation to these things was cooperation. <u>President Young told us it was the will of God that we should enter into it</u> . . . - President John Taylor, September 22, 1878

Our motives in taking up cooperation matter

[In reference to cooperation:] In temporal administration, the same as in spiritual, one should exhibit in his labors a self-sacrificing principle when necessary, that is, he should show that he labors for the interests of the people rather than for building up himself. Lorenzo Snow, October 1873 General Conference

It is not great dividends that are going to make either the United Order, or any of our cooperative associations prosperous, permanent and successful, but honesty and straightforward business habits, and contentment with reasonable profits and rewards for our labors. - Erastus Snow, April 1875 General Conference

I will tell you, Latter-day Saints, that unless we can enter into our cooperative institutions and the United Order with singleness of heart and pure motives, as the Elders do when they go forth to preach the Gospel, because it is God's command, your efforts will be of small avail. We do not want to stop and ask, Is there money in it? Is it his will, his law and principle? When we combine our interests on this principle, and work to it, we will succeed and prosper. - President John Taylor, March 1879

The Brethren Directed the Saints to Sustain the Co-Operatives

And then, after awhile, when co-operation is taught unto us we will receive that also in a like spirit and faith; and if our minds are possessed of the Spirit of God we will say, "There is light in this principle; I see its advantages, <u>I will sustain it by carrying it out myself, and I will try and exercise influence with my friends and induce them to do the same</u>, that it may become universally practiced in the midst of the Saints." - George Q. Cannon, November 1870

Let us not be weary in well doing; let us not slacken our hands, either in cultivating the earth or in the manufacturing of what we need.

Cooperate in agricultural and mercantile matters, also in our tanneries, and in the making of butter and cheese. One man may engage in these branches of business with advantage if he have skill and experience to guide him; but in cooperation the wisdom of all is combined for the general good. - Wilford Woodruff, April 1872 General Conference

We must have experience in order to properly understand how to sustain temporal institutions, and manage financial concerns, and wisely use concentrated means. <u>Cooperation is of little benefit unless the people understand, appreciate, and feel disposed to sustain it</u>; and in order for this we must be taught and instructed in regard to its object and advantages. "Wait a little season, for the redemption of Zion, that my people may be taught more perfectly, and have experience, and know more perfectly concerning their duty and the things which I require at their hands". - Lorenzo Snow, October 1873 General Conference

This is a comparison with regard to our cooperative stores and every cooperative institution we have; **we expect that the whole people will support them and give them their influence**; that the whole people will work for the whole, and that all will be for the kingdom of God on the earth. - Brigham Young, May 1874

We took a vote at the Priesthood meeting, yesterday, and so far as I could discern, <u>the brethren all voted to sustain cooperation</u> . . . - President John Taylor, September 1878

Summary

The LDS leaders during the 1850s to 1880s taught these remarkable concepts about Cooperative Free Enterprise:

- Co-operatives are a stepping stone to Zion's United Orders.
- Co-ops help prepare us to build Zion by uniting us economically, and by helping to prevent the rise of social classes of rich and poor.

- Cooperation offers us advantages, leads to prosperity, helps us become self-sustaining, and is even a matter of self-preservation.
- Cooperation is God's will for us.
- Our motives in taking up cooperation should be pure—we should seek to bless our community and not just ourselves. [Perhaps this is what is really meant by "pure in heart"]
- The Brethren directed the Saints to sustain the co-operatives.

It is also appropriate to summarize this chapter the same way President John Taylor ended his April 9th, 1879 General Conference address:

We will strive to be one; and <u>if we cannot go so far as to sustain cooperation in regard to these things, how in the name of common sense are we ever going into the United Order</u>? But we will begin with this, and then cooperate in all the different Stakes, not only in your merchandising, but in your manufacturing affairs and in your producing affairs; and in everything it will be the duty of this general Board of Trade to regulate the interests of the whole community, honestly and faithfully, at least we will do it according to the best ability we have; and if there should any mistakes arise, we will try to correct them; if they are on the part of the people, we will talk to them about it, if on the part of the institution, we will talk to its management about it. **And we will keep working and operating until we succeed in introducing and establishing these things that God has desired, and until Zion shall be a united people** *and the glory of all the earth. God bless you and lead you in the path of life, in the name of Jesus. Amen.*

Challenge

In the spirit of doing "many good things of their own free will, and to bring to pass much righteousness" (D&C 58:26-29), I invite you to become a Champion for Zion yourself by joining an effort to begin building co-ops. This will start us back on the path of preparing ourselves for the economic unity required of those who live in a real Zion society.

12 - Cooperation is a Stepping Stone to Zion

As President Taylor just mentioned above, "<u>if we cannot go so far as to sustain cooperation in regard to these things, how in the name of common sense are we ever going into the United Order</u>?" Let's unite together with one heart and use the "stepping stone to the Order of Enoch" to prepare ourselves for Zion by learning to master Cooperative Free Enterprise. Come visit ZionBuilders.org.

Chapter Thirteen – Afterthoughts: Zion Shrugged

So . . . where's the Zion they were building?

It's been over 130 years since the early LDS leaders made the hundreds of statements about building Zion, and we still have no Zion. You would think, by now, we would have long since been well on our way to a City-of-Enoch style Zion right here in Utah. Why isn't there one?

Should we blame our current Church leaders?

I believe this would be a poor choice. From the records, it appears that the problem wasn't the leaders. It was the rank and file members. Our Champions for Zion kept preaching cooperation and economic unity until well after the Saints started drifting away towards Babylon's model.

Blaming others is never the solution. If we members want our leaders to pick up the cause of building Zion today, <u>we must first show we're ready by our actions</u>. We members must take responsibility for preparing ourselves to live in a Zion-level economy. We must show our determination to prepare to be worthy to move to a higher level before our leaders will even consider rolling out such a move church-wide. (Hence, ZionBuilders.org).

The LDS Church *is* taking baby steps towards Zion. Are we?

Before we presume to criticize our church leaders for not pushing Zion, are we helping the programs succeed that they *are* rolling out?

- The Perpetual Education Fund introduced by President Hinckley in 2001 is definitely a higher level of economic organization. Saints in poor countries are able to attend school by drawing on monies from the Fund. Then after graduating college and landing good-paying jobs, they pay their loans back into the Fund. That's economic cooperation.
- The new Self-Reliance program is two steps in one. First, the outward goal of the program is to help families achieve economic self-reliance. As wards and communities, it's much easier to build Zion with people who have the training or skills to provide for themselves. Second, the team focus of the program gets members used to working together for their mutual benefit—a very Zion-like value.
- The Church has also been involved in poorer countries with programs to give their members economic training and even micro-loans to start their own businesses. They usually do this through LDS Charities and by partnering with non-government organizations.

The Forces arrayed against Utah's Zion-building effort

From reading Leonard J. Arrington's book "Great Basin Kingdom", it appears there were three great forces working against the Church leaders and their efforts to fulfill the prophecies about a last days Zion being built "in the mountains of Israel". The three were: the Members, the Immigrants, and the Government.

The Members

The leaders simply tired of trying to "herd cats" and finally threw in the towel. Just after all the United Orders crumbled, Brigham Young passed away. John Taylor took up the Zion-building gauntlet with gusto. However, the Saints' patience with cooperative free enterprise was beginning to wane. Many Saints wanted to go their own way and do their own thing. They whined that cooperation limited their freedom.

Finally, John Taylor caved to the pressure. In what today would be called a First Presidency Message, President Taylor gave permission to the Saints to launch businesses that were not founded on cooperative principles—though he did continue to preach that the Saints had come to Utah to build the prophesied Zion. This was the beginning of the end of their Zion-building efforts.

When I explained this to a friend, she said, "Like the children of Israel!" Yes, our brave Utah pioneer ancestors were unable to live the not-all-that-higher higher law. Although their spiritual legacy is remarkable-- sacrificing life and limb to join the Church and move West—their economic legacy haunts us to this day. We are awash, along with the rest of society, with the unpleasant effects of Babylon's dis-unified economics—Materialism, Class conflict, Crime, along with Political & Moral Corruption.

The Immigrants

The constant influx of immigrants with old-world economic values also worked against Zion-building. Brother Brigham's inspired Perpetual Emigrating Fund (PEF) was very effective in helping new converts "Come to Zion". Unfortunately, it appears from quotes reviewed in Chapter One that they came too quickly to be properly absorbed into the fledgling culture of cooperation. Often Saints arrived in Utah only to reject the stewardships they were offered and chose to go their own way.

The Government

The death knoll rang for the Mormon Zion-building effort when the United States Government conquered the Church in the late 1880s. The non-member merchants, who lost dearly when they refused to join forces with Zion's Co-operative Mercantile Institute, riled up the Eastern newspapers, who in turn riled up the social warriors, who then riled up the US Government to shut down polygamy. Besides the dis-incorporation of the Church and the confiscation of its assets, the government's anti-polygamy crackdown forced the leaders of most of the co-ops, the surviving United Orders, and the Zion Boards of Trade into prison or into hiding. Those entities then either collapsed or drifted into private hands. Under these kinds of pressure, it's hard to blame them.

. . . and Brigham may have rushed things a tad much

In my opinion, Brigham Young rushed things. After converting the entire Utah economy from Competitive to Cooperative Free Enterprise, the Saints only had about 10 years for the values of cooperation, mutual benefit, and economic unity to soak into the local culture. After those brief 10 years, Brigham believed the Saints were ready to make the step up to celestial economics. So he organized them all into United Orders. Sadly, the vast majority of the Saints weren't ready, and Brigham's efforts met with drastic failure. Nearly all of the 200+ Orders he established failed within a year of launching.

It is my belief that if President Young had been satisfied for the Saints to remain on the terrestrial level of economics for *at least* a generation, the chances of the Saints being able to then successfully make the shift to celestial-level economics would have been greatly increased.

Remember the children of Israel and how many problems they had with the generation that had been used to the way things had been done in Egypt? Same problem. The older generation had to die off before the new values could be completely embraced on a community level. Economic values and traditions can't be changed overnight, or even, apparently over-decade.

Hindsight . . .

Were the early LDS Leaders simply wrong?

We saw numerous quotes in chapter three where our Champions for Zion came right out and said that their newly-built Zion society would not fail because God had decreed it would rise. As Wilford Woodruff so vehemently affirmed in 1889, "We have a great future before us. Zion will arise and shine, and the glory of God will rest upon her. Israel will be gathered, Jerusalem will be rebuilt, Zion [will] be established and thrown down no more forever. These things are in the record of divine truth. Not one of them will ever fail of fulfillment. They were given by revelation."

God had decreed Zion would rise and by darn they were building it! Then, it all fell apart. So, were they wrong? Were they uninspired? I don't think so, and here's one reason why: Chiasmus.

Introduction to Chiasmus

Chiasmus is a literary technique where a string of words or topics are spoken of and then repeated in reverse order. Frequently in scripture we'll see topics A, B, and C discussed in this order: A B C C B A. Sometimes the chiasmus will have ten or twenty words or topics that are stated and then repeated in reverse order. This literary device is reminiscent of the Lord's statement, "The first shall be last and the last shall be first."

This technique is used apparently by God himself, as well as ancient and modern prophets. In a 1972 article entitled, "Chiasmus in the Book of Mormon", LDS scholar John W. Welch gave a good explanation and plenty of examples you can google, if you're interested. And more recently, I noticed that all but the first paragraph of President Monson's April 2017 General Conference talk entitled, "The Power of the Book of Mormon", was a single chiasmus:

13 - Afterthoughts: Zion Shrugged

A. We live in <u>a **time** of great trouble</u> and wickedness.

B. What **will protect us** <u>from the sin and evil</u> so prevalent in the world today?

C. I maintain that <u>a strong **testimony**</u> of our Savior, Jesus Christ, and of His gospel <u>will help see us through to safety</u>.

D. If you are not reading the Book of Mormon each day, please **do** so.

E. If you will read it prayerfully and with a sincere desire to know the truth, <u>the Holy Ghost will manifest its truth to you</u>.

F. <u>If it **is true**</u>—and I solemnly testify that it *is*—then Joseph Smith was a prophet who saw God the Father and His Son, Jesus Christ.

F'. <u>Because the Book of Mormon **is true**</u>, The Church of Jesus Christ of Latter-day Saints is the Lord's Church on the earth, and the holy priesthood of God has been restored for the benefit and blessing of His children.

E'. If you do not have <u>a firm testimony</u> of these things,

D'. **do** <u>that which is necessary</u> to obtain one.

C'. <u>It is essential for you to have your own **testimony**</u>

B'. for the testimonies of others **will carry you** only so far.

A'. <u>in these difficult **times**</u>,

A possible Last Days Chiastic Timeline suggests Utah's Zion-building effort was no "failure".

There seems to be a chiastic pattern pairing the events of the Restoration with those prophesied of the Last Days. To the point—I believe there is a last days prophecy chiasmus and that the Utah Zion-building effort was simply an element in the first half of a chiastic pattern. I believe the Saints "failure" to establish Zion was simply God arranging a foreshadowing of the prophesied rise of Zion before Christ returns.

In 2014, I noticed a *possible* Last-Days Chiastic Timeline:

A through K are historic events listed in order. K' through A' are prophesied Last Days events that may possibly align with historic events, but in reverse order.

Note: the grayed entries are those that seem the most obvious counterparts of each other.

A. Christ appears to Joseph Smith. (1820)

B. Translation of the Book of Mormon completed. (1829)

C. First missionaries called to preach to the Lamanites. (1830)

D. Location of the New Jerusalem revealed to Joseph Smith. (1831)

E. Joseph Smith leads Zion's Camp to help Saints expelled from Jackson County. (1834)

F. Twelve Apostles ("traveling councilors") are called and sent to preach to all nations. (1835)

G. Christ, Moses, Elias, & Elijah give keys to Joseph Smith & Oliver Cowdery. (1836)

H. Joseph & Hyrum Smith martyred at Carthage Jail. (1844)

I. Brigham Young leads many Saints into Salt Lake Valley. (1847)

J. Saints are gathered to Utah to **build Zion** for 40 years. (1850s-1880s)

K. Babylon makes war against the Saints & its economy absorbs them. (1887+)

K'. Babylon falls and releases its economic hold on the Saints. (Rev.18)

J'. Some **Zion society will be built** for people to flee to for safety. (D&C 45:68)

I'. Man "like as Moses" leads Saints "out of bondage". (D&C 103:16-17)

H'. Two witnesses killed & resurrected in Jerusalem. (OR, Joseph & Hyrum resurrect)

G'. Christ & Patriarchs take back the keys at Adam-ondi-Ahman. (TPJS, p.157)

F'. 144,000 High Priests sent out for last time, 12,000 from each tribe. (D&C 77:11)

E'. Redemption of Zion by the "armies of Israel". (D&C 105:28-31)

D'. New Jerusalem established. (Moses 7:62)

C'. Lamanites embrace the Gospel (and/or Return of Lost Tribes?).

B'. Sealed portion of the Book of Mormon translated and/or published.

A'. Christ appears in glory.

Now, IF (and that's a big IF) this chiastic last days timeline is anywhere close to being accurate, it suggests that the Saints' roughly 40 years of Zion-building was simply a foreshadowing of "the real event"—the prophesied building of Zion "in the mountains of Israel" even before the New Jerusalem Zion is built. If that's the case, then the Lord never intended them to succeed at it. (Maybe that is why He allowed polygamy to be introduced as part of the Restoration, because the Lord foresaw that it would be the excuse used by the U.S. Government to torpedo their Zion-building efforts.)

Before constructing this timeline, I often wondered why the Lord would allow Zion's Camp to fail. Perhaps this chiastic timeline also "explains" that as well. Zion's Camp was essentially an army led by Joseph Smith to reclaim lands taken by Missouri mobs. Just before they arrived, a miraculous storm arose and scattered their enemies, but Joseph's "army" left without "redeeming Zion". They did not retake the lands from those who had pushed the Saints out. But, if this timeline is anywhere near accurate, it's possible that the first Zion's Camp was merely a foreshadowing of the "real" Zion's Camp prophesied in D&C 105:28-31.

Guess we'll see.

Chapter Fourteen – Objections & Rebuttals

"*We* can't build Zion, only Jesus can build Zion"

In the High Priests group in my ward, I heard this exact statement made by one particular, highly-influential brother every time the topic of establishing Zion was brought up (which was often). I believe that his statement was possibly rooted in one quote by one apostle given in the October 1882 General Conference. I have not found a single additional quote supporting the idea that his statement suggests—that we have to wait for Jesus to do all the heavy lifting. Here's Apostle Joseph F. Smith's statement:

Zion will be built up, for God will do it; and no man should deceive himself by entertaining the opinion, the thought or the feeling in his heart that it is he that will build up Zion, for men cannot do it. God has said: "I will do it; it is my work; it is my kingdom; I have cut the stone out of the mountain with mine own hands, and I will roll it forth; I will accomplish my purposes and my designs and my people shall triumph." God hath said it, and He will do it, and man will not do it, for he cannot do it . . .

Without knowing the context, one would think that Elder Smith was saying that "We can't build Zion, only Jesus can build Zion". However, if we read the entire quote, in context, with the idea that Elder Smith was saying something else, we can see plenty of evidence to the contrary:

May He bless all who are assisting to build up Zion and the good of the earth everywhere. Zion will be built up, for God will do it; and no man should deceive himself by entertaining the opinion, the thought or the feeling in his heart that it is he that will build up Zion, for men cannot do it. God has said: "I will do it; it is my work; it is my kingdom; I have cut the stone out of the mountain with mine own hands, and I will roll it forth; I will accomplish my purposes and my designs and my people shall triumph." God hath said it, and He will do it, and man will not do it, for he cannot do it, **though he will be the agent in the hands of God in accomplishing much good**. God will bestow great power upon His servants and will bless them with light and wisdom, knowledge and understanding, power and authority, and the keys of the Priesthood to accomplish a great and mighty work. <u>But He will have the honor and the glory; for it is he that will give the power to accomplish the work; man has no power in and of himself to do so.</u>

That last sentence makes the whole quote make more sense. Elder Smith was NOT saying we can't build Zion, he was saying that we may *assist* God in building *his* Zion, and God is the one who gets the credit, not us. We have "no power in and of [ourselves] to do so." We are the tools in God's hands to build his Zion. Is God likely to pick us up and use us as tools if we are rusty in regards to building Zion? Not likely. We should be qualifying ourselves by working together in the preparatory level of Cooperative Free Enterprise.

This statement, made in April 1870 by Brigham Young expresses the perspective better that building Zion IS God's work, but WE are the ones who will do the labor:

*Are we prepared now to establish the Zion that the Lord designs to build up? . . . "Well," says one, "I thought the Lord was going to do this." So He is **if we will let Him**. That is what we want: we want the people to be* *willing for the Lord to do it. But He will do it by means. He will not send His angels to gather up the rock to build up the New Jerusalem. He will not send His angels from the heavens to go to the mountains to cut the timber and make it into lumber to adorn the city of Zion.* **He has called upon us to do this work**; *and if we will let Him work by, through, and with us, He can accomplish it; otherwise we shall fall short, and shall never have the honor of building up Zion on the earth. Is this so? Certainly. Well, then, let us keep the commandments.*

"We can't build Zion until the prophet commands it"

True. We can't build THE "center stake of Zion", the New Jerusalem, until God directs us through his prophet. No argument there.

However, the quotes in previous chapters suggest we have everything we need to build a Zion society in the here and now, no waiting required. Brigham's quotes all make it blatantly clear that we can build a Zion society <u>any time we want</u>. We simply have to want it bad enough to take action.

Besides, in this book I am *not* calling on the Saints to build Zion-like communities (although some Gentiles are successfully doing it), but to PREPARE to build Zion by getting involved in its stepping stone—cooperative free enterprise. We have to learn the lessons we simply cannot learn here in Babylon's schools and businesses. So, we need to take baby steps in the direction of building Zion so that, when the time comes, we will be *able* to assist the Lord in his official effort.

"Since our prophets today aren't calling for Zion to be built, we aren't obligated to do so."

Also true . . . sort of. We aren't *obligated* to build Zion. In 1888, Bishop Orson F. Whitney concurred:

The command of Noah to build an ark does not make it obligatory upon you or me to build one. This Church is based upon immediate and direct revelation. It is what God says today, not what He said yesterday to someone else, that must be considered. We must not take the dead letter and with it judge the living oracle. We must not sit in judgment upon God and say, "I can not do this, because yesterday you told someone else to do differently." We can only escape His wrath by being willing to do everything that He requires at our hands, and acknowledge His hand in all things.

About our non-obligation, Elder Abraham O. Woodruff (Wilford's son), said in the October 1899 General Conference:

We ought to desire to build up the material Zion; and while we may not be commanded in these things, we should, as the revelation . . . says, be willing to do many things of our own free will and choice.

So, according to Elder Woodruff, we may not be obligated by commandment to build the "material Zion" but we can do it under the Good-Cause Clause of D&C 58:26-29.

Here's the thing, "prophets, seers, and revelators" today HAVE called for Zion to be built. Have we heard the call? Consider these calls-to-action:

As we sing together "Come to Zion," we mean . . . come to the ward, the branch, the mission, the stake, and give assistance to build up Zion. – President **Spencer W. Kimball,** Paris Area Conference, 1976

My dear brethren and sisters, we must prepare to redeem Zion. It was essentially the sin of pride that kept us from establishing Zion in the days of the Prophet Joseph Smith. It was the same sin of pride that brought consecration to an end among the Nephites. Pride is the great stumbling block to Zion. I repeat: Pride is the great stumbling block to Zion. We must cleanse the inner vessel by conquering pride. - President Ezra Taft Benson, April 1989 General Conference

If we are to build that Zion of which the prophets have spoken and of which the Lord has given mighty promise, we must set aside our consuming selfishness. We must rise above our love for comfort and ease, and in the very process of effort and struggle, even in our extremity, we shall become better acquainted with our God. – Apostle Gordon B. Hinckley, October 1991 Conference

If we would establish Zion in our homes, branches, wards, and stakes, we must rise to this standard. It will be necessary (1) to become unified in one heart and one mind; (2) to become, individually and collectively, a holy people; and (3) to care for the poor and needy with such effectiveness that we eliminate poverty among us. **We cannot wait until Zion comes for these things to happen—Zion will come only as they happen**. *In our families and in our stakes and districts, let us seek to build up Zion through unity, godliness, and charity, preparing for that great day when Zion, the New Jerusalem, will arise.* - Elder D. Todd Christofferson, October 2008 General Conference

"I'm waiting for the *current* prophet to tell us."

True, we haven't been commanded by our current prophet to build Zion. But should we wait to be commanded in all things Zion? D&C 58:26-29 suggests otherwise:

26 For behold, it is not meet that I should command in all things; for he that is compelled in all things, the same is a slothful and not a wise servant; wherefore he receiveth no reward.

27 Verily I say, **men should be anxiously engaged in a good cause, and do many things of their own free will, and bring to pass much righteousness***;*

28 For the power is in them, wherein they are agents unto themselves. And inasmuch as men do good they shall in nowise lose their reward.

29 But <u>he that doeth not anything until he is commanded</u>, and receiveth a commandment with doubtful heart, and keepeth it with slothfulness, <u>the same is damned</u>.

I agree that the call to build the New Jerusalem itself should come from the Lord directly, through his anointed servant. However, *I also believe we can implement principles of a Zion society in our homes, businesses, schools, and governments without any direction whatsoever, as part of the Good-Cause Clause of D&C 58. The Gentiles are doing it, why can't we as "children of the covenant"?*

Why wait? Who benefits if we delay?

Chapter Fifteen – No Need to Wait

Admittedly, most of the following are one-off quotes—these are the only statements I found where these LDS leaders made these specific points. Therefore, we cannot conclude that each of these statements on its own is doctrinally sound. However, when considered as a whole they give us the clear understanding that they believed there was no need to wait to begin building Zion.

The Lord is willing

I was present at the time the revelation came for the brethren to give their surplus property into the hands of the Bishops for the building up of Zion. . . . If we are disposed to enter into covenant one with another, and have an agreement made according to the laws of our land, and we are disposed to put our property into the hands of trustees, and work as we are directed . . . the Lord has not the least objection in the world, and would be perfectly willing for us to do it, and I should like, right well, for us to try it. - Brigham Young, April 1873 General Conference

We are called to do it

The kingdom of God is before us; we have it to build up, and to establish the Zion of our God upon this land. And if I am right in my

views and feelings, the Latter-day Saints cannot labor too fast nor too diligently to accomplish the work they are called to do. Then let us go to with our might, and labor faithfully to establish that kingdom which is all and in all to us. May the Lord help us. Amen. - Brigham Young, April 1862 General Conference

We have everything we need

There is not one thing wanting in all the works of God's hands to make a Zion upon the earth when the people conclude to make it. We can make a Zion of God on earth at our pleasure, upon the same principle that we can raise a field of wheat, or build and inhabit. There has been no time when the material has not been here from which to produce corn, wheat, &c.; and by the judicious management and arrangement of this ever-existing material a Zion of God can always be built on the earth. - Brigham Young, February 1862

We have the authority

I say to you, and I bear testimony to it, that all the keys, all the authority, all the power, and all the Spirit that were necessary to build up Zion were bestowed upon the Prophet Joseph; and by him conferred upon his fellow-servants, and are in existence and held and exercised at the present time by the Apostles of this Church. - George Q. Cannon, March 1889

We have the privilege

Wherever there is a people of God, the principles of the United Order are applicable, if they would receive and obey them. Some have thought that the United Order was to be kept only by the people who should go up to the land of Missouri. Now this, I believe, is incorrect. It would seem very singular that the Latter-day Saints, when they receive the Gospel, should not have the privilege of uniting themselves, according to the principles of the celestial law, and that Jackson County should be the only place where this law might be observed. - Lorenzo Snow, April 1878

We have the determination

We are not going to wait for angels, or for Enoch and his company to come and build up Zion, but we are going to build it. We will raise our wheat, build our houses, fence our farms, plant our vineyards and orchards, and produce everything that will make our bodies comfortable and happy, and in this manner we intend to build up Zion on the earth and purify it and cleanse it from all pollutions. - Brigham Young, February 1862

We have the opportunity

I consider that we are in a position in which we have every chance to do a great deal of good in our day and generation, we have every chance to work with the Lord, every chance to fulfil our mission and calling here on the earth. We have every chance to build up the Zion of God. - Wilford Woodruff, May 1870

We have the power

The Lord has put into our hands the power to build up his Zion and kingdom on the earth, and we have more to encourage us than was ever possessed by any generation that has preceded us. - Wilford Woodruff, January 1873

We have the priesthood

You are literally and lawfully heirs of the Priesthood through the lineage of your fathers, and that Priesthood will continue throughout eternity, therefore you have received your appointment, and the Lord looks to you to build up his Zion and kingdom upon the earth. - Wilford Woodruff, September 1875

We have the resources

The elements are here to produce as good a Zion as was ever made in all the eternities of the Gods. Here are the elements to produce grain which is good for the food of man, as also the fruit of the vine, and that which yieldeth fruit, whether in the ground or above the ground. - Brigham Young, February 1862

And, we have the right to do it

It is for us, as children of our heavenly Father, to arise and <u>assume the right the law of the Holy Priesthood gives us</u>, and organize the elements for a Zion, and bring it forth, no matter where we are. I would not give much for a religion that is not thus practical. - Brigham Young, February 1862

Brigham called for a model Zion community

Suppose we should say to a few of the Latter-day Saints, if we could find those who would answer the purpose, "How *would* you like to build up a stake of Zion, a little city of Enoch? How would you like this? Would you like to enter into a covenant, and into bonds, according to the law of our land, and <u>let us bind ourselves together to go into a systematic cooperative system, not only in merchandising, but in farming and in all mechanical work, and in every trade and business there is</u>; and we will classify the business throughout, and we will gather together a few hundred families, and commence and keep the law of God, and preserve ourselves in purity." How would the Latter-day Saints like it? Do you think there could any be found who would be willing to do this?

Let me say to you, my brethren, I have a very fine place to start such a society as this that would probably sustain from five to ten thousand persons. I would like to make a deed of this property to such a society, and enter into a covenant with men of God and women of God that we *would go to and show the world and <u>show the Latter-day Saints how to build up a city of Zion</u>, and how to increase intelligence among the people, how to walk circumspectly before our God and before one another, and classify every branch of labor, taking advantage of every improvement, and of all the learning in the world, and direct the labor of men and women, and see what it would produce; follow it out for ten years, and then look at the result.* - Brigham Young, October 1872 General Conference

Afterthoughts:

Though the above quotes suggest we can build Zion anytime, as a people, it is unlikely that we are actually *ready* to build Zion. But we can follow in their footsteps by preparing ourselves to be ready by doing what they did. They saw cooperatives as a stepping stone to help the Saints learn to achieve economic unity and to eliminate poverty from among them. We can certainly do *that* of our own free will "to bring to pass much righteousness" for the power is within us and we are agents unto ourselves. Hence comes the challenge again to prepare as our Utah forefathers prepared, by building and operating co-operatives:

Champion Challenge Renewed

Again, I invite you to become a Champion for Zion yourself by joining an effort to build co-ops. By doing so, we can better prepare ourselves for the economic unity required of those who are to live in a real Zion society. As President Taylor was quoted in chapter 13, "if we cannot go so far as to sustain cooperation in regard to these things, how in the name of common sense are we ever going into the United Order?" Let's unite together with one heart and use the "stepping stone to the Order of Enoch" to prepare ourselves for Zion by learning to master Cooperative Free Enterprise.

Come visit ZionBuilders.org.

CHAMPIONS FOR ZION

·—·

Now we are brought face to face with this question,
shall we take these counsels to heart,
shall we listen to the voice of God through his servants
which we have heard now these 42 years in these valleys,
and follow the direction which they have given
concerning the people of Zion,
or shall we make a new departure?
Shall we throw aside all that we have heretofore been taught
as the correct course and policy
to be adopted in building up the kingdom of God,
shall we throw it aside, cast it behind us
and adopt some new principles,
some new policy and practice
concerning the Zion of our God in the earth?

• George Q. Cannon, September 1889

Appendix A

Chapter One - What Early LDS Leaders Said About Establishing Zion

2. Building Zion Was Considered a Core LDS Doctrine.

What has been said to you? What has been said to me? If we will preach this doctrine, the people almost universally will follow us and say, "Don't mention Joseph Smith—never mention the Book of Mormon or Zion, and all the people will follow you." I said, It would not do them any good, if we were to listen to their requirements. What I have received from the Lord, I have received by Joseph Smith: he was the instrument made use of. If I drop him, I must drop these principles: they have not been revealed, declared, or explained by any other man since the days of the Apostles. - Brigham Young, July 29, 1852

3. Building Zion is Central to the Church's Mission

What makes us so buoyant and joyful on occasions like this? Why is it that the Spirit and power of God is more visibly manifested at the time of our General Conference, when the authorities of the Church from all parts are assembled together to talk on the things of God, regulate the affairs of his kingdom, to put in order anything that may be wrong, and counsel together pertaining to the interests of Zion and the building up of Israel? - Elder John Taylor, October 1859 General Conference

This Gospel is meat to my soul; it affords me continual pleasure; I contemplate it with delight. If I had the tongue of an angel, or of the most eloquent upon the earth it would be my delight to speak of the goodness of God and of the work he is performing; for it appears very glorious to me. **The building up of Zion** *and the establishment of the kingdom of God are to me interesting in the highest degree: the work in which we are all engaged is a constant solace to my soul.* - Elder Daniel H. Wells, October 1860 General Conference

[I]f all the numbers that have been baptized into this Church since its first organization were added together I do not suppose that there would be less than a million, and but few of these have remained to the present time, the rest have built up cities for the Gentiles, and have populated such towns as St. Louis, San Francisco, and in fact almost all of the cities of California and the Western States. The rest are still laboring to [1] **build up Zion***, to [2] spread abroad the fulness of the everlasting Gospel and to [3] save all who will give heed to its teachings and the dictates of the Holy Spirit . . . .* - Elder George A. Smith, May 11, 1862

The Lord gives us possessions, and he requires of us one-tenth of the increase which we make by the putting to good use the means He has placed in our hands. I am sorry to see a disposition manifested in some to go to distant parts to trade and build up themselves and make money, while the ability which God has given them is not concentrated in [1] building up His kingdom, in [2] gathering the house of Israel, in [3] redeeming and <u>building up Zion</u>*, in [4] renovating the earth to make it like the garden of Eden, in [5] overcoming sin in themselves, and in [6] spreading righteousness throughout the land.* - President Brigham Young, October 1863 General Conference

While many are willing to admit that the servants of God understand everything connected with the work of God, and with the various departments of it on the earth, they think there are some kinds of knowledge which they possess in a superior degree to them who preside

*over us. They will admit that the servants of God may possess all the knowledge that is needed to [1] spread the Gospel and have it carried to the remotest regions, to [2] **build up Zion**; but there is something connected with their particular calling that, they think, they understand to a far greater extent than he or they who are appointed to preside over them.* - Elder George Q. Cannon, January 1, 1865

I testify that this work of God in which we are engaged has been commenced to gather the house of Israel and <u>establish Zion</u> in the last days . . . . - President Brigham Young, May 10, 1868

If we will faithfully mind our own concerns, live our religion, do good to all men, preach the Gospel to the nations of the earth, gather up the honest in heart, <u>build up and establish Zion in the earth</u>, send the Gospel to the House of Israel, and live and serve God in all things, all will be well with us, we have no cause for fear in the least. - President Brigham Young, April 29, 1877

We are called of God; we have been chosen, we have been ordained as men who have been called to bear the priesthood and to attend to the ordinances of the house of God, to preach the Gospel, to warn this generation, **to build up Zion***, to redeem the earth, to erect temples unto the name of the Most High God, to redeem the living and the dead, and to carry out those great purposes which have been foreordained before the world was.* - Elder Wilford Woodruff, October 1880 General Conference

We pay our Tithing and we pay Temple donations, we attend to the duties of the House of the Lord; we go forth and proclaim the Gospel of peace to the nations of the earth; we convert people, under the blessing of God, and they come to a knowledge of the principles of the Gospel, <u>and we continue our labors to build up Zion</u> . . . . - President John Taylor, January 9, 1881

It remains for us to continue to bear our testimony to the world, to build our Temples, in which to perform *the* work for ourselves and our dead, essential to salvation and exaltation in his kingdom, and to build up a Zion to the glory of God. That this may be our determined purpose to a faithful consummation, I humbly pray, in the name of Jesus, our Lord. Amen. - Franklin D. Richards, April 1882 General Conference

I fully realize what Elder Woodruff said this morning concerning the aged Elders of Israel passing away, and that the responsibility and labor of bearing off this kingdom will soon rest upon the generation which is growing up in our midst, upon which will devolve the work of carrying the Gospel to those who have not heard it among the nations of the earth, and gathering Israel and establishing Zion and building up and maintaining the Kingdom of God upon the earth . . . . - Erastus Snow, April 1883 General Conference

5. Building Zion Was a Primary Focus of LDS Leaders

Let us go, to work and build up Zion as well as build up ourselves, for when we build up Zion we build up ourselves, when we enrich Zion we enrich ourselves. - Heber C. Kimball, November 26, 1854

I want to live for this, to see Zion redeemed, and the Church and kingdom of God cover the face of the whole earth, and have one universal reign of peace. - Brigham Young, March 29, 1857

How the soul of the Prophet [Joseph] rejoiced when he beheld the work of God spreading abroad in the earth, the truth received by the children of men, and the promises of God verified to the letter in the gathering of the Saints, and a way prepared for the establishment of Zion upon the earth. - Wilford Woodruff, January 10, 1858

I have Zion in my view constantly. - Brigham Young, February 23, 1862

Appendix A – Chapter 1

The poet says—"Do what is right, let the consequence follow." This is the duty of the Latter-day Saints in their attempts and endeavors to build up Zion. - John Taylor, April 13, 1862

We are determined to build up the kingdom of God on the earth; to bring forth Zion, to promote the cause of righteousness on the earth, and to walk under foot sin and wickedness. - Brigham Young, August 31, 1862

Our course is onward to build up Zion, and the nation that has slain the Prophet of God and cast out his people will have to pay the debt. - Brigham Young, August 31, 1862

May the Lord multiply his blessings upon you, brethren and sisters, and upon all the faithful ministers and Saints throughout the world, and may He bless all those who do good, who love righteousness and desire the welfare and building up of Zion; I ask this in the name of Jesus Christ. Amen. - Heber C. Kimball, July 19, 1863

I have spoken this afternoon that you may see that I am living and in good health; and I intend to live, if I can, until the Zion of our God is established upon the earth, and until all wickedness is swept from the land. - Brigham Young, July 17, 1864

You and I have the privilege of serving God, of building up Zion, sending the gospel to the nations of the earth and preaching it at home, subduing every passion within us, and bringing all subject to the law of God. - Brigham Young, December 8, 1867

We have the right to do good, but not evil. The principles of the gospel of Jesus Christ which have been revealed in our day are the power of God unto salvation to all that believe, both Jew and Gentile, in this age of the world as well as any other; and inasmuch as we will be united in carrying out the counsel we have received, we can overcome every evil that lies in our path, build up the Zion of God, and place ourselves in a position that we may be saved therein, which, may God grant, for Christ's sake. Amen. - Wilford Woodruff, April 7, 1867

I delight to hear a person give an intimation of their having faith in God; to hear it said, "I believe in Jesus Christ. I believe in his crucifixion and atonement, and in his ordinances." These ordinances we are trying to live, that we may glorify God, and prepare ourselves to build up His Zion on the earth, that the world may be filled with peace, knowledge, and joy. God help us to do so! - Brigham Young, May 29, 1870

We have a Zion to build up, and we shall build it. We shall build it. WE SHALL BUILD IT. No power can stop it. - John Taylor, April 1872 General Conference, emphasis in the original.

I pray God, my heavenly Father that he will pour out his Spirit upon the daughters of Zion, upon the mothers in Zion, upon the Elders, and upon all her inhabitants, that we may listen to the counsels of the servants of God, that we may be justified in the sight of God, that we may be preserved in the faith, that we may have power to build Temples, build up Zion, redeem our dead, and be redeemed ourselves, for Jesus' sake. Amen. - Wilford Woodruff, Oct 1873 General Conference

If we have not the truth, that is what we are after, we want it. But we know that we have it, that the Gospel as restored, revealed through Joseph Smith, is the truth of God, and we know that the Lord has set to his hand to build up Zion, and he is going to do it. We bear record of this because we know it is true. - Wilford Woodruff, Oct 1874 General Conference

The full set time has come to build up and favor Zion, to build up the kingdom of God, to warn the world and prepare them for the judgments of the Almighty. - Wilford Woodruff, September 12, 1875

I think it a great blessing and privilege to stand in the midst of the people of God in this age of the world to preach the Gospel of Jesus, and

to labor to build up Zion, in obedience to his commandments, and to carry out his purposes in the day and age in which I live. - Wilford Woodruff, April 1878 General Conference

We will operate together, and with all Israel and with the gods in the eternal worlds, and with the patriarchs, prophets and apostles, and all the holy men of God who have lived before us, in assisting to bring to pass all the designs of God of which the prophets have spoken, and in building up the Zion of God, in redeeming the earth and establishing the kingdom of God thereon. - John Taylor, May 15, 1878

God had revealed himself to the human family and had restored the everlasting Gospel, and that with it came all these other things— apostles and high priests and elders and patriarchs and bishops and high councilors and all the various organizations of the Church and kingdom of God as they now exist upon the earth, all occupying their own peculiar place and position. What for? For the building up of a something that is called Zion or the pure in heart. - John Taylor, December 1, 1878

It shows that while God has revealed the Priesthood to us upon the earth and conferred upon us those privileges, that in former generations he revealed the same Priesthood to other men, and that those men holding that Priesthood ministered to others here upon the earth; and that we are operating with them and they with us in our interests and in the interests of the Church and kingdom of God, in assisting to build up the Zion of God, and in seeking to establish truth and righteousness upon the earth - John Taylor, July 24, 1882

It is upon President Taylor night and day, I know. Every thought and desire of his heart is for the salvation of this people, and to establish and build up the Zion of our God. - George Q. Cannon, October 29, 1882

I pray God to bless you with His Holy Spirit; I pray that he will give us power to fulfill our calling in the Priesthood, power to build up Zion, power to finish these temples in which we may redeem our dead. This is

my prayer in the name of Jesus Christ. Amen. - Wilford Woodruff, December 10, 1882

The Lord Almighty has set His hand to establish His Church and kingdom on the earth, to build up Zion in the mountains of Israel. - Wilford Woodruff, July 20, 1883

If you will give me your attention and your faith and prayers I will endeavor to address you. It always affords me pleasure to meet with the Saints of God. In company with my brethren we have been traveling up and down lately, associating with the Saints in the different conferences, trying to speak of things in which we are all interested, things pertaining to the building up of the kingdom of God, and the establishing of His Zion upon the earth. - John Taylor, December 9, 1883

[T]he keys of the Holy Priesthood . . . [bring] life and salvation to the dead as well as to the living. Having these keys committed unto us, we proceed to establish Zion; to build up her Stakes; to build her temples; to gather together those who purify themselves before the Lord - Erastus Snow, February 2, 1884

Chapter Two - What *IS* Zion?

It has been seen by thinking men that there is something radically wrong in the organization of society in this respect, but they have not known how to remedy the evils. It is so in the religious world. - George Q. Cannon, April 1869 General Conference

Why are men tempted, to be thieves? Why do they steal—take property that does not belong to them? Would they do this if society was properly constituted? No, they would not be tempted to do it. The temptations that we are exposed to are the result, in a great degree, of the false organization of society. - George Q. Cannon, June 29, 1873

What is it, then, that produces the misery that we read about, and that we sometimes see? What is it that produces the destitution among the nations of the earth, and, to some extent, among us? It is because **there is something lacking in the organization of society**. *These anarchists feel it; these societies of various kinds feel it; but their methods of reaching the desired end are not from God; therefore they fall.* - George Q. Cannon, March 11, 1894

Zion as One of Three Foundations of a God-centered Society

This Church *has continued to rise. It is the only true church upon the face of the whole earth. Its history is before the world. It has continued to grow and increase from the day it was organized until the present time.* **This is the Zion of God.** *We see an embryo of it in these valleys of the mountains, and it is designed by the Most High God to stand on the earth in power and glory and dominion, as the prophets of God saw it in their day and generation.* **This is the kingdom** *that Daniel saw, and it will continue to roll forth until it fills the whole earth. These are eternal truths, whether the world believe or disbelieve them, it matters not, the truths cannot be made of non-effect. This is certainly a strange work and a wonder. There has been every exertion made to stay it. Armies have been sent forth to destroy this people, but we have been upheld and* *sustained by the hand of the Lord until today.* - Wilford Woodruff, June 6, 1880

We are here as the representatives of God upon the earth to accomplish his purposes, and to carry out his designs, to spread forth his Gospel [i.e. **Church***], to build up his* **kingdom***, to establish his* **Zion** *. . . This is what we are here for, as I understand it, and this is what we will do . . .* - President Taylor, August 20, 1882.

We live, in fact, in the dispensation of the fullness of times, the last dispensation in which the Lord will reveal his mind and will to the inhabitants of the earth, the last time in which the Lord will prune his vineyard, the last time in which he will set up his **kingdom** *upon the earth, establish His* **Church***,* <u>and</u> *build up His* **Zion***, to prepare for the coming of the Son of Man.* - Wilford Woodruff, December 10, 1882

[T]he day will come when all peoples will mourn who take a stand against the kingdom of God, the Zion of God, the Church of God, and the Lord's anointed . . . . - Wilford Woodruff, December 10, 1882

We are here for the purpose of becoming acquainted with the will of God, with the law of God, with the order of God, with the dominion of God; and we are here to establish **the kingdom of God***. We are here to be taught in things pertaining to* **the Church of God***, and its purification. We are here to build up* <u>a</u> ***Zion of God****, which implies the pure in heart.* - President John Taylor, October 19, 1884

Specifically, Zion is the God-given, True *Economic* Organization of Society [as opposed to Babylon, the false organization of society]

The world is more or less controlled all the time by influences that Lucifer evidently is not opposed to; he has little objection to the present organization of human society, from the fact that everything passes along in the wake that agrees with his religion, and rather tends to forward his purposes. - Jedidiah M. Grant, February 19, 1854

Nearly 37 years ago the Prophet Joseph, or rather the Lord, through him, gave revelations upon the Order of Enoch. Those revelations were taught to the people in plainness so far as they went. They were simple and easily understood; but they embodied within themselves what might have been termed new principles, and indicated a new course of action and a new organization of society. I say new, because they were new so far as this generation is concerned. The principles taught by those revelations were as old as eternity; and the Order sought to be introduced by their means was called the "Order of Enoch," in consequence of its having been revealed to and practiced by Enoch; and through its practice he and his people were prepared for translation and, as we read in the Scriptures, were taken from the earth. The Lord inspired the Prophet Joseph Smith to once more communicate these principles unto the children of men; but, as I have remarked, the people were not prepared to carry them out. - George Q. Cannon, April 1869 General Conference

It has been seen by thinking men that there is something radically wrong in the organization of society in this respect, but they have not known how to remedy the evils. It is so in the religious world. - George Q. Cannon, April 1869 General Conference

Why are men tempted, to be thieves? Why do they steal—take property that does not belong to them? Would they do this if society was properly constituted? No, they would not be tempted to do it. The temptations that we are exposed to are the result, in a great degree, of the false organization of society. - George Q. Cannon, June 29, 1873

What is it, then, that produces the misery that we read about, and that we sometimes see? What is it that produces the destitution among the nations of the earth, and, to some extent, among us? It is because there is something lacking in the organization of society. These anarchists feel it; these societies of various kinds feel it; but their methods of reaching the desired end are not from God; therefore they fail. - George Q. Cannon, March 11, 1894

Chapter Three - God's Will

God Intends Zion to be Built

Do we [LDS] think that we shall be shielded from the judgments of the Almighty if we lay ourselves liable by the same acts as the world? If we do we are mistaken, for if we are guilty of the same crimes and wickedness the results will be the same with us as with the world, with the exception perhaps that the judgments will overtake us a little quicker, for they will commence with us. For it would thwart the purposes of the Almighty to let the wicked get a foothold and predominate in the midst of Israel, where <u>he intends to prepare his people for the building up of Zion</u> and the New Jerusalem. - Daniel H. Wells, 1862

The Zion of God is before his face continually. He has laid a foundation and He will build upon it, and his Saints will build upon it; and thousands and tens of thousands of the meek of the earth will yet take hold and become co-workers in the great work of God. - Wilford Woodruff, May 6, 1870.

The Lord Almighty has set His hand to gather His people, and to build up his Zion . . . . - Wilford Woodruff, May 14, 1882

I say to those who are able to see and comprehend these things, it is clear and plain that God has had His eye upon this American continent as the place where He first commenced His great work on the earth . . . <u>where He has determined ultimately to establish His Zion</u> and gather together His people . . . . - Erastus Snow, April 1883 General Conference

Building Zion is part of God's work

Appendix A – Chapter 3

*Some men have had visions concerning things that were to come relative to the restoration of Israel; <u>the building up of Zion</u>; the establishment of the Kingdom of God upon the earth . . . There are a great many curious sayings in the Scriptures in relation to these things. Where did they all come from? Where did these ideas, theories, and notions, so numerous in what we call the Word of God, originate? We all believe they come by inspiration, "that holy men of God," as the Scriptures say, "spake as they were moved upon by the Holy Ghost." I believe they were men who knew how to approach God, and that when they did they obtained visions, revelations and the ministering of angels, and could look through the dark vista of future ages and see **the purposes and designs of God** rolling on to their accomplishment.* - John Taylor, February 24, 1867

*And God will bless and protect Israel; he will lead us forth in the paths of life—not all of us, for as we have heard, we are not all of us doing just right. <u>But he will accomplish his purposes and roll forth his work **and** build up his kingdom **and** establish Zion</u>, and bring to pass all the things spoken of by the holy prophets since the world began.* - President John Taylor, November 30, 1879

We are told to build up Zion, shall we do it? I tell you in the name of Israel's God we will do it with the help of the Almighty; we cannot do it without, but with his help we will do it. We will build up the Zion of our God, and help to roll on the work which <u>God</u> has commenced. - President John Taylor, March 21, 1880

*[F]or God has ordained this [American] form of government in this age of the world, and **has chosen His own instruments to further His great purposes on the earth**—the organization of his Church, the proclamation of the everlasting Gospel, <u>the establishment of His Zion</u>, and bringing to pass His wonderful works which He predicted by the mouths of the ancient Prophets.* - Erastus Snow, April 1883 General Conference

And we testify of these things, that God has reserved to Himself this right to command His people when it seemeth to Him good and to accomplish the object He has in view—that is, to raise up a righteous seed, a seed that will pay respect to His law <u>and will build up Zion</u> in the earth. - Erastus Snow, June 24, 1883

God Has Declared Zion, So It <u>Must</u> Rise

We shall pass away and go to the other side of the veil, and the burden of the building up of Zion will rest upon our sons and daughters. Then rejoice in the Gospel of Christ. Rejoice in the principles of eternal life. I am looking for the fulfillment of all things that the Lord has spoken, and <u>they will come to pass as the Lord God lives</u>. Zion is bound to rise and flourish. Wilford Woodruff, January 12, 1873

No man or woman on the face of the earth will ever be disappointed with regard to the fulfillment of the word of the Lord, for he has uttered decrees, made covenants, and through his servants the Prophets has declared his word and will concerning the world and its inhabitants, and not one of his sayings will fail, all must be fulfilled. If it could be otherwise, the Zion of God would never be built up; but <u>God has decreed that his kingdom will be established, that Zion will arise and shine</u>, and that every weapon formed against her will be broken. - Wilford Woodruff, October General Conference, 1874.

The Lord is Working Through His Church to Build Zion

[T]he Lord has set his hand to accomplish his designs in these last days; he has opened the heavens and revealed his purposes to his servants the Prophets, and <u>has called his people from the ends of the earth to gather together, that he might establish his Zion</u> upon the earth, and bring to pass these things which have been spoken of by all the holy Prophets since the world was. - John Taylor, January 10, 1858

We [Church members] must build up the Zion and kingdom of God on the earth, or fail in the object of our calling and receiving the Priesthood of God in these latter days. The full set time has come, which the Lord decreed before the foundation of the world—the great dispensation of the last days, and a people must be prepared for the coming of the Son of Man. How can they do it? By being gathered out from Babylon . . . we have gathered together that we may be taught by Prophets, Patriarchs and inspired men, and we are endeavoring, under their instructions, to throw off the trammels with which we and our forefathers have been bound for generations. We are not prepared for the coming of the Son of Man, and if he were to come today we could not endure it. There is no people on the earth prepared for that. But the Lord is laboring with us, he has carried us through a school of experience now for forty years, and we should certainly have been dull scholars if we had not learned some wisdom. - Wilford Woodruff, April Conference 1862

It is for us all [in the Church] to take a course that we may secure the favor and approbation of the Almighty, that we individually may be led by him, having his spirit always with us. Then if the Presidency be under the guidance of the Almighty, and God direct the Priesthood through them in all its ramifications, carrying out his will in the building up of Zion on the earth, then we shall be one with them and one with God. This is what we are after, and may God help us to carry out his purposes and designs. - Elder John Taylor, November 5, 1876

God expects me to talk plainly. . . . I tell you the truth. And while He has called us to high privileges, to thrones and principalities and dominions, and to be saviors on Mount Zion . . . while God has ordained us for this, in the name of Israel's God we will try and carry it out. And we will find enough [men] that will be true and faithful to God and to His Holy priesthood. And the work of God will roll on, Zion will be established, and the kingdom of God built up, and no man will stay its progress. Amen. - President John Taylor, August 28, 1881

We are *Called* by God to Build Zion

[W]e are not here to attend to our own personal affairs merely, but, <u>we are called to look after the interests of God, to build up his Zion</u> and establish his kingdom on this his earth. *"For as I have said,* **we are not here to build up ourselves, but to build up Zion** *and establish the principles of righteousness upon the earth.* <u>That is our calling</u> *. . . and it behooves us to magnify it and honor our God.* - John Taylor, President of the Quorum of the Twelve Apostles, October 21, 1877 (seven weeks after Brigham's death)

<u>*God has set us apart to do His will and to build up His Kingdom and His Zion*</u>*. Zion means the pure in heart, and we have to be pure in heart and pure in life. We have to be honest. We must not steal. What, do Saints steal? I hope you have no thieves among you here. And then there are covetous men, men who conceive all kinds of plans to get possession of other people's property.* - President John Taylor, June 24, 1883

We have been called to gather, not to scatter; ***we have been called by the Lord to build up Zion.****"* - George Q. Cannon, April 1889 General Conference (the day after being set apart as First Counselor to President Woodruff).

Two Prophets and One Apostle Declare It's God's Will We Build Zion

What does the Lord want of us up here in the tops of these mountains? <u>*He wishes us to build up Zion*</u>. - Brigham Young, January 12, 1868

What has He told us? *He has told us, and it is recorded in the revelations contained in the New Testament, that in the latter days He would send His angel flying through the midst of heaven, having the everlasting Gospel to preach to those who dwell on the earth. That angel has flown, the Gospel is delivered, the kingdom is established, and* <u>*Zion has to be built up*</u>. - Brigham Young, April 17, 1870

I have labored nearly forty years to get the people to believe and to embrace, in their faith and practice, what the Lord has told us to do. **The**

Lord wants to build up His Zion, and He wants to build it up through you and me. - Brigham Young, April 17, 1870

We are required/commanded to build Zion

The commandment has gone forth for the Saints to gather and build up Zion. - Brigham Young, September 2, 1860

We have a great Work laid upon us, and we are responsible to God for the manner in which we make use of these blessings. **The Lord requires of us to build up Zion**, *to gather the honest-in-heart, . . . establish universal peace and prepare a kingdom and a people for the coming and reign of the Messiah. When we do all we can to forward and accomplish this Work then are we justified. This is the work of our lives, and it makes life of some consequence to us.* - Wilford Woodruff, June 12, 1863

Do we know and understand that it is our business to build up Zion? To have seen the way this people have conducted themselves in years past, one would not have had the least idea that such was our business; but it made no difference whom we built cities for; many would build for Jew or Gentile, Greek, Mahommedan, or Pagan, every class of men on the earth, as readily, apparently, as they would build up Zion. Yet the word of the Lord to us is to build up Zion and her cities and stakes. Lengthen her cords and strengthen her stakes, O ye House of Israel; add to her beauty and add to her strength! Why, to have seen the conduct of the people you might have supposed they knew no more about Zion than about a city of the Chinese, or a city in France, Italy, Germany, or Asia; just as soon build up a city in Asia or Africa as anywhere else, "no matter whom we build for if we only get the dollar, only get our pay for our work." Yet the commandment of God to us is to build up Zion and her cities. - Brigham Young, February 10, 1867

My brethren and sisters, we are commanded not to give the whole of our attention to the accumulation of earthly things; we are commanded also to lay up treasures in heaven. We are **required** to build up Zion on *the earth; then let us take a course that will ensure to us the blessing and favor of God our Heavenly Father, that our prayers and thanksgiving may be acceptable before Him.* - George Q. Cannon, 7July 21, 1867

The ordinance of sealing must be performed here man to man, and woman to man, and children to parents, etc., until the chain of generation is made perfect in the sealing ordinances back to father Adam; hence, we have been <u>commanded</u> to gather ourselves together, to come out from Babylon, and sanctify ourselves, and build up the Zion of our God, by building cities and temples, redeeming countries from the solitude of nature, until the earth is sanctified and prepared for the residence of God and angels. - Brigham Young, February 16, 1868

But we are not called upon to build an ark to save ourselves; we are called to build up Zion. God has spoken from the heavens, and given us revelations, and it is for you and me to obey. The **command** *has been given, it is recorded, and you can all read [it] for yourselves.* - Brigham Young, April 17, 1870

These are some of the grand events spoken of in this Bible; these are events that the Latter-day Saints believe in, and that so far as it lies in their power, they are trying to fulfill. If we are not Jews we are not required to go to old Jerusalem, but we are <u>required</u> to build up a Zion; that is spoken of as well as the building of Jerusalem. Zion is to be built up in the mountains in the last days, not at Jerusalem. - Orson Pratt, July 25, 1875

[I]t seems as though we have almost lost sight of our calling, of the object of our being gathered together, and the purposes which God requires at our hands. There is a good deal for us to do if we build up Zion; and if we do that and sanctify ourselves before the Lord, it has got to be done through obedience to the commandments of the Lord. The Lord has **commanded** *us, and we have got to obey his commandments if we receive the blessings of obedience.* - Wilford Woodruff, April 1876 General Conference

I think it a great blessing and privilege to stand in the midst of the people of God in this age of the world to preach the Gospel of Jesus, and to labor to build up Zion, <u>in obedience to his commandments</u>, and to carry out his purposes in the day and age in which I live. - Wilford Woodruff, April 1878 General Conference

*Now then, if Zion—**we were talking about building up Zion**—I am not going to enter into the whys and wherefores of these things, but will say it is a test to the people of God, or for us who profess to be, that we may know whether people will observe **a certain specific law** given by the Almighty or not, and thus have a proof of their fidelity and obedience.* - President John Taylor, January 9, 1881

Chapter Four - Prophecies About Zion

Prophets foretold of a latter-day Zion

"When the Lord shall bring again Zion, and the watchmen shall see eye to eye, and Zion shall be established, saviors will come upon Mount Zion and save all the sons and daughters of Adam that are capable of being saved, by administering for them. [Isaiah 52:8]" - Brigham Young, April 1860 General Conference

Said he, "Sing, O heavens; and be joyful, O earth; and break forth into singing, O mountains: for the Lord hath comforted his people, and will have mercy upon his afflicted." What do you see, Isaiah, that should cause you to break forth in such language as this? I see what the Gods of eternity see. I <u>see what all the prophets and patriarchs before me have seen—that the Lord Almighty will build up his Zion upon the earth in great power and glory in the latter days</u>. - Wilford Woodruff, October 22, 1865.

Some men have had visions concerning things that were to come relative to the restoration of Israel; **the building up of Zion;** *the establishment of the Kingdom of God upon the earth; the reign of righteousness, when iniquity should be swept from the face thereof, when the "law should go forth from Zion, and the word of the Lord from Jerusalem;" when all men should be subject to that law, and when to Jesus every knee shall bow and every tongue confess. There are a great many curious sayings in the Scriptures in relation to these things.* - John Taylor, February 24, 1867

Isaiah and Jeremiah and nearly all the prophets since the world began have foretold the gathering of the people in the last days to establish Zion, *from which the law of the Lord should go forth to rule the nations of the earth, while the word of the Lord should go forth from Jerusalem.* - Wilford Woodruff, July 19, 1868

The words contained in the 7th verse of the 52nd chapter of the prophecies of Isaiah are brought to my mind. While contemplating <u>the great work of building up the Zion of God in the last days</u>, *he says— "How beautiful upon the mountains are the feet of him that bringeth good tidings, that publisheth peace; that bringeth good tidings of good, that publisheth salvation; that saith unto Zion, Thy God reigneth!"* - Wilford Woodruff, September 5, 1869

<u>*Isaiah and other prophets saw in vision much concerning the building up and establishment of the latter-day Zion of God upon the earth*</u>. *They saw the people gathering from the nations of the earth to the mountains of Israel; they speak of a great company coming up to Zion, the women with child and her that travailed with child together . . .* - Wilford Woodruff, May 6, 1870

The revelations of Isaiah concerning the building up of the Zion of God in the last days will have their fulfillment. *The house of God will be established upon the tops of the mountains, and all nations must flow unto it. Zion must arise and put on her beautiful garments, she must be*

clothed with the glory of her God . . .
Adam, our first great progenitor and father, after the fall, received this Gospel, and he received the holy Priesthood in all its power, and its keys and ordinances. He sealed these blessings upon his sons—Seth, Enos, Jared, Cainan, Mahaleel, Enoch and Methusaleh. All these men received this high and holy Priesthood. They all professed to give revelation. They all had inspiration and left their record on the earth; <u>and not one of them but what saw and prophesied about the great Zion of God in the latter days</u>. And when we say this of them, we say it of every Apostle and Prophet who ever lived upon the earth. Their revelations and prophecies all point to our day and that great kingdom of God which was spoken of by Daniel, that great Zion of God spoken of by Isaiah and Jeremiah, and that great gathering of the house of Israel spoken of by Ezekiel and Malachi and many of the ancient Patriarchs and Prophets . . .

As I before remarked . . . holy men of old spoke as they were moved upon by the inspiration of the Holy Ghost, and when any of those Prophets and Patriarchs for the last six thousand years spoke, when wrapped in prophetic vision, **of the Zion of God being established in the last dispensation**, those decrees had to be fulfilled to the very letter . . . <u>Isaiah speaks of the foundation of this great Zion, and writes the whole of her history and travels up to the present day</u>, and from this time on until the winding-up scene. If we had not been driven from Nauvoo we would never have come up the Platte River, where, Isaiah says, he saw the Saints going by the river of water wherein went no galley with oars; a great company of women with child and her that travailed with child would never have come here to the mountains of Israel if we had not been driven from that land, and a whole flood of prophecy would have remained unfulfilled, with regard to our making this desert blossom as the rose, the waters coming forth out of the barren desert, our building the house of God on the tops of the mountains, lifting up a standard for these nations to flee to; all this and much more would have remained unfulfilled had we not been guided and led by the strong arm of Jehovah, <u>whose words must be fulfilled though the heavens and the</u>

earth pass away. - Wilford Woodruff, October General Conference, 1873.

[T]he Lord answered that in the dispensation of the fulness of times the earth would fill the measure of its days, and then it would rest from wickedness and abominations, for in that day he would establish his kingdom upon it, to be thrown down no more forever. Then a reign of righteousness would commence and the honest and meek of the earth would be gathered together to serve the Lord, and upon them would rest power **to build up the great Zion of God in the latter days**. - Wilford Woodruff, October General Conference, 1874.

Now, how is it pertaining to the last days? As it was in the days of Noah, so shall it be in the days of the coming of the Son of Man. *As it was in the days of Lot, so shall it also be in the days of the coming of the Son of Man. In what respect? In the days of Noah did they have the Gospel preached unto them? Yes. Did the people generally reject it? Yes.* Did the people gather together and build up a Zion? Yes. - President John Taylor, December 14, 1884

Zion is to be built before Christ returns

We are told in the prophecies of Isaiah that **before the time of the second advent**, *when the glory of the Lord should be revealed and all flesh should see it together,* **there should be a Zion built up on the earth**. - Orson Pratt, April 1872 General Conference

We find, in the 40th chapter of the prophecies of Isaiah, that the people of Zion are to be raised up preparatory to the second advent of the Son of God. - Orson Pratt, June 15, 1873

[The great shepherd] will stir up his strength and will save the house of Joseph. But it will be in his own time and way. First, a remnant will be converted; **second, Zion will be redeemed, and all among the Gentiles who believe will assist this remnant of Jacob in building the New**

219

Jerusalem; *third, a vast number of missionaries will be sent throughout the length and breadth of this great continent, to gather all the dispersed of his people in unto the New Jerusalem;* **fourth, the power of heaven will be made manifest in the midst of this people, and the Lord also will be in their midst** *. . . This is what we must look for . . . not asking God to establish this people upon their inheritances in Jackson County, until the other things are fulfilled in their order, and in their times and seasons.* - Orson Pratt, February 7, 1875

Prophecies about Zion are to be fulfilled in our day

Here, you Latter-day Saints *must be prepared to carry out and fulfill his purposes in the last days pertaining to the redemption of the desert, that joy and thanksgiving may be offered up in all parts of it in fulfillment of the prophecy of Isaiah, which has often been sung by the Christian world—"The Lord shall comfort* Zion, *he shall comfort all her waste places, make her wilderness like Eden, and her desert like the garden of the Lord. Joy and gladness shall be found therein, thanksgiving and the voice of melody."* You here see the beginning of the fulfillment of this ancient prophecy *. . .* Zion in the midst of the great American desert is beginning to redeem it and make it blossom as the rose, *making it like the garden of Eden, that joy and thanksgiving and songs of praise and prayer and gladness may ascend up from all her habitations and settlements throughout the length and breadth of this desert, and thus the prophecies will be fulfilled. Amen.* - Orson Pratt, November 27, 1870

In the last chapter of the first book of Nephi, the Lord, through the Prophet, speaks concerning the building up of Zion **in the latter days** on the earth. He says his people should be, as it were, in great straits, at certain times, *but said the Prophet, "The righteous need not fear, for I will preserve them, if it must needs be that I send down fire from heaven unto the destruction of their enemies." This will be fulfilled if necessary. Let the righteous among this people abide in their righteousness, and let them cleave unto the Lord their God; and if there are those among them* who will not keep his commandments, they will be cleansed out by the judgments of which I have spoken. <u>But if the majority of **this** people will be faithful, the Lord will preserve them from their enemies</u>, from sword, pestilence and plague, and from every weapon that is lifted against them . . . God will shield us by his power, if we are to be led forth out of bondage as our fathers were led, at the first. This indicates that there may be bondage ahead, and that <u>the Latter-day Saints</u> may see severe times, and that unless we keep the commandments of God, we may be brought into circumstances that will cause our hearts to tremble within us, that is, those who are not upright before God. <u>But if this people should be brought into bondage</u>, as the Israelites were in ancient days, <u>Zion must be led forth out of bondage, as Israel was at the first</u>. In order to do this God has prophesied that he will raise up a man like unto Moses, who shall lead his people therefrom. - Orson Pratt March 9, 1873

There never was a generation of the inhabitants of the earth in any age of the world who had greater events awaiting them than the present. As I before remarked, <u>the fulfillment of this whole volume of revelation points to our day</u>. The building up of the kingdom of God, <u>the building up of the Zion of God</u>, in the mountains of Israel, the erection of a standard for the Gentiles to flee unto, the warning of the nations of the earth to prepare them for the great judgments of our God . . . <u>all these things are to be performed in our day</u>. And an age fraught with greater interest to the children of men than the one in which we live never dawned since the creation of the world. - Wilford Woodruff, September 12, 1875.

Isaiah prophesied Zion to be built in the mountains of Israel

But we have been rolling up hill for the past ten years, in fulfillment of the predictions of Isaiah, which says -- "O Zion, that bringest glad tidings, get thee up into the high mountain . . ." - Orson Pratt, January 24, 1858

All the Saints of God among the nations, who have been faithful, have been inspired by the same spirit to gather home to Zion. Why have we *gathered to Zion? To fulfill the revelations of God. Isaiah and Jeremiah and nearly all the prophets since the world began have foretold the gathering of the people in the last days to establish Zion, from which the law of the Lord should go forth to rule the nations of the earth, while the word of the Lord should go forth from Jerusalem. We are here to do these things, and to receive teachings and instructions that we may be prepared for the coming of the Son of Man. We are here to be shut up a little while in these chambers of the mountains, while the indignation of the Almighty passes over the nations. For this the Lord through his ancient servant said, "Come out of her, my people, that ye be not partakers of her sins, and that ye receive not of her plagues."* - Wilford Woodruff, July 19, 1868

The Prophet [Isaiah] gives the following exhortation to that Zion—"O Zion, thou that bringest good tidings, get thee up into the high mountain." Here then is a prophecy that, in the latter days, God would have a Zion on the earth before he should reveal himself from heaven and manifest his glory to all people; and the people called Zion are exhorted, in the 40th chapter of Isaiah, to get up into the high mountain. Here we are in this great mountain region, in a Territory called the mountain Territory. Here we are on the great backbone, as it were, of the western hemisphere, located among the valleys of this great ridge of mountains, which extends for thousands of miles—from the frozen regions in the north, almost to the southern extremity of South America. **Here are the people called Zion, gone up into the high mountain, according to the prediction of the Prophet Isaiah.** *Isaiah uttered the prophecy;* **Joseph Smith also prophesied the same thing**, *but died without seeing it fulfilled.* - Orson Pratt, April 1872 General Conference

We find, <u>in the 40th chapter of the prophecies of Isaiah</u>, that the people of Zion are to be raised up preparatory to the second advent of the Son of God. Isaiah uses an exclamation something like this—"<u>O Zion</u>, that bringest good tidings, <u>get thee up into the high mountain</u>." It seems by this, that the people called Zion, wherever they might be, were to be *removed from the regions they originally inhabited, and were to be located in a high mountain, or in a very elevated region. If you wish to know the time which this prophetic exhortation to the people of Zion had reference to, read the whole of the 40th chapter of Isaiah, and you will find that, at that period, the glory of God is to be revealed and all flesh is to see it together, evidently referring to the great day when the Son of God shall come in his glory . . . .* - Orson Pratt, June 15, 1873

Territorial Utah Saints were working to fulfill the prophecies about Zion.

All the Saints of God among the nations, who have been faithful, have been inspired by the same spirit to gather home to Zion. **Why have we gathered to Zion? To fulfill the revelations of God. Isaiah and Jeremiah and nearly all the prophets since the world began have foretold the gathering of the people in the last days to establish Zion,** *from which the law of the Lord should go forth to rule the nations of the earth, while the word of the Lord should go forth from Jerusalem.* <u>We are here to do these things</u>, *and to receive teachings and instructions that we may be prepared for the coming of the Son of Man. We are here to be shut up a little while in these chambers of the mountains, while the indignation of the Almighty passes over the nations. For this the Lord through his ancient servant said, "Come out of her, my people, that ye be not partakers of her sins, and that ye receive not of her plagues."* - Wilford Woodruff, July 19th, 1868

These are some of the grand events spoken of in this Bible; <u>these are events that the Latter-day Saints believe in, and</u> *that so far as it lies in their power,* <u>they are trying to fulfill</u>. *If we are not Jews we are not required to go to old Jerusalem, but* <u>we are required to build up a Zion</u>; *that is spoken of as well as the building of Jerusalem. Zion is to be built up in the mountains in the last days, not at Jerusalem.* - Orson Pratt, July 25, 1875

*One thing is certain, that **if God accomplishes with the Latter-day Saints what the prophets have foretold, and establishes his Zion**, and he makes them a holy nation, a kingdom of priests, a peculiar people to himself, as he has promised, it will not be by our clinging to Babylon and to her foolish ways . . .* - Erastus Snow, June 3rd, 1877

The Lord has sent forth angels out of heaven. He has delivered the fulness of the Gospel to Joseph Smith. <u>He was raised up as a Prophet of God, by the power of God . . . to build up that Zion which Isaiah, Jeremiah and Ezekiel said should be built up in the latter days</u>. We believe this with every sentiment of our hearts. - Wilford Woodruff, October 23rd, 1881

*<u>The work before **us** is a great one, and very much remaineth to be accomplished according to the prophecies</u>—Israel is to be gathered, Jerusalem rebuilt, <u>Zion established</u>, the vineyard of the Lord pruned and the corrupt branches cut off and cast into the fire, while the good branches shall be grafted in and partake of the root and fatness of the tame olive tree.* - Erastus Snow, February 2nd, 1884

Chapter Five – Our Obligations Regarding Zion

Building Zion is the work we've been given to do.

*That is our errand in the world, and **we have no business but to** build up the kingdom of God, and preserve it and ourselves in it. Whether it is ploughing, sowing, harvesting, building, going into the canyons, or whatever it is we do, it is all within the pale of the kingdom of God, to forward his cause on the earth, to redeem and **build up his Zion**, and prepare ourselves, that when the Lord shall usher in the morning of rest.*
- Brigham Young, December 27, 1857

Joseph, the Prophet, told us to go to work and build up the cities of Zion, and not to build up strange cities. - George A. Smith, December 29, 1867

My brethren and sisters, we are commanded not to give the whole of our attention to the accumulation of earthly things; we are commanded also to lay up treasures in heaven. **We are required to build up Zion** *on the earth; then let us take a course that will ensure to us the blessing and favor of God our Heavenly Father, that our prayers and thanksgiving may be acceptable before Him.* - Elder Wilford Woodruff, January 12, 1873

We have no business here other than to build up and establish the Zion of God. - Brigham Young, April 1877 General Conference (his last).

We have no time to throw away, or spend in the foolish things of the flesh; what time is at our disposal should be used in building up the Zion of God - Wilford Woodruff, August 1st, 1880

I want to say to my brethren and sisters, that we are placed upon the earth to build up Zion, to build up the kingdom of God. - Wilford Woodruff, October 1881 General Conference

It is not my business; God has not required it of me that I should build up anything that is opposed to Zion, but on the contrary that I should always keep in my thoughts and be influenced by it in my actions that which will advance the cause of Zion, and that which will not retard it or operate against it in any manner. - George Q. Cannon, August 26, 1883

As they in [Enoch's] day were placed under the guidance of the Almighty, so are we. As they had a work to perform associated with the welfare of the human family, so have we. As they had the Gospel to preach, so have we. **As they had a Zion to build up, so have we**. - John Taylor, October 1884 General Conference

Appendix A – Chapter 5

It is our duty & responsibility to build up Zion

There is no time allotted to us to use outside of the limits of <u>duty</u>. But in doing our <u>duty</u>, in serving our God, in living our religion, in using every possible means to send forth the Gospel of salvation to the inhabitants of the earth, to gather Israel, and <u>establish Zion</u>, and build up the kingdom of heaven upon the earth are incorporated all blessings, all comforts that men can desire. - Brigham Young, July 5, 1857

Perhaps those who thus become disaffected may not say anything about it for a time; but they will say in their hearts and souls that they do not like this, they disapprove of that, and they despise the other . . . This is because <u>they forget that upon themselves rests the responsibility of making that Zion</u> about which they talked, prayed, and preached. It is because they forget that it is their business to labor for the establishment of righteous principles, and to walk wickedness under their feet. This is the duty, and this should be the labor of all that come up here. - Daniel H. Wells, September 30, 1860

[Jesus Christ] leans upon no other people; he expects from no people but those who have obeyed his Gospel and gathered here, the accomplishment of his great work, <u>the building up of his latter-day Zion</u> and kingdom. And, as I have said, <u>this responsibility rests not only upon Prophets and Apostles, but upon every man and woman who has entered into covenant with him</u>. - Wilford Woodruff, January 12, 1873

*If we are in the line of our **duty**, we are engaged in a great and glorious cause. It is very essential to our individual welfare that every man and every woman who has entered into the covenant of the Gospel, through repentance and baptism, should feel that as individuals **it is their bounden duty to use their intelligence, and the agency which the Lord has given them, for the promotion of the interests of Zion and the establishment of her cause, in the earth**.* - Joseph F. Smith, April 1876 General Conference

Now, brethren and sisters, I do not wish myself to occupy all your time this morning, but I want to say to you that our position, our calling, our religion embrace the noble work of God, both temporal and spiritual, which rests upon us. We <u>have to</u> go forth with our hands and build up Zion. - Wilford Woodruff, April 1878 General Conference

It is difficult, as has been remarked, for us sometimes to realize the position we occupy—the relation we sustain to our heavenly Father—the responsibility that rests upon us, and the various duties we have to perform in the fulfillment of the purposes of God; in the interest of a world lying in wickedness; in the building up of the Zion of our God. - John Taylor, August 31, 1879

[P]ray also for my brethren of the Twelve that they may be guided by the inspirations of the Most High, and be led and that they may lead others in the paths of life; that we may magnify the calling God has given unto us and honor it and do good among men, and <u>help to build up His Zion. This work devolves upon you in your sphere as much as upon President Smoot and his counselors and the several bishops. Everyone has his duties to perform</u>; and if we all do them we will do pretty well. - John Taylor, November 30, 1879

*[I]**t is our duty to build up Zion**. From my childhood I have vowed in my heart—and I have endeavored to keep the vow—that not one cent of mine would ever go to build up anything that was opposed to Zion. At the same time I have spent years, as others have done, traveling without purse or scrip and preaching the Gospel to those who were in darkness; but so far as working to sustain that which is opposed to Zion I have determined, and I did so determine in my childhood, not to do that . . . .* - George Q. Cannon, October 1881 General Conference

Building Zion is one of our callings from God

This should be uppermost in our minds, we should look for the building up of the kingdom, and secure not only blessings for ourselves, but seek

to become saviors of men on Mount Zion, and try to do all the good we can, **laboring to promote the cause and interest of Zion in every department thereof where we are all called to act**. - Wilford Woodruff, February 22, 1857

In this case the Mission to which <u>you, brethren, are called is to build a city</u>; it calls for wives, children, for machinery, for mechanics, for everything that is calculated to add to the comfort and happiness of the citizens of a city. We are not going to be a great while isolated from our brethren, but <u>we are going to assist in building up Zion</u>. - George A. Smith, October 20, 1861

I rejoice in this work because it is true, because it is the plan of salvation, the eternal law of God that has been revealed to us, and <u>the building up of Zion is what we are called to perform</u>. I think we have done very well considering our traditions and all the difficulties which we have had to encounter; and I look forward, by faith, if I live a few years, to the time when this people will accomplish that which the Lord expects them to do. If we do not, our children will. Zion has got to be built up . . . - Wilford Woodruff, May 19, 1867

<u>We are called to build up Zion</u>, and to establish righteousness and truth . . . - Wilford Woodruff, July 19, 1868

Our calling is to perfect ourselves, to purify Zion, and make it a fit habitation for the Son of God when he comes; to build Temples, and in them perform the rites and ordinances for the living and the dead, and accomplish all that God designs us to do. And that we may be faithful in the performance thereof, is my prayer in the name of Jesus. Amen. - Wilford Woodruff, August 13, 1876

We are called of God; we have been chosen, we have been ordained as men who have been called to bear the priesthood and to attend to the ordinances of the house of God, to preach the Gospel, to warn this generation, **to build up Zion**, to redeem the earth, to erect temples unto *the name of the Most High God, to redeem the living and the dead, and to carry out those great purposes which have been foreordained before the world was.* - Wilford Woodruff, October 1880 General Conference

The Priesthood obligates us to build Zion

God expects these things at our hands, and they are things which we have a right to expect from one another; it is expected that we all will do our duty, and <u>God the Father of Jesus, and all the eternal Priesthood in the heavens expect</u> the Presidency, the Twelve, the Presidents of Stakes, the High Priests, High Councils, the Seventies and Elders, the Bishops, Priests, Teachers and Deacons and <u>all the Priesthood</u> and all the people to be governed by the law of God, and <u>to help faithfully to build Zion</u> and establish the kingdom of God <u>that we may be one in all things temporal and spiritual</u>; that we may be welded and united together on earth and not only on the earth but in the heavens also. - John Taylor, President of the Quorum of the Twelve, June 17, 1877

<u>*I feel therefore to say to my brethren who bear the holy priesthood*</u>, *and I say it to myself and to all—I do not think we have much time to lie down and slumber. We have no time to speculate in trying to get rich, in trying to accumulate gold and silver. What we have got to do is to build up the kingdom of God. As apostles, high priests, elders, seventies and the lesser priesthood, we are bound together by this new and everlasting Gospel and covenant; <u>we are called to perform the great and mighty work of building up Zion</u> . . . and we should live in that way and manner that we may be governed and controlled at all times by the Holy Spirit.* - Wilford Woodruff, June 6, 1880

But we are here in a school to learn, and **it is for the Elders of Israel** *who are desirous to do the will of God, and keep His commandments, to put themselves in the way of doing so, to seek to the Lord for His guidance and direction, to repent of their follies, their nonsense and wickedness of every kind, and to come out for God and His kingdom, and* **to seek to build up the Zion of God** *and the kingdom of God upon the earth, and if* *we do this, God will bless us and exalt us in time and throughout the eternities that are to come. Amen.* - President John Taylor, June 15, 1884

The whole point of receiving the Priesthood is to build Zion

We are the only people to whom this holy Gospel, <u>Priesthood</u>, and covenants have been committed in our day; and we shall be held responsible for the use we make of them. Then we should be diligent and faithful in offering this great salvation unto the children of men, and in <u>building up Zion</u> and the kingdom of our God. - Wilford Woodruff, April 1857 General Conference

I pray that the blessing of God may rest upon [the former counselors of Brigham Young], and lead them in the paths of life, and that they with the Twelve may unite together as a grand phalanx, not in our own individual interests, but in the interests of the Church and kingdom of God, and the building up of his Zion on the earth; for <u>the Priesthood is not instituted for the purpose of personal aggrandizement or personal honor, but it is for the accomplishment of certain purposes</u> of which the Lord is the Author and Designer, and in which the dead, the living, and the unborn are interested. <u>We ought, brethren, all of us, to feel and act as though we were the servants of the living God, feeling in our hearts an honest desire to do his will and establish his purposes</u> on the earth. <u>If we can be united in our faith, our acts and labors</u>, as we have been in our voting, as manifested at this Conference, the heavens will smile upon us, the angels of God will manifest themselves to us, the power of God will be in our midst, and <u>Zion will arise and shine</u>, and the glory of God rest upon her. - John Taylor, President of the Quorum of the Twelve, October 1877 General Conference (a few weeks after Brigham Young's death).

[G]od had revealed himself to the human family and had restored the everlasting Gospel, and that with it came all these other things — apostles and high priests and elders and patriarchs and bishops and high

councilors and all the various organizations of the Church and kingdom of God as they now exist upon the earth, all occupying their own peculiar place and position. **What for? For the building up of a something that is called Zion** *or the pure in heart.* - President John Taylor, December 1, 1878

It shows that while **God has revealed the Priesthood to us** *upon the earth and conferred upon us those privileges, that in former generations he revealed the same Priesthood to other men, and that those men holding that Priesthood ministered to others here upon the earth; and that* **we are operating** *with them and they with us in our interests and in the interests of the Church and kingdom of God,* **in assisting to build up the Zion of God,** *and in seeking to establish truth and righteousness upon the earth* - President John Taylor, July 24, 1882

<u>*We are here as the representatives of God upon the earth to accomplish his purposes,*</u> *and to carry out his designs, to spread forth his Gospel, to build up his kingdom,* <u>*to establish his Zion*</u> *. . . This is what we are here for, as I understand it, and this is what we will do . . .* - President John Taylor, August 20, 1882

This is the position that **we as Priests of the Most High God** *ought to occupy. We should feel that we are not living for ourselves, but that we are living for God—living to accomplish His purposes. We are here to build up His Church and to purify it from all evil, that it may be presented before the Father as the bride, the Lamb's wife without spot or wrinkle.* **We are here to build up a Zion unto the Lord of Hosts—a Zion**, *which signifies the pure in heart—a people who will be prepared for the great events that are about to transpire upon this earth, and who will be able to stand the convulsions that will overthrow the world—and He has given us the Priesthood for that very purpose.* - President John Taylor, 1883

Chapter Six - The Saints were Actively Building a Zion in Utah

God wants a Zion built in Utah

The Lord has led the people carefully along, and dictated according to his pleasure. Brother Heber says we have been going from place to place, until, finally, we have come into these valleys in the mountains. Why? Because we were obliged to. <u>The Lord has had his eye on this spot from the beginning—upon this part of the land of Joseph . . . He has known, from the beginning of creation, that this is the land whereon to build this Zion.</u> - Brigham Young, June 3, 1860

God has set his hand a second time *to build up that kingdom which Daniel was permitted to see in vision, and* **to establish that Zion in the mountains which Isaiah saw.** - Wilford Woodruff, June 30, 1878

But that we might be a peculiar people full of the light of truth and intelligence and revelations of God; that we might be a people having no longer need of the oral law or the written law, but a people upon whose hearts the law of God shall be written and engraven as in characters of living fire, being under the inspiration and guidance of the Almighty, walking according to the principles of eternal truth, and being led in the paths of life; being united with God and his Son Jesus Christ and with the ancient patriarchs and apostles and men of God, operating with them in the <u>building up of Zion</u>*, in establishing the kingdom of God upon the earth, and in spreading salvation to the ends of the earth.* <u>This is what he has brought us here for.</u> - President John Taylor, November 28, 1879

<u>The Lord Almighty has set His hand to</u> *establish His Church and kingdom on the earth, to* <u>build up Zion in the mountains of Israel</u>. - Wilford Woodruff, July 20, 1883

This is the work devolving upon us. We have to build up **here** *a Zion unto God.* - President Taylor, May 18, 1884

We can, want to, and WILL build Zion here in Utah

*We **can** make Zion, or we can make Babylon, just as we please. We **can** make just what we please of <u>this place</u>. The people **can** make Zion: they can make a heaven within themselves. When people gather here, they should come with a determination to make Zion within themselves, with the resolution that, "I will carry myself full of the Spirit of Zion wherever I go; and this is the way in which I will control evil spirits; for I mean that my spirit shall have control over evil:" and do you not see that such a course will make Zion?* - Brigham Young, July 5, 1857

*We would have a pure people <u>here</u>; we **would have** a Zion such as the Bible describes, if we were allowed; we would have a city in which angels might walk in the streets all day, if we could have our way; but Satan says: "You shall not."* - George Q. Cannon, January 6, 1884
[In this quote it appears Elder Cannon is using the older use of the word "would", meaning "want to".]

*We read of the Zion that was built up by Enoch . . . We have been **expecting** all along to build up a similar Zion <u>upon these mountains</u> . . .* - John Taylor, August 31, 1875

We know that the world is angry at us, and that we cannot help. <u>We mean to pursue our course, build up the kingdom of God on earth, and establish Zion.</u> - Brigham Young, June 7, 1857

*If [the mobs] will not let us alone, we **will** take the musket and the sword in one hand, the trowel and the hammer in the other, and build up the Zion of our God; and they cannot prevent it.* - Brigham Young, March 4, 1860

*The work we are engaged in is not a phantom. We are **going to** build up the Zion of God; and the kingdom of God will continue to grow and increase, until "the kingdoms of this world are become the kingdoms of our Lord, and of His Christ; and He shall reign forever." If we will be* *faithful, God will bless us and prosper us, and all things spoken in the Prophets will be fulfilled.* - John Taylor, November 23, 1882

*This is my testimony in relation to this matter. God has led His people out of bondage, and he has given them these strong mountain fastnesses for an inheritance. <u>This</u> **will** be a land of Zion unto us. We shall rejoice in it and prosper exceedingly, if we continue to do our duty. Amen.* - Joseph F. Smith, December 3, 1882

Building Zion was the whole point of gathering to Utah

*[Their converts] are not worth bringing across the Plains; for, after their arrival, they annoy and disturb the peace of others. **Do such come here to build up Zion?** Did such persons love the Gospel? **No**; or, if they did, they lost that love while coming here.* - Brigham Young, April 22, 1860

***We have come out from among the world, for the express purpose of** serving God and keeping His commandments, **building up Zion**, and establishing His Kingdom upon the earth.* - John Taylor, July 21, 1867

*The Latter-day Saints gather together for the express purpose, they say, to establish Zion. Where is Zion? On the American continent. **Where is the gathering place? For the present, in the mountains. What are you going there for? To help to build up Zion**.* - Brigham Young, November 14, 1869

***We have come here to build up Zion**, to be taught of the Lord, to establish righteousness, and to prepare a people for his coming. Certainly, **we have come here for the purpose of building up <u>a</u> Zion**, and we ought to use all diligence for its accomplishment.* - John Taylor, January 5, 1873

[W]e have been wandering about from place to place, and the Lord has blessed us in a remarkable degree. <u>And we are gathered together, as I</u>

have said, for the purpose of building up Zion . . . - John Taylor, September 21, 1878

We are now gathered together to Zion. For what? To build up Zion, and to accomplish the purposes of the Lord pertaining to the human family upon the earth. - President John Taylor, April 13, 1879

We are talking about building up Zion. Here is where the thing applies itself with great force to me as well as to you, when you comprehend it as it exists and see it by the light of the Spirit of Truth. For it is written: "And I say unto you, if my people observe not this law, to keep it holy, and by this law sanctify the land of Zion unto me, that my statutes and my judgments may be kept thereon, that it may be most holy, behold, verily I say unto you, it shall not be a land of Zion unto you." Well, we are talking about building up the land of Zion, which is one of the things we are here for. And God has said that if we do not obey this law, it shall not be a land of Zion unto us. Does this apply to us? I will read a little further: "And this shall be an ensample unto all the stakes of Zion." - President John Taylor, January 9, 1881

But as a people we are not of the spirit of the world; ***we are here not to pattern after the follies of the world, but to build up Zion****, the Church and Kingdom of God upon the earth;* - President John Taylor, January 9, 1881

We are here to build up Zion, and to establish the kingdom of God - President John Taylor, June 27, 1881

And as ***we are here for the purpose of building up Zion****, He [God] expects that we will be upright and honorable in all our dealings with one another and with all men.* - President John Taylor, April 1882 General Conference

We are here to do the will of God, to build up the kingdom of God, and to establish the Zion of God. - President John Taylor, November 23, 1882

235

We are here to build up the Zion of God, and to this end we must subject our bodies and our spirits to the law, to the word, and to the will of God. - President John Taylor, Oct 1883 General Conference

This is what we are gathered here for—to build up the Zion of our God, to establish the Kingdom of God, and to purify and exalt the Church of the living God. - President John Taylor, February 10, 1884

While it is well with us here, and we are enjoying all these blessings, it is but right, I think, that we should ask our Father in heaven that the day of [the Israelites'] affliction and sorrow may soon come to an end, and that they may come, as we have come, with obedient hearts to help build up Zion and Jerusalem. - Franklin D. Richards, May 17, 1884

We are here to build up the Zion of God, and not to build up ourselves. - President John Taylor, July 20, 1884

It has pleased God to call us to these lands and to make use of us for certain purposes in the interest of humanity and for the welfare of a fallen world. This is the object of our being gathered together, and that we might build up a Zion unto the Lord, and be instructed in all the principles of righteousness, truth, integrity, and everything associated with our present and future happiness, and thus become the blessed of the Lord, and our offspring with us. - President John Taylor, October 19, 1884

We are here really to build up and purify the Church of the living God. We are here to build up and establish the kingdom of God. We are here also to build up a Zion unto our God . . . - President John Taylor, November 30, 1884

Evidence the Saints were anxiously engaged in building a Zion in Utah

I rejoice that I am happy to meet with you and my family: you are my friends, and you are the friends of God, and we are building up the *kingdom of God, and by and by the kings and princes of the earth will come, and gaze upon the glory of Zion.* - John Taylor, August 22, 1852

I do not expect to be with you forever, neither will brother Brigham in these bodies; they are nearly worn out; they have stood a long and violent siege and will soon go the way of all the earth. Still we may live many years yet to assist in making permanent the foundations of Zion. There are thousands of good men in the earth who can act in the same capacity we do, after we he passed through the veil of death. - Heber C. Kimball, March 19, 1854

If I feel at our approaching Conference as I now do, I shall ask to move that our home missions be not diminished, but increased, if possible; and all set to raising wheat, and make Zion a house and city of refuge for the Saints and for the sons of strangers, that they may come and build up our walls, even as the old Prophet hath spoken. - Orson Hyde, March 18, 1855

But we desire to appear before thee [Lord] with clean hands and hearts, to call upon thee for thy blessing and do thy will, that our inheritance may be blest and all we have, and that all the efforts we make to build up Zion and rear temples to thy name may be blest, that the people of God may flock to the mountains by tens of thousands - Jedediah M. Grant, July 24, 1856

But so long as they remain upon the earth in the flesh, they remain under the same obligation to serve the Lord today as much as yesterday, and then continue the next day and the next week as they were at first to repent and be baptized for the remission of their sins, when the commandment of the Lord comes to them in England, Australia, Denmark, Switzerland, and the islands of the sea, to gather up their substance, come to the gathering place, and assist in building up the Zion of our God, and to assist in establishing his kingdom in the tops of the mountains. - Erastus Snow, August 26, 1860

And every true, faithful Latter-day Saint—yes, every mother and wife in Israel do feel this, and under no consideration would they throw an impediment in the way of their father, husband, or brother, to prevent their going to bear this message of life, or, if required to build up the temples of our God, to establish the cities of Zion, to cultivate the earth, and make it produce that which is necessary for the sustenance of the people of God; and if their duties are to labor physically while in this tabernacle, they should be willing to do it, and do it with the same missionary zeal and the same good feeling that they would preach the Gospel. - Erastus Snow, August 26, 1860

I want our sisters that are called to go with their husbands, to cultivate a spirit of joy, cheerfulness and satisfaction, and feel a pleasure in going. They ought to feel that they are honored in being called to go and build up the cities of Zion. - George A. Smith, October 20, 1861

I presume now that in speaking at the present time, I am addressing a considerable portion of those brethren who have been called on to strengthen the stakes of Zion on the southern borders of our Territory . . . A man who has come into this Valley to make Zion his home, has gone to work and by untiring industry has surrounded himself with comforts, and probably with wealth and an abundance of this world's goods; he can proclaim himself an Elder in Israel who is ready for anything. Such a man would go into the mountains to hedge up the way of our enemies, go abroad and preach the Gospel, and in fact he will find himself constantly called to assist in establishing Zion. - George A. Smith, October 20, 1861

And if we should wait for the rotten-hearted kings and queens of the wicked nations to gather us home, we shall have to wait a long time. Possibly some of them may come and look at the place, but they will never come to stay and assist in building up Zion. - Heber C. Kimball, February 17, 1861

I will prophesy in the name of the Lord God of Hosts that if we continue to walk in the light of truth, to labor to build up Zion, that cup of trembling spoken of by the Prophet Isaiah shall never return to your lips nor to our habitations, but we will float along increasing in power and strength from day to day, continually rejoicing in the truths of our holy religion. - Orson Hyde, October 1862 General Conference

Quite a number of young men have been called to go to the southern portion of our Territory for the purpose of developing the resources thereof and building up Zion. - Lorenzo Snow, October 1867 General Conference

We are engaged in the great latter-day work, of preaching the Gospel to the nations, gathering the poor and building up Zion upon the earth. - Joseph F. Smith, November 25, 1868

But I am not discouraged; I have no feelings to linger or flag, but feel to persevere and to do all I can for the building up of the Zion of our God. - Orson Hyde, October 1869 General Conference

Consequently our teachings during Conference will be to instruct the people how to live and order their lives before the Lord and each other; how to accomplish the work devolving upon them in building up Zion on the earth. - Brigham Young, October 1870 General Conference

In fact there is no dispensation that has been looked upon with as much interest by all the prophets of God and inspired men, from the day of Joseph Smith, as that in which we live, in which the Zion of God is being built up, and the earth is being prepared for the coming of the Son of Man. - Wilford Woodruff, May 6, 1870

Endeavor, brethren, to build up Zion, and not Babylon. I think very often, when I am speaking to the people, of a remark to President Young. He has been in the Church a great many years. On one occasion, only a very few years after the Church was organized, the Prophet Joseph counseled

him and others never to do another day's work to build up Babylon, and he has obeyed that counsel. I know he has for twenty-five years past, and I am satisfied he has from the time the counsel was given. - Brigham Young, Jr., October 1872 General Conference

We are trying to unite the people together in the order that the Lord revealed to Enoch, which will be observed and sustained in the latter days in redeeming and building up Zion; this is the very order that will do it, and nothing short of it. We are trying to organize the Latter-day Saints into this order; but I want to tell you, my brethren and sisters, that I have not come here to say that you have got to join this order or we will cut you off the Church, or you must join this order or we will consider you apostates; no such thing, oh no, the Saints are not prepared to see everything at once. They have got to learn little by little, and to receive a little here and a little there. - Brigham Young, June 21, 1874

We do not see today what we saw twenty-four years ago, and we do not see today what will be seen twenty-four years hence; there will be no stoppage to the building up of the Zion of God, or to the carrying out of his work. - Wilford Woodruff, October 1874 General Conference

Many of us have spent considerable of our time in preaching the Gospel at home and abroad, and in otherwise assisting to establish the kingdom of God upon the earth, and we are still engaged in this work. We have donated towards the deliverance of the poor from foreign lands, bringing them here, where they have the privilege of being taught further in the plan of salvation, and <u>where they can assist more materially in the establishment of Zion in the earth</u>. - Brigham Young, August 15, 1876

Now, sisters, take hold; do this that we ask you to do. It is for your own benefit, and health, and life, and for the comfort of the people, and the building up of Zion. And let us go to, and establish the Zion of God upon the earth, that we may be prepared to enjoy it, which I most earnestly

pray for every day, in the name of Jesus, Amen. - Brigham Young, July 20, 1877 (5 weeks before his passing)

President Young labored hard and faithful during the last few years of his life in organizing and building up Zion. We have to continue the work they were engaged in, and when our time comes to take our departure for that life behind the veil, none of us will regret having devoted our time, talents, and labor for the accomplishment of this great object. The riches of the world will appear as the dust under our feet compared with the eternal reward before us. - Wilford Woodruff, October 13, 1877

There are facilities for many fine, flourishing settlements in [southern Colorado]; and we are establishing some colonies in that [area], consisting mostly of emigrants from the Southern States, with a few from Utah, to counsel and instruct them in the art of irrigating the soil and establishing settlements after the order of Zion. - Erastus Snow, August 7, 1880

I am happy to say that the people are being led to examine their own hearts, and to ask themselves what they are doing individually towards building up the Zion of God, and towards influencing others to do likewise. - Brigham Young, Jr., April 1884 General Conference

Chapter Seven – What is Required of Us to Establish Zion?

Zion in our hearts

Let there be an hallowed influence go from us over all things over which we have any power; over the soil we cultivate, over the houses we build, and over everything we possess; and if we cease to hold fellowship with that which is corrupt and <u>establish the Zion of God in our hearts</u>, in our own houses, in our cities, and throughout our country, we shall ultimately overcome the earth, for we are the lords of the earth; and, *instead of thorns and thistles, every useful plant that is good for the food of man and to beautify and adorn will spring from its bosom.* - Brigham Young, February 23, 1862

It is not an easy thing to serve God and mammon. If the Saints comprehend what they have to do in order to establish Zion, and go to work <u>with ready hands and willing hearts</u> to accomplish the labor, they will find it a comparatively easy matter; but unless there is a unity of action on the part of those who are engaged in the work it is not very easily performed. - Brigham Young, November 14, 1869

*[I]t would be an easy matter to bring their hands to join in the establishment of the Zion of God upon the earth. But, herein lies our labor. The weakness and shortsightedness of man are such, and he is so prone to wander and give himself up to the groveling things of the world, having had so little knowledge with regard to God and godliness for hundreds of years, that it is literally a breaking up of the fallow ground **of his heart** to prepare him to see the holy city that the Lord will establish.* - Brigham Young, November 14, 1869

*It occurs to me what I heard President Young say many times, that when he arrived at Kirtland the Prophet Joseph told him from that time forth he should labor for the building up of Zion; and from that time forward, he said, he never did any work that did not pertain to the building up of Zion. This is the spirit that every man who labors should have; and all who are imbued with this spirit will seek the welfare of his brothers, for charity and love will be **in his heart**.* - George Q. Cannon, September 2, 1889

We must desire it

*If we could only get to **the affections of the people** and could plant within them the principles of the kingdom of heaven, it would be an easy matter to bring their hands to join in the establishment of the Zion of God upon the earth.* - Brigham Young, November 14, 1869

Eye single to building Zion, not Babylon

Brethren, **your eye should be single to the glory of God, to hearkening to the counsel of brother Brigham, and to the building up of Zion,** *then your bodies would be filled with spirit, and your understandings with light, and your hearts with joy, and your souls would be quickened into eternal life with the power of the Holy Ghost, you would then become the depositories of that wisdom and knowledge which would qualify you to be saviors unto your brethren and your posterity.* - Lorenzo Snow, January 4, 1857

Suppose we bring a few illustrations in regard to the present feelings and knowledge of the elders of Israel. We need not go back to Nauvoo or Kirtland, to find illustrations among our merchants, but take them as we find them here. If they enter upon their business without God in their thoughts, it is "How much can I get for this? And how much can I make on that? And how much will the people give for this and for that? And how last can I get rich? And how long will it take me to be a millionaire?" Which thoughts should <u>never</u> come into the mind of a merchant who professes to be a Latter-day Saint. But it should be, **"What can I do to benefit this people?"** *And when they live, act, and do business upon this principle, and think, "What can I do to benefit the kingdom of God on the earth, to establish the laws of this kingdom, to make this kingdom and people honorable, and bring them into note, and give them influence among the nations,* <u>so that they can gather the pure in heart, build up Zion</u>, *redeem the House of Israel, and perhaps assist (though I do not thinks there will be any need of it), to gather the Jews to Jerusalem and prepare for the coming of the Son of Man?"* - Brigham Young, February 3, 1867

And our mechanics [i.e. tradesmen], **do they labor for the express purpose of building up Zion** *and the kingdom of God? I am sorry to say that I think there are but very few into whose hearts it has entered, or whose thoughts are occupied in the least with such a principle; but it is, "How much can I make?" If our mechanics would work upon the* *principle of establishing the Kingdom of God upon the earth, and building up Zion, they would, as the prophet Joseph said, in the year 1833, never do another day's work but with that end in view.* - Brigham Young, February 3, 1867

As to the riches of the world they belong to the Lord, and He gives them to whom He will. <u>If we are determined to devote our lives to the kingdom of Heaven, and not to this world</u>, we shall in due time inherit all that is good for us to inherit; and unless we realize the objects of our existence, and learn to govern and control our spirits so as to devote ourselves and our energies and all the means given to us <u>to build up Zion</u>, then the good things of this life would be wasted upon us comparatively. - Erastus Snow, April 1868 General Conference

In building up the Zion of God on this land **we must become very different from what we are now, in many respects and particularly in financial matters** *. . . There are many men who are so anxious for wealth, that if they cannot make a fortune in a few months, they feel they are not succeeding according to their desires, and they turn to something else. I do not do this; nor am I anxious to spend a dollar as fast as I make it. Some people feel as if a dollar would burn a hole in their pockets; and you will see a great many almost crazy to spend whatever they have.* - Brigham Young, May 17, 1868

I felt thankful to learn that our brethren in the cotton country were filled with the spirit and were zealous for the accomplishment of their work, and that they were progressing very satisfactorily in the accomplishment of their mission, or at any rate that portion of them who **have taken hold of it with the zeal which becomes men who are honored with the privilege of laboring in any department for the building up of Zion.** - George A. Smith, April 1869 General Conference

A man is as much on a mission at home, building up Zion, as he is when abroad preaching the Gospel, and <u>he should esteem his labors under the direction and dictation of the servants of God</u> just the same. Here is

where a good many make mistakes. They think that unless they are called to go on a mission to preach the Gospel they are not on a mission at all, but their only business is to look after their own individual interests. - Daniel H. Wells, February 23, 1873

Forsake Babylon's Values

Let there be an hallowed influence go from us over all things over which we have any power; over the soil we cultivate, over the houses we build, and over everything we possess; and if we **cease to hold fellowship with that which is corrupt and establish the Zion of God in our hearts**, *in our own houses, in our cities, and throughout our country, we shall ultimately overcome the earth, for we are the lords of the earth; and, instead of thorns and thistles, every useful plant that is good for the food of man and to beautify and adorn will spring from its bosom.* - Brigham Young, February 23, 1862

[W]hen reflecting upon the great work to be done in molding the children of God, gathered from the various nations and denominations, <u>with all their prejudices, traditions, and varied habits of living</u>. They come here filled with ideas averse to those of God and differing from each other; and under these circumstances it is difficult for them to arrive at a oneness in their associations—to use an expression common amongst us at the present—it is difficult for them to cooperate to build up Zion in the last days. - George A. Smith, May 6, 1870

Some of the daughters of Zion do not seem willing to **forsake the fashions of Babylon**. *I to such would say hasten it, and let the woe that is threatened on this account come* [Isaiah 3], *that we may get through with it, then we can go on and build up the Zion of God on the earth.* - Wilford Woodruff, October 1873 General Conference

The Latter-day Saints have a work to do, not only in proclaiming the Gospel and warning the people, but to build up Zion right here upon the earth. Not afar off in some far distant sphere, but here, where the Lord

has planted their feet, in the valleys of the mountains. And we must be united and must operate together, as far as in our power lies, to bring to pass the purposes of the Almighty, because righteousness, and peace and harmony must dwell in the kingdom. A house divided against itself cannot stand. Is a reformation needed amongst the Saints? Yes, it is needed with us all. We must reform and continue to reform. <u>We have inherited lies from, and are full of the traditions of, the fathers. We have all imbibed errors in our infant years</u>, and the enemy is on the alert, ready to enter in and to lead into by and forbidden paths the footsteps of the young, that he may cause them to make shipwreck of their faith and go away from the truth, the eternal truth of heaven. - Daniel H. Wells, October 1875 General Conference

Gather

When you had obeyed the first ordinances of the Gospel, then you discovered that the Lord and set his hand to gather Israel, <u>that Zion might be built up</u> and Israel gathered from the four winds. These doctrines have been taught and re-taught again and again. I think there is not a man here who did not fully understand them while in his native country. - Brigham Young, April 1852 General Conference

The Apostle John no doubt saw in vision, by the spirit of revelation, Zion in her beauty and perfection, and that Zion would have to be built up **by the gathering of God's people out of Babylon**. - Brigham Young, February 12, 1868

[T]he Lord has required His people to gather in the last days, that they might escape the sins of the wicked, and the plagues which shall be poured out upon them, and that they might be taught in His paths, taught to govern themselves, to correct their foolish habits and customs, and to train themselves and their offspring <u>that they may be able to build up Zion</u> according to the law and order of Heaven. We have already made a commendable advance in this direction. - Erastus Snow, April 1868 General Conference

*We say we are the people of God and are building up the kingdom of God. We say we are gathered out of the nations **to establish Zion**. Let us prove it by our works . . . .* - Brigham Young, January 2, 1870

Zion will be built up <u>by the gathering of the Saints</u> from all the nations and kingdoms of the earth. - Orson Pratt, March 10, 1872

*We have gathered here **for the express purpose of establishing Zion**, which, according to the Scriptures, must be before the Gospel can be sent to the Jews.* - Wilford Woodruff, August 13, 1876

We are now gathered together to Zion. For what? To build up Zion, and to accomplish the purposes of the Lord pertaining to the human family upon the earth. - John Taylor, April 13, 1879

<u>This is what we are gathered here for—to build up the Zion of our God</u>, to establish the Kingdom of God, and to purify and exalt the Church of the living God; that His people may be presented without spot or wrinkle, as spoken of in the Scriptures; that they may be prepared to have an inheritance among those that are sanctified; and that the principles of eternal truth may go forth from the land of Zion, and extend to the ends of the earth, that the honest in heart may be gathered together to help establish the principles of truth upon this land of Zion. Shall we accomplish this? I think we shall. - John Taylor, February 10, 1884

Unity

We can see that the people of the world are becoming more and more divided every day, and the evils resulting therefrom are everywhere apparent. <u>We are called to build up Zion, and we cannot build it up unless we are united</u>; and in that union we have got to carry out the commandments of God unto us, and we have got to obey those who are set to lead and guide the affairs of the Kingdom of God. - Wilford Woodruff, April 1867 General Conference

Appendix A – Chapter 7

*It is not an easy thing to serve God and mammon. If the Saints comprehend what they have to do in order to establish Zion, and go to work with ready hands and willing hearts to accomplish the labor, they will find it a comparatively easy matter; but **unless there is a unity of action on the part of those who are engaged in the work it is not very easily performed**.* - Brigham Young, November 14, 1869

But when He speaks from the heavens and says, "Now, my children, gather out from the wicked," some consent to this, and actually go so far as to gather, and that is why we are here in these mountains. But our labor is not done: <u>we must still progress until we become one</u>. The Lord says, "Be one; except ye are one ye are not mine, be united." But do we take a course to become so? I will ask, have we, as a general thing, obeyed the first revelations, to gather to Zion, and when there, to consecrate our property and devote all our substance, time and talents for the building up the kingdom? Have we obeyed the commandments and requirements of Heaven in yielding up everything to the will of God, and being dictated, as we should be, by the spirit of revelation? No, we have not. - Brigham Young, April 17, 1870

*The feeling that was manifested here yesterday, is most creditable to Israel, it is approved of by the Gods in the eternal worlds; and if we carry out in our practice and daily lives that union which we manifested in our voting, the Lord God will continue to pour upon us his blessing **until we shall be united in all things, temporal and spiritual, which unity we have got to come to.** <u>When this is achieved, Zion will arise and shine</u>, and then the glory of our God will rest upon her, then his power will be made manifest in our midst.* - John Taylor, October 1877 General Conference

*Let us cultivate the spirit of love and kindness, and let every little unpleasantness be buried, let us forget the election difficulty and our neighbor's difficulty, and be one, brethren and sisters together, **united in building up Zion** and establishing the Kingdom of God upon the earth.* - John Taylor, March 2, 1879

For instance, if there were two stores in this town, one occupied by a man who is not of our faith, and another occupied by a man who is of our faith, a man whose whole interests were identified with Zion, whose whole thought was to build up Zion and to advance the cause thereof on the earth, would I be an enemy of the man not of us because I did not patronize him, but patronized and sustained the man who is of us? Certainly not; it would be no mark of enmity on my part to him. <u>I might have and would have a preference for my brother, for the man who was identified with me and who was laboring for the same end; and this is the spirit we should have</u>. - George Q. Cannon, August 26, 1883

Inspiration/Revelation

You can read in the writings of the ancient Prophets that <u>the Lord is going to bring again Zion</u>. The Prophet said that very quickly: it took him not more than half a minute. Let me ask the Latter-day Saints, How long will it take this people to fulfil that short sentence? How can they, unless they live in the light of revelation, and God leads them day by day? Then can they do it in a moment, in an hour, in a week, in a month, or in a year? No. It will take years to perform that saying of the Prophet that he wrote down so soon [quickly]. And it will take more than one Prophet or person; it will take hundreds and thousands of them to fulfil that saying; and <u>they cannot begin to fulfil one part of it without the power of revelation</u>. - Brigham Young, July 28, 1861

Take the people in the east, west, north, and south who have obeyed the gospel, and, so far as the spiritual gifts are concerned, they are all of one heart and one mind, but not one soul knows how to build up Zion. Not a man in all the realms and kingdoms that exist knows how to commence the foundation of the Zion of God in the latter days without revelation. If the people in the world could sanctify themselves and prepare themselves to build up Zion they might remain scattered, but they cannot, they must be gathered together to be taught, that they may sanctify themselves before the Lord and become of one heart and of one mind. - Brigham Young, April 14, 1867

This is one thing I want to say to my friends and to the Saints of God, that without the Holy Ghost, without direct revelation and the inspiration of God continually, Brigham Young could not lead this people twenty-four hours. He could not lead them at all. Joseph could not have done it, neither could any man. This power is in the bosom of Almighty God, and he imparts it to his servants the prophets as they stand in need of it day by day to build up Zion. - Wilford Woodruff, 1870

I know that, without the power of God, we should not have been able to do what has been done; and I also know that we never should be able to build up the Zion of God in power, beauty and glory were it not that our prayers ascends into the ears of the Lord God of Sabaoth, and he hears and answers them. - Wilford Woodruff, January 12, 1873

And above all other things, teach our children the fear of God. Let our teachers be men of God, imbued with the Spirit of God, that they may lead them forth in the paths of life . . . Teach them how to approach God, that they may call upon him and he will hear them, and by their means we will build up and establish Zion, and roll forth that kingdom which God has designed shall rule and reign over the nations of the earth. We want to prepare them for these things; and to study from the best books as well as by faith, and become acquainted with the laws of nations, and of kingdoms and governments, and with everything calculated to exalt, ennoble, and dignify the human family. - John Taylor, September 22, 1878

And he will have to give more revelation on other things equally as important, for we shall need instructions how to build up Zion; how to establish the center city; how to lay off the streets; the kind of ornamental trees to adorn the sidewalks, as well as everything else by way of beautifying it, and making it a city of perfection, as David prophetically calls it. - Orson Pratt, November 13, 1879

Here we are. We are organized under the direction of the Almighty; and as I before said, not according to our ideas and notions, but according to the word and will and revelations and law of God. And none of us can do anything only as God permits us. What are we going to do? We are going to build up Zion. What then?...then we will build up our Zion after the pattern that God will show us, and we will be governed by his law and submit to his authority and be governed by the holy priesthood and by the word and will of God. - John Taylor, March 21, 1880

Obedience

Whenever we are disposed to give ourselves perfectly to righteousness, to yield all the powers and faculties of the soul . . . <u>when we are swallowed up in the will of Him who has called us</u>; when we enjoy the peace and the smiles of our Father in Heaven, the things of His Spirit, and all the blessings we are capacitated to receive and improve upon, <u>then are we in Zion, that is Zion</u>. - Brigham Young, January 16, 1853

When our Elders go out to preach the Gospel, they tell the people to gather to Zion. Where is it? It is at the City of the Great Salt Lake in the Valleys of the Mountains, in the settlements of Utah Territory—there is Zion now. But you perceive when you come here the same covetous feelings imbibed in the hearts of many, as in other places, the same tempter is here, and there are plenty of allurements; and unless the people **live before the Lord in the obedience** *of His commandments, they cannot have Zion within them. They must carry it with them, if they expect to live in it, to enjoy it, and increase in it. If they do not do this, they are as much destitute of Zion here as they are in other places.* - Brigham Young, April 1855 General Conference

<u>When the law is revealed to us and the ordinances committed to our charge, if we exercise ourselves therein according to the best knowledge and wisdom that we have, and continue so to do, God will add to us, until we shall know how to establish Zion in perfection</u>, and have the kingdom of God, in the fulness thereof, in our midst and within us, and enjoy the society of holy beings. - Brigham Young, June 14, 1857

*I know the world oppose us because we are united; they say we are governed by one man. <u>I would to God that all Israel would obey the voice of one man as the heavens obey the voice of God.</u> **Then** we would have power to build up Zion and to obtain all things necessary for us before the Lord.* - Wilford Woodruff, April 1867 General Conference

*We can see that the people of the world are becoming more and more divided every day, and the evils resulting therefrom are everywhere apparent. We are called to build up Zion, and we cannot build it up unless we are united; and **in that union we have got to carry out the commandments of God unto us**, and we have got to obey those who are set to lead and guide the affairs of the Kingdom of God.* - Wilford Woodruff, April 1867 General Conference

*We have either to build up Zion in its beauty, power, and glory, to the order which has been received by the servants of God, or else give it up. We must do one or the other. If we do this we must advance, and **whatever God requires at our hands we must carry out**.* - Wilford Woodruff, April 1867 General Conference

The Lord has put into our hands the power to build up this great Zion, which all the ancient prophets rejoiced in and prophesied about. What manner of people ought we to be who are called to carry out this work? We ought to be the Saints and children of God in very deed. <u>Our hearts ought to be open and prepared to receive instruction, light and truth, and to carry out all principles which may be communicated unto us by the servants of the Lord</u>. The counsels we have had today are of great value to the Latter-day Saints. - Wilford Woodruff, May 6, 1870

I will now ask a question of the Latter-day Saints, and I can ask it of the aged, middle-aged and the youth, for it is a matter that comes within the range of the understanding of the entire community, even the children—How long will it take us to establish Zion, the way we are going on now? You can answer this question . . . I suppose, and say, "If forty years has brought a large percentage of Babylon into the midst of *this people, how long will it take to get Babylon out and actually to establish Zion?" . . .You can say, "I do not know," and it is true, you do not know; but I can inform you on that subject—**Until the father, the mother, the son and the daughter take the counsel that is given them by those who lead and direct them in building up the kingdom of God, they will never establish Zion**, no never, worlds without end. When they learn to do this, I do not think there will be much complaining or grumbling, or much of what we have heard about today—improper language to man or beast. I do not think there will be much pilfering, purloining, bad dealing, covetousness or anything of the kind; not much of this unruly spirit that wants everybody to sustain its possessor and let him get rich, whether anybody else does or not.* - Brigham Young, August 18, 1872

What kind of a Zion would we build if called this present season to go back to Jackson County? We would have to begin altogether a new order of things. Are we prepared for it? I think not. <u>If the people had faithfully complied with these inferior laws they would be better prepared</u>: but, when I see the backwardness of many of the people of this Territory calling themselves Latter-day Saints, about paying their tithing, refusing to do so or being careless about it, I say in my heart, "Oh Lord, when will thy people be prepared to go back and build up the waste places of Zion according to celestial law? - Orson Pratt, March 9, 1873

*Besides there are a great many circumstances, transpiring from time to time, which render it necessary that we should be conversant with one another's feelings; that **we should understand the mind and will of the Lord, and that, we should be prepared to operate with Him in the interests of the human family, in the establishment of Zion** and in the building up of the Kingdom of God on the earth.* - President John Taylor, November 30, 1879

I hope we live our religion. <u>I hope we strive to keep the commandments of God.</u> We occupy a very important position in the world. <u>There are very

<u>few of the inhabitants of the earth who are laboring to build up Zion.
There are very few, apparently, who are able to abide the law of God.</u>
There are very few who are willing to sacrifice anything for eternal life
and salvation . . . . - Wilford Woodruff, December 10, 1882

Now, my brethren and sisters, I feel that it is a matter, as I have said, of
vital importance that we should have this that I have spoken of—faith
and confidence in the Priesthood of the Son of God, and we cannot build
up Zion without we have it, and **we cannot build up Zion without we
are willing to do all we have been taught by the inspiration of God**—I
know that as well as I do that I live. - George Q. Cannon, August 12,
1883

We are here to build up the Zion of God, and to this end <u>we must subject
our bodies and our spirits to the law, to the word, and to the will of God.</u>
- President John Taylor, October 1883 General Conference

It was by an **obedience** to the same [gospel] principles that Enoch
succeeded in gathering out the honest in heart unto the city of Zion. He
was 365 years in building up that Zion and in gathering into it a people
on the same principles that have been revealed to us in these latter
days. - Franklin D. Richards, April 1885 General Conference

Chapter Eight – Building Zion Is Spiritual AND Temporal!

Building Zion has a strong temporal element

Do not haul off the straw to burn, but save it all, and all the manure you
can produce. In this way Zion can be made to blossom as a rose, and the
beauty of Zion will begin to shine forth like the morning - George A.
Smith, April 1856 General Conference

In this case the Mission to which you, brethren, are called is to build a city; it calls for wives, children, for machinery, for mechanics, for everything that is calculated to add to the comfort and happiness of the citizens of a city. We are not going to be a great while isolated from our brethren, but we are going to assist in building up Zion. We want all necessary and important improvements, and if we build a telegraphic line from here to Santa Clara, it won't cost more than fifty thousand dollars. But you need not be afraid of leaving headquarters, for although we cannot all live at headquarters we expect that headquarters will be connected with every part of the world, and when Zion is not big enough for us, the Lord will be willing to stretch it so as to make room for his Saints. - George A. Smith, October 20, 1861

I do not arise with any desire to interfere with the call of brother George A. Smith for brethren to go to the cotton district of our Territory, for I am very much in favor of brethren going to locate in the different settlements of Washington County to raise cotton and such other staple articles as are necessary for the welfare and prosperity of the Saints, and for the building up of Zion in the last days. - Ezra T. Benson, March 8, 1862

I sometimes think that I would be willing to give anything, to do almost anything in reason, to see one fully organized Branch of this kingdom— one fully organized Ward. "But," says one, "I had supposed that the kingdom of God was organized long ago." So it is, in one sense; and again, in another sense it is not. **Wheresoever this Gospel has been preached and people have received it, the spiritual kingdom is set up and organized, but is Zion organized? No. Is there even in this Territory a fully organized Ward? Not one.** *It may be asked, "Why do you not fully organize the Church?" Because the people are incapable of being organized. I could organize a large Ward who would be subject to a full organization, by selecting families from the different Wards, but at present such a Branch of the Church is not in existence. - Brigham Young, October 1862 General Conference*

Let us train our minds until we delight in that which is good, lovely and holy, seeking continually after that intelligence which will enable us effectually to build up Zion, which consists in building houses, tabernacles, temples, streets, and every convenience necessary to embellish and beautify, seeking to do the will of the Lord all the days of our lives, improving our minds in all scientific and mechanical knowledge, seeking diligently to understand the great design and plan of all created things, that we may know what to do with our lives and how to improve upon the facilities placed within our reach. - Brigham Young, May 24, 1863

What is my feeling today? The same as it has been for years concerning houses, lands and possessions. I say to the people, "If you will give me for my property half what it has cost me I will devote that means for the gathering of the poor and the building of Zion upon the earth, and will start again with nothing. I have done it before, and I am willing to do it again . . . - Brigham Young, November 13, 1870

The building up of the Zion of God in these latter days includes, I may say of a truth, every branch of business, both temporal and spiritual, in which we are engaged. - Wilford Woodruff, April 1872 General Conference

In speaking of the affairs of this world, it is often asked by many—"Why, should we not attend to them?" Of course we should. Do we not talk of building up Zion? Of course we do. Do we not talk of building cities and of making beautiful habitations, gardens and orchards, and placing ourselves in such a position that we and our families can enjoy the blessings of life? Of course we do. God has given us the land and all the necessary elements for this purpose, and he has given us intelligence to use them. - John Taylor, January 5, 1873

I say, let us gather and accumulate the things of the earth in the manner indicated by the Lord, and then devote it to God and the building up of his kingdom. What little property I have I wish it to be devoted to the

building up of Zion, and I suppose I have as much as any other man in the Church. - Brigham Young, April 1877 General Conference

And if we, as Latter-day Saints, were to strictly observe the Sabbath day, and pay our tithes and offerings, and meet our engagements, and be less worldly minded, be united in temporal and spiritual things, Zion would arise and shine, and the glory of God would rest upon her. - President John Taylor, July 7, 1878

There are a great many things associated also with this Kingdom that it is proper should be presented to us from time to time, that we may be enabled to act and to operate together and be one in our feelings religious, one in our feelings social, and one in our feelings political; for all these things are mixed up and intimately connected with the position we occupy as the Saints of the Most High God in the building up of His Zion here upon the earth. There are things spiritual, there are things denominated temporal, there are things also spoken of as being eternal in their nature, and all these subjects, in all their various ramifications, demand more or less of our attention. - President John Taylor, November 30, 1879

We must be ready to physically build the New Jerusalem

It is the duty of the brethren to know how to build a house, how to make a garden, and how to do everything that can be accomplished by the ingenuity given to man. Why? That we may know how to build and beautify Zion. - Brigham Young, June 3, 1860

What do you know about building the great Temple that is yet to be built, upon which the glory of God will rest by day and by night? Where is the man that knows how to lay the first rock in that Temple, or to get out the first stick of timber for it? Where is the woman that knows how to make a single part of its interior decorations? That knowledge is not now here; and unless you wisely improve upon your privileges day by day, you will not be prepared, when called upon, to engage to the best advantage in building up Zion. - Brigham Young, June 3, 1860

Building Zion requires physical labor

Do not think you will be without your trials here, that you are to be a stereotyped edition to sit upon stools, singing glory to God, and that that is all you have to do.
I have often said to the English brethren and sisters that were I in England . . . I would tell them the first things they might expect to meet in Zion, viz: to leap into the mire and help to fill up a mud hole, to make adobies with their sleeves rolled up, and be spattered with clay from head to foot; and that some would be set to ditching in Zion, to making ditch fence ankle deep in mire; and that they might expect to eat their bread by the sweat of their brow, as in their native country. - Jedediah M. Grant, September 25, 1854

Go to work and say nothing about wages, but feel that "this is Zion; and what can I do to build it up, without asking any man to pay me one dollar?" Let that be your chief joy and delight, and you will never lack for work, food, or raiment. - Brigham Young, September 2, 1860

I want salvation, I wish to inherit eternal life, I wish to get back to the presence of God from whence I came, when I have finished my probation in the flesh. And I believe that I desire nothing in this respect but what you also wish. Then I know that it requires my diligence and my constant labor and study, the little time I have to spend in the flesh, to do all I can to build up Zion and to establish the Church and the kingdom of God upon the earth. - Wilford Woodruff, April 1878 General Conference

Building Zion requires our full-time labor

The word of the Presidency is, brethren, it is necessary to strengthen the southern border of our thriving Territory, and this is for the general good of all. Now you go down south and raise cotton and you will be blessed

more than you ever have been heretofore, and know that in doing this you are doing your part to build up Zion - George A. Smith, October 20, 1861

Supposing that the property of the whole community were divided today equally amongst all, what might we expect? Why a year from today we should need another division, for some would waste and squander it away, while others would add to their portion. The skill of building up and establishing the Zion of our God on the earth is to take the people and teach them how to take care of themselves and that which the Lord has entrusted to their care, and to use all that we command to glorify his holy name. This is the work of regenerating, of elevating mankind to the higher plane of the Gospel; in other words, of simply teaching them their duty. - Brigham Young, April 1877 General Conference

I can say with all propriety that, if we had strictly followed the counsels that have been given from the commencement until today, instead of being in such poverty, as we are in one sense, we would be a self-sustaining, independent people, commanding millions just as easy as we now command thousands. But how unwise, how foolish some of our brethren are! I am ashamed of them, and their condition is deplorable. Instead of beautifying their homes and improving their farms, and helping to reclaim the community and build up the Zion of the latter days, they have done—what? Dug holes in the ground? [i.e. become miners] - Brigham Young, June 17, 1877

We can't think, talk, or sing Zion into existence

But a person may merely think until he goes down to the grave, and he will never be the means of saving one soul, not even his own, unless he adds physical labor to his thinking. He must think, and pray, and preach, <u>and toil and labor with mind and body, in order to build up Zion in the last days</u>. - Brigham Young, October 1855 General Conference

Appendix A – Chapter 9

Chapter Nine - Babylon, Zion's Opposite.

What is Babylon?

The world is going to the devil just as fast as it can go. Corruption, fraud, chicanery, deception, evil and iniquity of every kind prevail, so that you cannot trust a man in any place, you cannot rely upon his word, you cannot rely upon any instrument of writing that he gets up, and there is nothing you can rely upon. Every day's news brings accounts of defalcations, frauds, infamies, rottenness and corruptions of every kind, enough to sink a nation from the presence of God and all honorable beings. And this is not only so in the United States, but other nations, in ours especially.
We, as a people, have come out from Babylon, but we have brought a great amount of these infernal principles with us, and we have been grabbing, grasping, pinching, squeezing, hauling, horning and hooking on every side, and it seems as though every man was for himself and the devil for us all. That is about the position we are in today. - John Taylor, 1874

Every Man for Himself

*We, as a people, have come out from Babylon, but we have brought a great amount of these infernal principles with us, and we have been grabbing, grasping, pinching, squeezing, hauling, horning and hooking on every side, and it seems as though **every man was for himself** and the devil for us all. That is about the position we are in today. We want a change in these things. <u>We have come to Zion</u>.* - John Taylor, April 19, 1874

*The grand principle upon which the Gospel of life and salvation is founded and on which Zion is to be built, is brotherly love and good will to man . . . Hitherto, under our old systems, it has been **"every man for himself**, and the devil for us all;" but the principle which the Lord proposes is that we should square our lives by a higher and holier one,* *namely, everyone for the whole and God for us all.* - Erastus Snow, May 8, 1874

The United Order is designed to help us to be self-reliant and to teach us to understand what it costs to produce that which we consume. One of the chief obstacles in the way of our progress towards becoming a self-sustaining people is the lack of this understanding among the people. They cling to the habits and customs of Babylon that they have learned abroad—the laborer wishing to eat up the <u>capitalist</u>, and the capitalist constantly guarded for fear he should . . . succumb to the demands of [labor's] operatives. This is the way of the world, and the warfare that is going on all the time; and why? Because they comprehend not how to promote their mutual interests; <u>covetousness of capital</u> on one hand, and <u>covetousness of labor</u> on the other, each trying to <u>enrich</u> itself at the expense of the other. - Erastus Snow, June 3, 1877

Babylon is self-focus mixed with avarice

The southern settlements were at first considered rather orderly, more so than some of those nearer this city, but in the spring of 1858, there was an influx from California of a large number of persons, who had gone there because they were not contented to live in this country, and who could not enjoy the liberty that was here. Many of them went to California to get rich, but a spirit came over some of them that the Lord was going to destroy all the Gentiles, and that if they came up here for a while they could go back after the Gentiles were killed off, and find better diggings . . . Several hundred persons came into the southern counties under these and similar influences, and intended to stay, no doubt, until the vengeance was over and the Gentiles swept off from the earth, then some thought they could go back and keep tavern . . . In this way there was grumbling, and a kind of daredevil influence scattered all through the settlements. We saw much of it here, but where the settlements were small, an influence of this kind took deeper hold and had a far more powerful effect. The spirit of avarice was not gratified, the Lord had not designed to cut off the wicked to please a few avaricious Mormons. - George A. Smith, October 20, 1861

[T]he Elder who has dreamed of preaching the Gospel to the nations, of building up Zion and laboring for the Gospel all night in his mind and feelings, being filled with the Holy Ghost, rejoices in his sleep; his slumbers are sweet to him and he rises in the morning filled with the good Spirit, and with him it is, "God bless you wife, God bless you my children." He feels to bless his house and his gardens, his orchards, his flocks and his herds, and everything looks pleasant to him and he rejoices exceedingly in the works of God's hands. He cherishes no malice, no anger; the spirit of the enemy has no place in him. How happy is such a person when compared with the man who is constantly laboring to amass gold and property, making this his only end and aim. How the Devil will play with a man who so worships gain. - Brigham Young, May 24, 1863

If you have the right to buy and sell and get gain, to go here and there, to do this and that, to build up the wicked and the ungodly, or their cities, you have rights that I have not got. I have the right to build up Zion, but I have no right to build up a city in wickedness. - Brigham Young, April 1867 General Conference

We have gone just as far as we can be permitted to go in the road on which we are now traveling. One man has his eye on a gold mine, another is for a silver mine, another is for marketing his flour or his wheat, another for selling his cattle, another to raise cattle, another to get a farm, or building here and there, and trading and trafficking with each other, just like Babylon, taking advantage wherever we can, and all going just as the rest of the world. Babylon is here, and we are following in the footsteps of the inhabitants of the earth, who are in a perfect sea of confusion. Do you know this? You ought to, for there are none of you but what see it daily; it is a daily spectacle before your eyes and mine, to see the Latter-day Saints trying to take advantage of their brethren. There are Elders in this Church who would take the widow's last cow, for five dollars, and then kneel down and thank God for the fine bargain they had made. - Brigham Young, April 18, 1874

Now the question is, how can we keep oil in our lamps? By keeping the commandments of God, remembering our prayers, do as we are told by the revelations of Jesus Christ, and otherwise assisting in building up Zion. When we are laboring for the kingdom of God, we will have oil in our lamps, our light will shine and we will feel the testimony of the spirit of God. On the other hand, if we set our hearts upon the things of the world and seek for the honors of men, we shall walk in the dark and not in the light. - Wilford Woodruff, January 9, 1881

The Saints Left Babylon for Utah

Does it not make your souls rejoice in the Lord, that He has established His people, and to realize that you are blessed above measure in having a name and a place in this city or territory? You are better off this afternoon in this place, in rags, and begging your bread, than in England, Scotland, or Wales, earning one hundred pounds per annum. **You would there be dwelling among the cloudy mists of Babylon**, *where you dare not say your souls were your own. You could make but little advancement in your holy religion there; but here* [in Utah] *you can receive words of life from those whom God has appointed to lead His people into the way of salvation.* - Franklin D. Richards, October 1853 General Conference

That angel delivered the keys of this apostleship and ministry to Joseph Smith and his brethren, and commanded them to blow the Gospel trump through all the nations of the earth, and to cry to all who love and wait patiently for the appearing of our Lord Jesus Christ, "Come out of her, my people, that ye may not be partakers of her sins and that ye receive not of her plagues." This was the doctrine of Jesus; this was the cry of John when on the Isle of Patmos. That angel has flown through the midst of heaven having the everlasting Gospel to preach to those who dwell on earth, and his cry was and is, "<u>Come out from Babylon</u>, from *pride, from the foolish fashions of the world; come out from the spirit of the world, from the spirit of hatred, anger, malice, wrath, selfishness and every feeling but that is honorable and justified of the heavens. Gather yourselves together! Sanctify the Lord God in your heart." <u>This was the cry, and it is the cry today</u>, and it will be until the pure in heart are gathered together.* - Brigham Young, July 17, 1870

We are told by the Revelator John, that a time would come when **the people of God should be commanded to come out of Babylon**, *out of confusion, when they should be gathered out from every nation, from the remotest parts of the earth, and when he should make of them a great and mighty people.*
 We see a partial fulfillment of this prediction in this Territory—*this people are gathered from various lands, and are dwelling together in peace and in union, without litigation, animosity or strife, all harmonizing together—their interests blended in one.* - George Q. Cannon, October 1872 General Conference

What are you here for? What did you come for? Virtually you all say <u>you left Babylon and came here</u> to build up the kingdom of God - Brigham Young, October 1872 General Conference

We must overcome the traditions of Babylon to build Zion

Suppose that every person who comes into these valleys should come with a determination to be led by the Lord, from day to day; suppose they should say, "I will serve my God and keep His commandments . . . and this will I do from this time, henceforth and forever;" and then let each one faithfully maintain such a determination, and we could truly say that we have the Territory of Zion, and the spirit, light, glory, and power thereof, and that the God of Zion dwells with this people. **But if we bring our old traditions with us** *. . . and say, "I will do so and so, this is the path I will pursue, and I am determined to walk in it, regardless of everything else," then we may expect to be overthrown, and the spirit of the holy Gospel will depart from us. Then you would soon learn that* *there was no temporal, no natural prospect for this people to escape from utter destruction* - Brigham Young, April 1855 General Conference

But you know that property is the Gentiles' god; it is sought after more eagerly than any other thing by the Gentile nations; it is worshipped by them, and their hearts are set on their treasures; and their treasures are of the earth and of an earthy nature; and <u>it will take a long time for the Saints to get rid of their old idols</u>—their idolatrous notions and traditions. The Gentile god has great influence even over the Saints; consequently it will take years to eradicate covetousness from our hearts; as our President has told us that the law relating to a full consecration of our property would perhaps be one of the last laws that would be fulfilled before the coming of Christ. Much patience and forbearance will need to be exercised before the Saints will get completely rid of their <u>old traditions, Gentile notions</u>, and whims about property, so as to come to that perfect law required of them in the revelations of Jesus Christ. But the day will come when there will be no poor in Zion, but the Lord will make them equal in earthly things, that they may be equal in heavenly things; that is, according to His notions of equality, and not according to our narrow, contracted views of the same. - Orson Pratt, April 1855 General Conference

Babylon *will* fall

By and by the earth becomes corrupted again, and the nations make themselves drunken with the wine of the wrath of great Babylon; but the Lord has reserved the same earth for fire; hence He says by the prophet Malachi, "Behold, the day cometh that shall burn as an oven, &c." A complete purification is again to come upon the earth, and that too, by the more powerful element of fire; and the wicked will be burned as stubble. - Orson Pratt, July 25, 1852

What man is there who reads the Scriptures, and believes that God means what He says, and says what He means, but what can see a flood of dreadful events ready to be poured out upon this generation with the

rapidity of lightning? No man can escape the influence of these events that are about to burst upon the heads of this generation. The Gospel has gone forth, and when the nations are warned, another angel will cry, "<u>Babylon is fallen</u>." War, and famine, and the plague will overwhelm the nations of the earth, and none can escape . . . But this is only the beginning of sorrow and trouble; the heavens are full of great judgments which are about to be poured out on the world. The words of the Prophets cannot have their fulfillment unless these things take place. Read the Revelation of Saint John, touching <u>the fall of Babylon</u>, and you there have a faint picture of what is about to transpire. - Wilford Woodruff, February 25, 1855

Chapter Ten – Building Zion Includes Economic Independence from Babylon.

Economic dependence on the world invites trouble

Let the people consider for themselves whether we have, so far as we could have done, been taking a course to become that kingdom that we anticipate, or whether we have not been more or less dependent upon our enemies for many things that we could have produced, or done without. - Brigham Young, March 28, 1858

See how dependent we are, when we have got no bread, clothing, sugar . . . and those who possess these articles hold us in servitude. It is the duty of every man to go to work and raise or make what he needs for his own consumption. This is one thing that causes President Young to go down south, so that he may ascertain if that country is capable of producing our cotton, sugar . . . and grapes. I know that we can make the sugar as well in this country as they can in the Southern States. The reason it is not done is because we have got men here who are so anxious to get a large quantity of molasses from their crops of sugar cane. I am satisfied that we can make good sugar here, if we will only take a little time to do it. I design to do it myself, if nothing happens to prevent. We make our flour, we saw our lumber, card our wool, we spin a great deal of yarn, and make a great deal of cloth; but still there are but very few of this people who dress in homemade cloth. We are dependent upon the States and the various nations of Europe for our clothing. - Heber C. Kimball, May 12, 1861

We raise a large amount of wool here, what do we do with it? We export a great deal of it to the States. We have got a large amount of excellent timber here, what do we do for our furniture? We send to the States for a great deal of it. Where do we get our pails and our washtubs, and all our cooper ware from? We send to the States for it. Where do we get our brooms from? From the States; and so on all the way through the catalogue, and millions on millions of dollars are sent out of the Territory every year, for the purchase of articles, most of which we could manufacture and raise at home. This is certainly very poor economy, for we have thousands and thousands of men who are desirous to get some kind of employment, and they cannot get it. Why? Because other people are making our shoes, hats, clothing, bonnets, silks, artificial flowers, and many other things that we need. This may do very well for a while in an artificial state of society; **but the moment any reverse comes that kind of thing is upset, and all our calculations are destroyed**. - John Taylor, May 7, 1874

Independence through local manufacturing

It should be our aim as individuals, as families and as a community to dispense with everything that we cannot manufacture. I am told that thousands of dollars a year are expended in supplying our tables with mustard imported from the East. I have no means of knowing the truth of this, but it seems incredible, that we, with the facilities we have for its production, should depend upon importation for the supply of a common article like mustard.

But this is only one article. When we sit down to our tables, and take a survey, we find many articles that are thus imported. It may be, and frequently is said by a certain class of persons that articles can be imported much cheaper than they can be manufactured here. This is urged by them as a reason for importing; but it is a delusion and a snare, and the man who utters such a sentiment is an ignoramus. He knows nothing about the true principles of building up a people and kingdom. That which is manufactured here, though it cost ten times the amount it would cost in the east, is the cheaper, for that is the commencement of independence. The man or the family who carries on home manufacture is laying the foundation for true and lasting independence. - George Q. Cannon, April 1868 General Conference

I would urge the brethren of the southern country to plant cotton sufficient to supply the wants of the factories that are now in the country, and let us continue our labors until we can manufacture everything we want. All this is embraced in our religion, every good word and work, all things temporal, and all things spiritual, things in heaven, things on earth, and things that are under the earth are circumscribed by our religion. We are in the fastnesses of the mountains, and if we do these things, and delight in doing right, our feet will be made fast and immovable like the bases of these everlasting hills. - Brigham Young, April 1868 General Conference

But let us unite closer together, and harmonize our temporal interests, until we shall manufacture everything we need to make us independent of the world. - Pres. John Taylor, September 22, 1878

Why is economic independence so important?

*And I know another thing, that a great many people are becoming so proud—well, perhaps it is not pride, but they have got so that they cannot dress and clothe themselves with anything that is not brought here by the merchants. Many will bring in their wool, and their linsey, and their good clothing that they make here from the wool, and give it to clothe the Indians, for they are too proud to wear it themselves. But **the day will come when the merchants of the earth will lift up their heads and their voices, and cry out, "We have no place to sell our merchandise."*** - Heber C. Kimball, November 26, 1854

I would like to see the people take a course to make their own clothing, make their own machinery, their own knives and their own forks, and everything else we need, for <u>the day will come when we will be under the necessity of doing it, for trouble and perplexity, war and famine, bloodshed and fire, and thunder and lightning will roll upon the nations of the earth, insomuch that we cannot get to them, nor they to us.</u> If you do not believe me I want you to believe the Prophets; read the revelations that came through brother Joseph Smith, and through Daniel and Moses, and through Jesus, and through all the ancient Prophets. They spoke of these things, and declare they shall come to pass in the latter days. - Heber C. Kimball, November 26, 1854

Are you going to prepare for [Babylon's fall]? *We say we are the people of God and are building up the kingdom of God. We say we are gathered out of the nations to establish Zion. Let us prove it by our works, and we will then manufacture that which we wear. Do we make clothing enough for me and you to wear? Yes; plenty.* - Brigham Young, February 2, 1870

<u>By and by Babylon will fall</u>; in a little while "no man will buy her merchandise," and the sooner we are prepared for the changes which are about to take place in our nation and in the nations of the earth the better for us. - Wilford Woodruff, May 6, 1870

The time will come when the thread will be cut, but I think we could live if the thread were cut tomorrow. We can produce everything, except perhaps what are called the luxuries; still we would suffer much inconvenience. There are a great many things we would have to do without, and if the thread were cut we would have to do a great many things that we now neglect to do. **We should not be forever dependent on Babylon**. Call them little things if you please, but they are as essential to the building up of the kingdom as they are to any other kingdom on the earth. - Daniel H. Wells, June 1, 1878

<u>We read in the Scriptures of a time that is coming when there will be a howling among the merchants in Babylon, for men will not be found to buy their merchandise.</u> This is in accordance with the prediction of John the Revelator. And the gold and the silver and the fine linen, etc., in Babylon will be of no avail. But before that time comes, <u>we as a people must prepare for those events, that we may be able to live and sustain ourselves when in the midst of convulsions that by and by will overtake the nations of the earth</u>, and among others, this nation. The time that is spoken of is not very far distant. "He that will not take up his sword against his neighbor, must needs flee to Zion for safety." And Zion herself must flee to the God of Israel and hide herself in the shadow of his wing, seeking for his guidance and direction to lead her in the right path, both as regards spiritual and temporal affairs; things social and things political, and everything pertaining to human existence. - President John Taylor, April 1879 General Conference

Zion and Her Saints Must Become Self-Sustaining

I am satisfied that the people now begin to learn that they can make their own clothing, and that those who do not learn will run the risk of being uncomfortably clad. But would this people, by their wisdom, ever have brought themselves to that independence that God will, by his providence, in a seeming chastisement? I say seeming, for it is no chastisement: it is a blessing to this people, and one of the greatest that can be bestowed upon us, to cut the thread between us and our enemies, and oblige us to sustain ourselves in everything that we can produce with our labor, skill, and economy. The Lord can bring this about, or cause the Devil to do it, just as he pleases. - Brigham Young, March 28, 1858

I wished to add my testimony to the things you have listened to. May the blessings of God rest upon us, and give unto us wisdom and ability to contribute our aid <u>to make the people of Zion self-sustaining</u>. - George A. Smith, February 6, 1862

*Many years ago efforts were made on the part of the Presidency to extend the settlements into the warm valleys south of the rim of the Basin. The country was very forbidding and sterile. Many were invited and called upon to go and settle there . . . the mass of those who went, confident that the blessings of God would be upon their labors, pushed forth their exertions and built up towns, cities and villages; they established cotton fields and erected factories, and supplied many wants which could not be supplied within the rim of the Basin. It has been my lot to visit these regions recently, and I have felt to rejoice to see . . . where men and women had taken hold with all their hearts to obey the commandments of God, and **to lay a foundation for Zion to become self-sustaining**.* - George A. Smith, 1870

I wish we would learn how to produce [goods] instead of purchasing them. I wish we could concentrate our energies, and organize all hands, old, middle-aged and young, male and female, and put them under proper directions, with proper materials to manufacture everything we need to wear and use. We have forgotten even how to make sorghum molasses, and our memories are getting short on other points. We can hardly make a hat or coat, or a pair of boots and shoes, but we have to send to the States and import these paper ones, which last a very short time and then drop to pieces, and you have your hands continually in your pockets to supply these wants, and by and by your pockets are empty. It is therefore necessary that we right about face, and begin to turn the other end to, and be self-sustaining. - John Taylor, May 7, 1874

Is there anything extraordinary or new in the doctrine that it is well for a community to be self-sustaining? Why, the Whigs, you know, of this country, have contended on that principle from the time of the organization of the government, and they have sanctioned it and plead in its behalf before Congress, in political caucuses, and before the people up to the present time. There is nothing new in the doctrine of a people being self-sustaining. The first Napoleon introduced into France what is known as the "Continental system," which encouraged the production of all necessary articles at home, and it is the results of this system which today gives stability to France, and has enabled her, after the severe trials of the late war, to pay off her indebtedness and stand independent among the nations. - John Taylor, May 7, 1874

The blessings of the Lord are not bestowed upon the Latter-day Saints to be placed by them in the hands of the wicked. When could the Lord establish his purposes with a people who will act in that way? Never in the world. The time will come and is now hastening when the people of God will not be a dependent people, that is, dependent upon the outside world; of course they will always be dependent upon the Lord, but the day will come when they, under the blessing of heaven, will be **an entirely self-sustaining people**, *and the Lord is ready and willing, as he ever has been and ever will be, to sustain the efforts of his people in this direction. They must put forth their hands to be self-sustaining, and then* *the blessings of the Almighty will attend them even more abundantly. - Daniel H. Wells, April 1875 General Conference*

The principles which have been laid before us this morning in regard to our becoming a self-sustaining people, are plain and easy to be comprehended. They are self-evident to every reflecting mind, and are worthy of our earnest attention, for while we are dependent upon others for this, that and the other which is indispensable to our well-being and comfort, we can plainly see that our course is not only not the most advantageous to ourselves, but also that it is not the most pleasing to our heavenly Father, for in the revelations given by him in the early rise of this Church, his Saints were requested to pursue such a course in their home affairs as would make them self-sustaining. We have seen times in our experience here in this Territory, when it has been extremely difficult for us to obtain from abroad many things which we needed, and there is little doubt that we shall see such times again in the future; hence the very great necessity to adopt a policy in regard to temporal matters that will free us from the inconveniences that would arise in such a contingency, and that can only be done by producing as far as possible, according to our circumstances and the possibilities of our climate and Territory, everything that we need to sustain ourselves in comfort and convenience. - Charles C. Rich, April 1875 General Conference

I can see, as clearly as it is possible for me to see the light of the sun, that if the instructions that were given here yesterday, and the day before, in relation to uniting ourselves together in temporal affairs, were carried out by the people, we would soon no longer be beholden to the world, and it would be said of us, that we were dependent upon no power upon the earth but the power of God. - Joseph F. Smith, October 1875 General Conference

*For my greatest desire is to see Zion established according to the revelations of God, to see her inhabitants industrious **and self-sustaining**, filled with wisdom and the power of God, that around us may be built a wall of defense, a protection against the mighty powers* *of Babylon; and while the disobedient of our Father's family are contending, and filling up their cup of iniquity, even to the brim, and thus preparing themselves for the burning, we, who are the acknowledged children of the kingdom, being filled with the righteousness and knowledge of God, may be like the wise virgins, clothed in our wedding garments, and properly prepared for the coming of our Lord and Savior.* - Lorenzo Snow, November 5, 1876

The Southern States in the late civil war were whipped by the Northern States, why? There may be some general reasons, but you may say, speaking on natural principles they were not sufficiently self-sustaining. They relied mainly upon their cotton, and a few other products of the earth, mainly fruits of their close labor; they had few manufacturing establishments. They sent the raw material to other States and countries, and these worked it up, sending back to them the manufactured articles. No nation under heaven can long thrive, and continue this state of things. Just as soon as their trade was interfered with, their domestic institutions broken into, and the country blockaded, preventing the export of their raw material, and the import of manufactured goods, they were brought to the verge of ruin. - Erastus Snow, June 3, 1877

Go into debt, and pauperize the whole community, instead of building up Zion. I want you to stop. When we are in a position to build up ourselves, we are building up Zion. Let us sustain ourselves. - Brigham Young, July 19, 1877

We should establish branches of industry from which we could at least provide for our own necessities and as soon as possible be able to export our home productions, and thus give employment to every faithful Latter-day Saint who is gathered to Zion, that individuals may not only become self sustaining but contribute their proportion to the general good.
Our manufactories should be fostered, patronized and protected, and their staple wares sought after and preferred by the people, even

though they were more costly at first. It needs no argument to prove to the sagacious and far seeing that this policy will pay the best in the end. While we continue to be purchasers and importers only, we will remain dependent to, and at the mercy of manufacturers and exporters from abroad; but when we can produce what we need by our own industry and skill, from the elements which so abundantly surround us, we cease to import, to be dependent upon Babylon, or the world, we approach independence, and begin to assume the position in the earth which God has designed we should, to lead and not be led, to teach and not be taught, to be the "head and not the tail." - Joseph F. Smith, April 1879 General Conference

Chapter Eleven – Zion Requires Economic Unity

We must be one temporally too.

It is a temporal kingdom that we are engaged in building up for our God upon the earth; and it becomes essentially necessary that we should be one in regard to temporal matters, as well as in spiritual. - Daniel H. Wells, September 10, 1861

We are agreed in the matter of our religion, and **we must be agreed in temporal matters**. *If we cannot become of one mind in all things, we shall not be that people called the people of the Lord.* - Brigham Young, July 17, 1864

This is the land of Zion; but we are not yet prepared to go and establish the Center Stake of Zion . . . Now, it is for you and me to prepare to return back again; not to our fatherland, in many cases, but to return east, and by-and-by to build up the Center Stake of Zion. We are not prepared to do this now, but we are here to learn until we are of one heart and of one mind <u>in the things of this life</u>. - Brigham Young, February 10, 1867

*There is no division among us so far as the principles of our religion are concerned; it is in relation to some things the world call **temporal** that we are not one. How are you going to build up Zion? In the hearts of the people? . . . We have to build up Zion, a **temporal** work here upon the face of the earth, and we have got to establish righteousness and truth. When I say a temporal work, I speak of temporal things. The Zion of our God cannot be built up in the hearts of men alone. We have to build up temples and cities, and the earth has to become sanctified and to be made holy by the children of God who will dwell upon it, and to do this **we must be united together**.* - Wilford Woodruff, April 1867 General Conference

We are the only people under heaven who are one, and we are not half as much one as we ought to be; we have to improve. We are the only people in the whole Christian world who make any pretensions to oneness in building up the Zion of God on the earth. We profess to be one in the Gospel, and we have to become so in temporal matters. We have to become of one heart and mind in giving attention and obedience to the counsel of God in all things, both spiritual and temporal. Zion has got to advance; she has got to rise and shine and put on her beautiful garments. She is advancing and has been from the time of the organization of this Church, and she will continue to do so until the winding up scene. - Wilford Woodruff, May 6, 1870

A unity must exist, the Latter-day Saints must love one another, they must cease to worship this world's goods, they must lay a foundation to build up Zion and to be one, in order that they may be prepared for the great day that shall burn as an oven. - George A. Smith, October 1873 General Conference

I will now ask the question, where is the individual who can draw the line and show us that, when Jesus prayed that his disciples might be one, he meant a oneness only in spiritual things, and that it was not to extend to temporal affairs? Will any of you draw the line and tell us? For I am

certain that I have not wisdom enough to define the line between spiritual and temporal things. - Brigham Young, April 18, 1874

We cannot build up a Zion unless we are in possession of the spirit of Zion, and of the light and intelligence that flow from God, and under the direction of the Priesthood, the living oracles of God, to lead us in the paths of life. We do not know them without, and we need all these helps to lead us along, that by and by we may come to such a unity in our temporal and in our spiritual affairs, and in everything that pertains to our interest and happiness in this world and in the world to come, that we may be prepared to enter a Zion here upon the earth . . . and so operate and cooperate with the Gods in the eternal worlds, and with the Patriarchs, Prophets, Apostles, and men of God . . . we want to be one with them, one with God, and one with each other, for Jesus said— "Except you are one you are not mine." - John Taylor, August 31, 1875

God the Father of Jesus, and all the eternal Priesthood in the heavens expect . . . all the Priesthood and all the people to be governed by the law of God, and to help faithfully to build Zion and establish the kingdom of God <u>that we may be one in all things temporal</u> and spiritual. - John Taylor, June 17, 1877

Brotherly love should prevail among all the people of God, and we should be more united in our temporal and spiritual matters, and thereby claim the promised blessings. - John Taylor, October 1877 General Conference

*I wish to make a few remarks in relation to what we term the United Order. We are united today with God, and with the holy Priesthood that existed before us, with Jesus the Mediator of the New Covenant, and with the ancient Prophets and Apostles and men of God, in building up the Zion of God upon the earth. They, in their different spheres and callings, are operating with us, and we with them, and the whole thing is a grand Cooperative Society; and everything we do here should be with the view of **uniting our earthly interests, that we may be one in things***

temporal *and one in things spiritual, one on the earth and one with those in the heavens, helping with our united efforts to roll on the Kingdom of God according to his purposes, and not according to our erratic notions.* - John Taylor, October 1877 General Conference

We are told by the Savior that we must be united, or we are not his. Does this concern us as Latter-day Saints? I think it does, but some do not seem in any way concerned about it, notwithstanding the word of the Lord, that otherwise we "are none of his." How can we be united so as to be acceptable to God? <u>We have to be united, not merely in doctrinal matters, but in every other way.</u> *So far as doctrine is concerned, we are pretty well united, but not so in our temporal affairs. But we may become united in our temporal affairs.* - Charles C. Rich, February 10, 1878

For I tell you we have a perfect organization in view, and nothing short of it will satisfy us. The Twelve have all had it at heart, and they are bound by the covenants of the Holy Priesthood and by the responsibility which rests upon them, and upon him, who is the President of the Twelve and of the Church. I say we are bound by these covenants and these signs of responsibility, and to labor today, and labor tomorrow, and labor continuously until eternity shall dawn upon us <u>for the more perfect organization of this people in their temporal affairs</u>. *And as for division, we want it not; disunion, we want it not. We do not want to see the Elders of Israel fall asunder, dividing this people and leading them away from the union that should characterize us. We say that any man that does it is not of God; the man that does it is not inspired by the Spirit of God, and has not the love and prosperity of this work at heart.* - George Q. Cannon, April 1878 General Conference

When all things are in proper working order, and when every bishop is living his religion, and has the spirit of his bishopric resting upon him, and he fully understands the nature of his duties, everything in regard to temporal affairs will move like clockwork, and there will be no running down, as it were, of the clock, no deranging of the machinery, but every part will fulfil that which is required of it in relation to its particular calling, and all these various quorums of priesthood will strive to stir up the people to a oneness in regard to spiritual things; thus we keep spiritual and temporal things running parallel to each other, connected more or less together. So that the whole church becomes like unto one body, they become equal. - Orson Pratt, September 22, 1878

And shall we, because of individual interests and personalities draw off from things that God has ordained? I say no, never! No, never! But let us unite closer together, and harmonize our temporal interests. - John Taylor, September 22, 1878

God has established His Zion, and He is building it up in the way He has revealed and that He communicates to His servants from time to time . . . We must see eye to eye; we must progress in this direction. It is true our progress in some things is not what it ought to be. We do not progress, for instance, in the proper Management of financial matters, and in **union** *as foreshadowed in the revelations of the Lord concerning temporal matters to the extent and with the rapidity that many of us hoped we would see. But nevertheless it is our duty to keep on doing the best we can,* **striving to come to the unity of the faith in regard to these affairs.** - George Q. Cannon, September 28, 1889

Economics Under God's Direction

Many wish for the time when President Brigham Young and his brethren will be relieved from attending to temporal matters, and attend to spiritual matters altogether. You will have to wait for this until we get into the spiritual world and have to deal with spirits. All things pertaining to this world, both spiritual <u>and temporal</u>, will be dictated by the Prophet of God—by our President. - Heber C. Kimball, July 16, 1854

The people of God could not understand, in the beginning, that Brother Joseph had wisdom sufficient to direct them **in their temporal affairs as well as in their spiritual affairs.** *While the Church was in Kirtland it was* *a lesson they had not learned; they could admit that Joseph was a prophet of God, and chosen of Him to establish His kingdom on the earth, but they would not admit that he had wisdom sufficient to direct them in temporal affairs, and they had to be whipped, scourged, and driven from place to place before they could really believe that the servants of God had this wisdom; but, by-and-by, this knowledge dawned upon them, and they began to see that men, chosen of God to establish righteousness and build up His kingdom, had also wisdom concerning temporal affairs, and that the same God who made the earth so beautiful for the habitation of His saints—He who organized the heavens and controls the movements of the heavenly bodies, that same God had power to give Brother Joseph Smith wisdom to guide them in temporal affairs. This is a lesson that we have had taught unto us from that time until the present; and today I feel as though we were but poor scholars, and that there are many things yet to be impressed upon our understandings connected with this lesson. - George Q. Cannon, November 13, 1864*

How many are there within the hearing of my voice who have felt infringed upon in their feelings when they were told to sustain Zion and not to trade with their enemies. This was a new feature, but it touched things of a temporal nature. Why a great many felt as though they could not submit to be dictated to, though it was by the servant of God, in regard to temporal affairs. Is not this true, and we, too, right in the midst of Israel? O, yes, we can't deny it, there has been considerable howling made concerning this item. But yet this is the kingdom of God, and the kingdom and the greatness thereof are to be given to the Saints of the Most High. <u>Can we expect anything else than that His servant will dictate us concerning our temporal matters?</u> I do not understand it in any other way. When, I would ask, can the kingdom of God be established on the earth, or in other words when can the kingdom and the greatness thereof be given to the Saints of the Most High? Never until a people is found possessing sufficient good, hard, sound sense to use the blessings of that kingdom to build it up and not to give it to the *devil just as fast as the Lord hands them over to them. We have come up to Zion that we may be taught in the ways of the Lord and that we may learn to walk in His paths.* - Daniel H. Wells, May 5, 1870

When we reflect upon these things I think we all should be willing to let the Lord guide us in temporal matters. - Wilford Woodruff, May 8, 1874

The greatest trouble that has ever been, probably that the Lord has had, with the people in any age, has been <u>in reference to their temporal affairs, their financial matters.</u> *The Latter-day Saints at the present day, are very united in reference to their spiritual principles and doctrines. We see eye to eye in regard to principles that pertain to the doctrinal portion of the religion we have espoused; but when it comes to our temporal, our earthly possessions, and our conduct in relation to them, we seem to be a little confused in reference to what is right and wrong and more or less, we feel disposed to pursue our own course in regard to these matters and, as in the days of judges, "every man is doing what seems right in his own eyes." We seem to forget that the Lord has distinctly pointed out our duties, and that there is a little book, Doctrine and Covenants, that God has given by direct revelation in regard to these matters, by which we should be governed.* - Lorenzo Snow, October 18, 1879

What Economic Unity Looks Like: Mutual Benefit

Now I could show, by sound argument and logic, the necessity for the people **to live and labor for the good of all**. *Anybody ought to be able to see that when one member of a family is pulling away from the others, and living for self alone, it injures himself or herself as well as the whole family. The necessity and beauty of union cannot be better illustrated than by the example of the chief who called his sons together just previous to his death, and, taking a bundle of arrows, asked them each to break it. This they were unable to do. "Now," said he, "unloose the bundle." They did so, and could take the arrows singly, one by one, and break them with ease. This will give us as good a proof as we can desire,* that when we are bound together as a unit, we are strong and powerful, but when we are divided we are weak, and our enemies can obtain power over us. Take our financial affairs, and they will show the same principle. But we are prone to unbelief, and have to learn by the childish principle—a little today and a little more tomorrow, and after a while perhaps we will become truly Latter-day Saints. We profess to be so now. - Brigham Young, May 18, 1873

We are here to build up Zion; and how ought we to feel? We want to make as good houses as we can. That is all right provided we come by them honestly. We want to lay a foundation for our children if we can. That's all right. But do not let our hearts and affections be placed upon these things, for there are other things we have to do. We have to pay our tithes and offerings, as we have been commanded. We have to build Temples. And that is all right. I was going to say, if we do that . . .But do we want to speculate out of our brethren and get something from them to build us up? That is not right. **We want to build one another up as well as ourselves**. - President John Taylor, June 26, 1881

Benefits of Economic Unity

2. Economic Unity results in a classless society

I rejoice exceedingly to hear, that the President has been moved upon, not only before he left Salt Lake City to go down South, but while he has been there, to alter the order of things that has existed for many years here in these mountains, among the Latter-day Saints. In what respect? To bring about a united order of things in regard to their property and labor, and the development of the resources of our farming land; in regard to raising flocks and herds, building, and developing the mineral resources of our mountains. In all these respects the President has seen the necessity of beginning to bring about, gradually, as the way may open, a different order of things **that will strike the axe at the root of this pride and distinction of classes**. - Orson Pratt, April 1874 General Conference

3. The Elimination of Poverty

Speaking about the Zion of the last days, Isaiah says that the Lord will bring for brass gold, for iron silver, for wood brass, and for stones iron to build up the Zion of God. When will that be done? When we are united, so that we shall not consume the wealth that God will give us upon our lusts, upon creating class distinctions, raising one class above another, one class living in luxury and another class groveling in poverty; but when we are so organized that there will be no rich and no poor, but all partaking alike of the bounties that God shall give unto us, then, and in my opinion, not till then, can he bestow upon us the wealth that he has promised. - George Q. Cannon, October 1874 General Conference

Chapter Twelve – Cooperation is a Stepping Stone to Zion

So . . . Co-ops Help Us Build Zion?

In February, 1831, just after the organization of the Church, we received a revelation through Joseph Smith, commanding the members of the Church to let the beauty of their garments be the workmanship of their own hands . . . This revelation was given almost forty years ago, but slowly, very slowly, have we advanced in fulfilling it . . . I realize the reason of this, when reflecting upon the great work to be done in molding the children of God, gathered from the various nations and denominations, with all their prejudices, traditions, and varied habits of living. They come here filled with ideas averse to those of God and differing from each other; and under these circumstances it is difficult for them to arrive at a oneness in their associations—to use an expression common amongst us at the present—it is difficult for them to cooperate to build up Zion in the last days. - George A. Smith, May 6, 1870

We are looking forward to the day when we shall return to Jackson County. The time will come when the Latter-day Saints will build, in Independence, Mo., a holy city. That will one day be the Center Stake of Zion, the center spot of the New Jerusalem which God is to build on this land. We can only be prepared for that work by being united. Can we not unite a little in building a Temple, in contributing a tenth of all our substance to that work? Can we not unite a little in erecting a factory, in establishing a store? Can we not learn, step by step, the principles of unity, which will enable us to be the people of God, like the Zion of Enoch, and prepare us for a dwelling with the blest? Let us consider these things, and sustain with all our powers all the efforts that are made to bring about a unity among the Saints. Every step we take of this kind is in the right direction. Sustain our Cooperative stores, and cease to sustain those who do not build up Zion. - George A. Smith, October 1873 General Conference

The United Order of Zion, proposed for our consideration, as will be seen from the remarks that have been made by former speakers, and from the articles which were read yesterday afternoon, is a grand, comprehensive, cooperative system, designed to improve us who enter into it, financially, socially, morally and religiously; it will aid us, as Latter-day Saints, in living our religion, and in building up Zion. - Erastus Snow, May 8, 1874

So . . . how do co-ops actually help prepare us to build Zion?

1. "No poor among them".

What I have in my mind with regard to this cooperative business is this—There are very few people who cannot get twenty-five dollars to put into one of these cooperative stores. There are hundreds and thousands of women who, by prudence and industry, can obtain this sum. And we say to you put your capital into one of these stores. What for? To bring you interest for your money. Put your time and talents to usury. We have the parable before us. If we have one, two, three or five talents, of what advantage will they be if we wrap them in a napkin and lay them away? None at all. Put them out to usury. **These cooperative stores are instituted to give the poor a little advantage** as well as the rich. - Brigham Young, April 1869 General Conference

If these wards will each establish a store and concentrate their influence, they will double their capital every three months. I know that the 10th ward, which started with 700 dollars, three weeks afterwards had a thousand dollars worth of goods paid for and considerable money in the drawer. Think of that, in that poor little ward, though I will give it the praise of being one of the best wards in the city. - Brigham Young, April 1869 General Conference

Before cooperation started, you doubtless saw and deplored the increase of wealth in some few hands. There was rapidly growing in our midst a class of monetary men composing an aristocracy of wealth. Our community was menaced by serious dangers through this, because if a community is separated into two classes, one poor and the other rich, their interests are diverse. Poverty and wealth do not work together well—one lords it over the other; one becomes the prey of the other. This is apt to be the case in all societies, in ours as well as others; probably not to so great an extent, but still it was sufficiently serious to menace us as a people with danger. God inspired his servant to counsel the people to enter into cooperation, and it has now been practiced for *some years in our midst with the best results. Those who have put in a little means have had that more than doubled since Z. C. M. I. started—three years last March. And so it is with cooperative herds, cooperative factories, and cooperative institutions of all kinds which have been established in our midst, and* **all the people can partake of the benefits of this system**. - George Q. Cannon, October 1872 General Conference

We ask concerning the rich, Do we want your gold and your silver? No, we do not. Do we want your houses and lands? We do not. What do we want? We want obedience to the requirements of wisdom, to direct the labors of every man and every woman in this kingdom to the best possible advantage, that we may feed and clothe ourselves, build our houses and gather around us the comforts of life, without wasting so much time, means, and energy. And instead of saying that I shall give up my carriage for the poor to ride in, <u>we will direct the poor so that every man may have his carriage</u>, if he will be obedient to the requirements of the Almighty. <u>Every family will have all that they can reasonably desire</u>. When we learn and practice fair dealing in all our intercourse and transactions, then confidence, now so far lost, but so much needed, will be restored; and we will be enabled to effectually carry out our operations for the friendly and profitable cooperation of money and labor, now so generally and so injuriously antagonistic. - Brigham Young, May 4, 1874

2. "Of one heart and one mind"

I do not expect to be able to speak much during this Conference, but I make a request of my brethren who may speak, to give us their instructions and views for or against this general cooperative system, which we, with propriety, may call the United Order. If any choose to give it any other name that will be applicable to the nature of it, they can do so. **A system of oneness** *among any people . . . is beneficial.* - Brigham Young, May 7, 1874

We have abundantly proved in our experience that if we do not sustain ourselves, no other people will sustain us, and that we must be united, as was said this morning, in our temporal as well as in our spiritual affairs; and that if we would build up and strengthen ourselves in the earth, it must be by union of effort, and by concentrating our means in a way that shall produce the best results for the work with which we are identified. Cooperation, or a union of effort, has been proved in our experience, when properly carried out, to be most successful. With small means and limited incomes we can accomplish, by wisely uniting our efforts, great results, and to bring about greater union should be our continual effort. - George Q. Cannon, April 1875 General Conference

We have had, the last week, considerable conversation with leading men from various parts of this Territory concerning this principle of cooperation. Notwithstanding some differences of opinion upon some points, upon this one point that I have endeavored to set before you in my last few sentences, there has been an unanimity of feeling and opinion, that is of the imperative necessity of our being united in our business matters, in our financial matters and work to sustain each other and build each other up. - George Q. Cannon, April 1878 General Conference

You all know, who have attended conferences in past times, how much President Young was interested in this matter; not so much in the sale of merchandise as in the principle of cooperation. And he and others have stepped forward repeatedly, and have sustained it in the midst of the people, when otherwise it would have gone down. I allude to this because it comes in the line of my remarks, in the thread of my argument, so to speak. To be successful we ought, instead of dividing asunder and drawing one from another, to cling closer together; it is of the utmost importance that all our financial matters should be conducted in a way to contribute to the influence of the whole people. - George Q. Cannon, April 1878 General Conference

There is one thing, however, I would here say about forming unions and partnerships in any line of manufacture: Let them be formed with the understanding that when the proper time shall arrive they can merge into cooperation, or the United Order. It is very important that in all of our undertakings we should have at heart this feeling and work to this end, and then we may reasonably expect that it can be but a question of time to bring out a grand consolidation of all individual interests. - President John Taylor, September 21, 1878

We have, for instance, Zion's Cooperative Mercantile Institution; it is called the Parent Institution, and it ought to be the parent of all these institutions and act as a father and protector and benefactor, doing all it can to promote the welfare and prosperity of the people. And then the people, on the other hand, ought to protect it and sustain it by doing their business through that institution and act prudently, wisely, orderly and unitedly in regard to these matters, that we may be one; for our revelations tell us, If we are not one, we are not the Lord's. And if we are not the Lord's, whose are we? - President John Taylor, April 1879 General Conference

Cooperation is a principle that President Young was very much concerned about, and that he endeavored, with his brethren, to impress upon the minds of the people throughout the land. Under his administration our cooperative institutions were established, and by his efforts, many of the people, especially in the southern part of Utah and in Arizona, became united together in organizations that were called "the United Order." The object was cooperation, that the principles of union in labor as well as in faith might be developed to its fullest extent in the midst of the Saints. - Joseph F. Smith, July 18, 1884

Cooperatives are a stepping stone to Zion's United Orders

I want to say a few words still further to the people with regard to their faith in temporal things. If the people called Latter-day Saints do not

become one in temporal things as they are in spiritual things, they will not redeem and build up the Zion of God upon the earth. This cooperative movement is a stepping stone. We say to the people, take advantage of it, it is your privilege. Instead of giving it into the hands of a few individuals to make their hundreds and thousands, let the people, generally, enjoy the benefit arising from the sale of merchandise. - Brigham Young, April 1869 General Conference

When we have practiced this principle [of economic cooperation] long enough, and are sufficiently advanced in it, there are other principles, now ahead, which we shall be prepared to enter upon and practice. - George Q. Cannon, November 13, 1870

Now then, is this cooperative institution one step towards bringing the people to a union? Yes - Brigham Young, April 28, 1872

Brethren, if you will start here and operate together in farming, in making cheese, in herding sheep and cattle and every other kind of work, and get a factory here and a cooperative store . . . and operate together in sheep raising, storekeeping, manufacturing and everything else, no matter what it is, by and by, when we can plant ourselves upon a foundation that we cannot be broken up, we shall then proceed to arrange a family organization for which we are not yet quite prepared. You now, right here in this place, commence to carry on your business in a cooperative capacity. In every instance I could show every one of you what a great advantage would be gained in working together . . . Well, we can do this and keep up cooperation, and, by and by, when we can, we will build up a city after the order of Enoch. - Brigham Young, August 31, 1873

Well, the time is passing, but before closing, I wish to say a word or two in regard to this cooperation in temporal things. They are very little things, but they form a kind of stepping stone towards other and more important events. A closer union which we shall expect to inaugurate by-and-by, but which we are not prepared to yet . . . We expect to see these things carried out in honesty and truth, because it is the order which God has introduced as a steppingstone to something in the future. - President John Taylor, December 8, 1878

We will strive to be one; and if we cannot go so far as to sustain cooperation in regard to these things, how in the name of common sense are we ever going into the United Order? But we will begin with this, and then cooperate in all the different Stakes, not only in your merchandising, but in your manufacturing affairs and in your producing affairs; and in everything it will be the duty of this general Board of Trade to regulate the interests of the whole community, honestly and faithfully, at least we will do it according to the best ability we have; and if there should any mistakes arise, we will try to correct them; if they are on the part of the people, we will talk to them about it, if on the part of the institution, we will talk to its management about it. And we will keep working and operating until we succeed in introducing and establishing these things that God has desired, and until Zion shall be a united people and the glory of all the earth. - President John Taylor, April 1879 General Conference

Cooperation leads to prosperity

Taking up the system of our cooperative method of merchandising, **it gives to the people ease and money.** *They are not obliged to run a mile or two through the mud to buy a yard of ribbon, they have it in their own Ward, and they can purchase it twenty or thirty percent cheaper than they ever could before.* - Brigham Young, April 1869 General Conference

You take the Lehi Cooperative Store, for instance: Bishop Evans started it there last summer. Suppose he had sent East for his goods in July; if he had had the same luck that others have had, they would have been landed about this time, and some of them by and by, and when they had been operating three months what would they have made?

Nothing. But they came down here and bought their goods and took them home, only a thirty miles' drive, and put them on the shelves, and they were soon bought up. They sent to Salt Lake City about once a week to replenish their store, and when five months had passed away they struck a balance sheet and every man that had put in twenty-five dollars—the amount of a share—had, in addition to that amount, a little over twenty-eight dollars to his credit. <u>*Have any of our city merchants who have traded from here to New York, made money like this? Not one*</u>*.* - Brigham Young, April 1869 General Conference

The people of Brigham City have been operating a number of years upon these principles, and are beginning to derive therefrom **various financial advantages***, as well as many spiritual blessings.* - Lorenzo Snow, October 1873 General Conference

[W]ith regard to our cooperative stores and every cooperative institution we have; we expect that the whole people will support them and give them their influence; that the whole people will work for the whole, and that all will be for the kingdom of God on the earth. All that I have is in that kingdom. I have nothing, only what the Lord has put in my possession. It is his; I am his, and all I ask is for him to tell me what to do with my time, my talents and the means that he puts in my possession. It is to be devoted to his kingdom. Let every other man and woman do the same, and all the surplus we make is in one great amount for accomplishing the purposes of the Lord. He says, "<u>*I will make you the richest people on the earth*</u>*." Now, go to work, Latter-day Saints, and make yourselves one, and all needed blessings will follow.* - Brigham Young, May 4, 1874

Our motives in taking up cooperation matter

I say that they who are opposed to cooperation are opposed to heaven, to their own welfare, to the welfare of their neighbors, to truth and to everything that is good. - Brigham Young, June 28, 1873

Honesty, ability and devotedness are required in order that cooperation may be successfully carried out, and the Spirit and wisdom of the Lord are necessary, as much so as in proclaiming the Gospel. - Lorenzo Snow, October 1873 General Conference

One of the Bishops remarked yesterday that the people liked cooperation very much . . . As Latter-day Saints we have to deal with the Lord; he knows our hearts and comprehends our thoughts, and we cannot cover up the secrets of hearts from him. What we do that is right will be approved; that which we do that is wrong will be disapproved. If we are willing and obedient we shall find very little trouble in cooperation. We have embraced it in a small way, and we are expected to handle it honestly; and if we do not handle it honestly, it would be better if we never embraced it at all. We should seek to the Lord for knowledge and wisdom that we may deal with each other righteously, that we may establish confidence in each other that cannot be shaken. The Lord wishes to introduce and perfect among his Saints the principles of union. - Charles C. Rich, November 11, 1877

But in too many instances our cooperative institutions have jumped the track. What, the big Co-op? Yes, and little Co-ops too. Have you got a Co-op here? No, you have not. Do you know of any? We find little institutions they call Co-ops in most of our settlements, but when you come to inquire into affairs connected with them we generally find, that, instead of their being run in the interest of the community, and with a view to build up the kingdom of God, a few individuals represent the Co-op, who are the ones, who are benefited by it. That is the trouble. But is the principle right? Yes, if you can live it, dealing honestly one with another; but if you cannot, you need not try it, for instead of giving satisfaction, it will only be a disappointment. But I will promise the Latter-day Saints that if they will go into these things allowing God to dictate in the interests of Israel and the building up of his Zion on the earth, and take themselves and their individual interests out of the question, feeling they are acting for him and his kingdom, they will become the wealthiest of all people, and God will bless them and pour out wealth and intelligence and all the blessings that earth can afford. - John Taylor, March 2, 1879

The Brethren directed the Saints to sustain the co-operatives

We have a cooperative mercantile institution; and it is the duty of these Latter-day Saints to sustain and uphold it; and so with everything else that is in the kingdom, for these are the stepping stones to us to a fullness of the celestial kingdom of God. - Wilford Woodruff, October 1875 General Conference

I have not come here to talk about any personal matters at all, but upon principle and upon some of those principles that we as Latter-day Saints, and as elders in Israel, profess to believe in. The question would be and my text would be today, if I wanted to take a text: Shall we sustain cooperation and the United Order, and work with that end in view in all of our operations, or shall we give it up as a bad thing unworthy of our attention? That is where the thing comes to, in my mind. At any rate, we wish to act honestly and honorably in this matter. If we believe that these principles are true, let us be governed by them. . . .if we believe that these are principles that are inculcated by the Lord, then let us be governed by them. - John Taylor, September 21, 1878

As I have said, we took a vote yesterday, and the brethren agreed to sustain cooperation, and I would like to know from this congregation, whether you will sustain cooperation as directed by the Priesthood or not. All that are in favor of doing so, hold up the right hand. [The congregation voted unanimously.] Let us stick to our covenants, and get as near to correct principles as we can, and God will help us. - John Taylor, September 22, 1878

We were talking about the principle of cooperation in our priesthood meeting; and I thought I would refer to it here. And we are getting up County or rather Stake organizations throughout Zion. And we want in

all of our temporal affairs to deal justly one with another. We want to sustain cooperation, and then we want cooperation to sustain us. It is not all on one side; there are two sides. If we sustain cooperation, we will call upon cooperation to sustain us . . . carrying out the principles of cooperation honestly and truthfully before God and man. This is what we expect and we expect it from your President, his Counselors and also from the Bishops and from all the people. And if you cannot do this never talk about making worlds. - John Taylor, December 8, 1878

Appendix B

NOTE: The following are talks given by some of the strongest Champions for Zion during Utah's territorial years. They are included here for several purposes. First, to show how focused they were on the topic of building Zion. Second, so the reader can see even more clearly how all of the ideas from the various chapters of this book are woven together by these men.

Appendix B - The Signs of the Coming of the Son of Man

The Signs of the Coming of the Son of Man—The Saints' Duties.

Discourse by Elder Wilford Woodruff, delivered in the 13th Ward Assembly Rooms, Salt Lake City, January 12, 1873. Source: Journal of Discourses, Vol. 15, No. 35

Note: This talk is the most representative of the categories of teachings of our early LDS leaders on the topic of building Zion. The italicized sentences reflect the various chapters in this book.

My address this afternoon will be intended for those who profess to be Latter-day Saints—those who have entered into covenant with the Lord our God. I am surrounded with those who know by experience that we are dependent upon the influence and inspiration of the Holy Ghost to enable us to teach the things of the kingdom of God. My faith is that no man, in this or any other generation, is able to teach and edify the inhabitants of the earth without the inspiration of the Spirit of God. As a people we have been placed in positions the last forty years which have taught, in all our administrations and labors, the necessity of acknowledging the hand of God in all things. We feel this necessity today. I know that I am not qualified to teach either the Latter-day Saints or the world without the Spirit of God. I desire this this afternoon, and also your faith and prayers, that my mind may be led in a channel which may be beneficial to you. In my public teaching I never permit my mind to follow in any channel except that which the Spirit dictates to me, and this is the position we all occupy when we meet with the Saints, or when we go forth to preach the Gospel. As Jesus told his Apostles, Take no thought what ye shall say, it is told us, Take no thought what we shall say; but we treasure up in our minds words of wisdom by the blessing of God and studying the best books.

We are told in the 24th chapter of Matthew that Jesus, on a certain occasion, taught his disciples many things concerning his Gospel, the Temple, the Jews, his second coming and the end of the world; and they asked him—Master, what shall be the sign of these things? The Savior answered them, but in a very brief manner. As my mind runs a little in that channel, I feel disposed to read a portion of the word of the Lord unto us, which explains this matter more fully than the Savior explained it to his disciples. That portion of the word of the Lord which I shall read, is a revelation given to the Latter-day Saints, March 7, 1831, forty-two years ago next March. It commences on the 133rd page of the Book of Doctrine and Covenants.

[The speaker read the revelation, and then resumed his remarks as follows]:

I want to ask who are looking for the fulfillment of these events, and who upon the earth are preparing themselves for the fulfillment of the word of the Lord through the mouths of Prophets, Patriarchs and Apostles for the last six thousand years? Nobody that I have any knowledge of, without it is the Latter-day Saints, and I for one feel that we are not half so much awake as we ought to be, and not half as well prepared as we ought to be for the tremendous events which are coming upon the earth in quick succession in these latter days. Who can the Lord expect to prepare for his second coming but his Saints? None. Why? Because, as is said in this revelation, light has come forth to the inhabitants of the earth, and they have rejected it, because their deeds are evil. This message has been proclaimed among the Christian nations of Europe and America, and in many other nations for the past forty years. Inspired men—the Elders of Israel—have gone forth without purse or scrip declaring the Gospel of life and salvation to the nations of the world, but they have rejected their testimony, and condemnation rests upon them therefor. As the Prophet said, "Darkness covers the earth, and gross darkness the minds of the people." Who believes in the fulfillment of prophecy and revelation? Who, among priests and people today, has any faith in the sayings of Jesus Christ? If there be any people besides the Saints whose eyes are open to the great events which will soon overtake the nations, I would like to know and visit them. *I would to God that the eyes of the Latter-day Saints were open far more than they are to those things that rest upon them! The Lord is looking to them alone to build up his Zion here in the mountains of Israel, and to prepare the bride, the Lamb's wife, for the coming of the Great Bridegroom.* I believe in the fulfillment of the revelations which the Lord has given to us, as much as I believe that I have a soul to save or lose, or as much as I believe in the shining of the sun in the firmament of heaven. Why? Because every word that God has ever spoken, whether by his own voice out of the heavens, by the ministration of angels, or by the mouths of inspired men, has been fulfilled to the very letter as far as time has permitted. We have fulfilled many of the sayings of the Prophets of God. The revelation I have read this afternoon was given forty-two years ago. Has there been any sound of war since then? Has there been any sound of war in our land since that period? Has there been any standard lifted up to the nations, any gathering together of the people into these mountains of Israel from nearly all nations? There has. We have had a beginning, the fig tree is leafing, putting faith its leaves in the sight of all men, and the signs in both heaven and earth all indicate the coming of the Lord Jesus Christ.

When my mind, under the influence of the Spirit of God, is open to comprehend these things, I many times marvel and wonder, not only at the world but also at ourselves, that we are not more anxious and diligent in preparing ourselves and our families for the events now at our doors, for though the heavens and the earth pass away, not one jot or tittle of the word of the Lord will go unfulfilled. There is no prophecy of Scripture that is of any private interpretation, but holy men of God spake as they were moved upon by the Holy Ghost, and their words will be fulfilled on the earth.

We are approaching an important time. As Jesus once said, The world hate me, and without a cause, therefore I have chosen you out of the world, and the world hate you also. The servant is not above his master, you are not above me, they have hated me and they will hate you. The

Lord has chosen the Latter-day Saints, and through them has sent a message to all nations under heaven. The Zion of God is opposed by priest and people in every sect, party and denomination in Christendom. The Elders of Israel have been called from the plow, plane, hammer and the various occupations of life, to go forth and bear record of these things to the world. We have followed this up until the present time for more than forty-two years—forty-three years next April. The kingdom has steadily grown, and while we have labored we have seen the fulfillment of the word of the Lord. The sea has gone beyond its bounds, there have been earthquakes in divers places, and there have also been wars and rumors of wars. These are only a beginning, their fullness had not yet opened upon the sons of men, but it is at their doors; it is at the doors of this generation and of this nation. And when the world rise up against the kingdom of God in these latter days, should the Saints have any fears? Should we fear because men, in their secret chambers, concoct plans to overthrow the kingdom of God? We should not. There is one thing we should do, and that is, pray to God. Every righteous man has done this, even Jesus the Savior, the Only Begotten of the Father in the flesh, had to pray, from the manger to the cross, all the way through; every day he had to call upon his Father to give him grace to sustain him in his hour of affliction and to enable him to drink the bitter cup. So with his disciples. They were baptized with the same baptism that he was baptized with; they suffered the same death that he died, being crucified as he was. They sealed their testimony with their blood. Nevertheless all that Jesus said concerning the Jews has had its fulfillment to the present day. This should be a strong testimony to the whole infidel world of the truth of Christ's mission and divinity. Let them look at the Jewish nation and the state of the world, in fulfillment of the words of the Savior eighteen hundred years ago in Jerusalem. It is one of the strongest testimonies in the world of the fulfillment of revelation, the truth of the Bible and the mission of Jesus Christ. The Jews have fulfilled the words of Moses, the prophets and Jesus, up to the present day. They have been dispersed and trampled under the feet of the Gentile world now for eighteen hundred years. When Pontius Pilate wished to release Jesus

Christ, saying that he found no fault in that just man, the high priests, scribes, Pharisees and other Jews present on that occasion cried, "Crucify him, and let his blood be upon us, and upon our children." Has it not followed them to this day, and been manifest in their dispersion, persecution and oppression through the whole Gentile world for eighteen hundred years? It has. And they have to fulfill the words of the Lord still further. As I have been reading to you today, the Jews have got to gather to their own land in unbelief. They will go and rebuild Jerusalem and their temple. They will take their gold and silver from the nations and will gather to the Holy Land, and when they have done this and rebuilt their city, the Gentiles, in fulfillment of the words of Ezekiel, Jeremiah, and other prophets, will go up against Jerusalem to battle and to take a spoil and a prey; and then, when they have taken one-half of Jerusalem captive and distressed the Jews for the last time on the earth, their Great Deliverer, Shiloh, will come. They do not believe in Jesus of Nazareth now, nor ever will until he comes and sets his foot on Mount Olivet and it cleaves in twain, one part going towards the east, and the other towards the west. Then, when they behold the wounds in his hands and in his feet, they will say, "Where did you get them?" And he will reply, "I am Jesus of Nazareth, King of the Jews, your Shiloh, him whom you crucified." Then, for the first time will the eyes of Judah be opened. They will remain in unbelief until that day. This is one of the events that will transpire in the latter day.

The Gospel of Christ has to go to the Gentiles until the Lord says "enough," until their times are fulfilled, and it will be in this generation. Forty years have passed since the revelation I have read was given to the sons of men. We are living in a late age, although it is true there are a great many vast and important events to transpire in these days. But one thing is certain, though the Lord has not revealed the day nor the hour wherein the Son of Man shall come, he has pointed out the generation, and the signs predicted as the forerunners of that great event have begun to appear in the heavens and on the earth, and they will continue until all is consummated. If we, as Latter-day Saints, want anything to stir us up, let us read the Bible, Book of Mormon and the Book of Doctrine and Covenants, they contain enough to edify and instruct us in the things of God. Treasure up the revelations of God and the Gospel of Christ contained therein.

As an individual, I will say that I feel a great responsibility resting upon me, and it also rests upon you. Joseph Smith and Brigham Young alone have not been called to build up in the latter day that great and mighty kingdom of God which Daniel foretold, and which he said should be thrown down no more forever. I say, they were not called to be the only ones to labor in building up that great and glorious Zion, which was to become terrible to all nations; nor their counselors; nor the Twelve Apostles; but this responsibility rests upon every one of the Lord's anointed upon the face of the earth, I do not care who they are, whether male or female, and the Lord will require this at the hands of all the Latter-day Saints. I therefore desire that we may be awake to these subjects, and to the position we occupy before God and in the world.

The inhabitants of the earth may hate and oppose us, as they did Jesus Christ, and as they have all inspired men, as they did Noah, Enoch, Abraham, Isaac, Jacob, Isaiah, Jeremiah, and all the prophets who ever lived. They have always been a thorn in the flesh to the world. Why? Because they had enough independence of mind to rebuke sin, to maintain the promises of God unto man, and to proclaim the declarations of the Almighty unto the inhabitants of the earth, fearless of consequences. The last song sung here was, "Do what is right, let the consequence follow." That is what I say to the Latter-day Saints. Let us do what is right, maintain our religion before God, be valiant in the testimony of Jesus Christ, and prepare ourselves for his coming, for it is near, and this is what God requires at our hands. He leans upon no other people; he expects from no people but those who have obeyed his Gospel and gathered here, the accomplishment of his great work, the building up of his latter-day Zion and kingdom. And, as I have said, this responsibility rests not only upon Prophets and Apostles, but upon every

Appendix B - The Signs of the Coming of the Son of Man

man and woman who has entered into covenant with him. I say that we are too near asleep, we are not half awake to the position that we occupy before God, and the responsibilities we are under to him. We should be on the watchtower.

Who is going to be prepared for the coming of the Messiah? These men who enjoy the Holy Ghost and live under the inspiration of the Almighty, who abide in Jesus Christ and bring forth fruit to the honor and glory of God. No other people will be. *There never was a more infidel generation of Christians on the face of the earth than there is today. They do not expect that God will do anything in a temporal point of view towards the fulfillment of his promises; they are not looking forward for the establishment of his kingdom, or for the building up of his Zion on the earth. Their eyes are closed to these things, because they have rejected the light.* When Joseph Smith brought this Gospel to the world, there was a great deal more faith in God, a great deal more faith in his revelations, and, according to the light they had, a great deal more pure and undefiled religion than there is now. We have carried the Gospel to all Christian nations who would permit us, and they have rejected it, and they are under condemnation. Our own nation is under condemnation on this account. *This land, North and South America, is the land of Zion, it is a choice land—and that was given by promise from old father Jacob to his grandson and his descendants, the land on which the Zion of God should be established in the latter days. We have been fulfilling the prophecies concerning it, for the last forty years.* We have come up here and established the kingdom. True, it is small today, it may be compared to a mustard seed, but as the Lord our God lives, the little one will become a thousand, and the small one a strong nation, and the Lord Almighty will hasten it in his own time, and the world will learn one thing in this generation, and that is, that when they fight against Mount Zion, they fight against the decrees of the Almighty and the principles of eternal life.

I rejoice before God that I have lived to hear the principles of eternal life proclaimed to the sons of men; I rejoice that I have lived to see this people gathered together, I rejoice in coming to the land of Zion with the Saints of God. When we came here twenty-four years ago, we were a little handful of men, pioneers; we came to a parched and barren desert. Since then we have built up six hundred miles of cities, towns, villages, gardens, farms and orchards; and while doing this we have had to contend with the opposition of both priest and people. Have they prevailed? They have not, and they will not. Why? Because he who sits in the heavens, the Lord our God, has decreed certain things and they will come to pass; because the Lord is watching over the interests of this people. He requires us to work with him, he is at work for us. It is our duty to build these temples here—this in Salt Lake City, another in St. George, in Logan or wherever they may be needed for the benefit of the Saints of God in the latter days. I think many times that many of us will get to heaven before we shall want to go there. If we were to go there today, many would meet their friends in the spirit world and it would be a reproach to them, for you, Latter-day Saints, in one sense of the word, hold in your hands the salvation of your dead, for we can do much for them. But I think many times that our hearts are too much set on the vain things of the world to attend to many important duties devolving upon us connected with the Gospel. We are too much after gold and silver, and we give our hearts and attention to temporal matters at the expense of the light and truth of the Gospel of Jesus Christ.

We have not much time to spare as a people, for a great work is required at our hands. I know that, without the power of God, we should not have been able to do what has been done; and I also know that we never should be able to build up the Zion of God in power, beauty and glory were it not that our prayers ascends into the ears of the Lord God of Sabaoth, and he hears and answers them. The world has sought our overthrow from the beginning, and the devil does not like us very well. Lucifer, the Son of the Morning, does not like the idea of revelation to the Saints of God, and he has inspired the hearts of a great many men,

Appendix B - The Signs of the Coming of the Son of Man

since the Gospel was restored to the earth, to make war against us. But not one of them has made anything out of it yet—neither glory, immortality, eternal life nor money. No man or people ever did make anything by fighting against God in the past, and no man or people will ever make anything by taking that course in the future.

This is the work and kingdom of God; this is the Zion of God and the Church of Christ, and we are called by his name. The Latter-day Saints have to abide in Christ, and we cannot do that unless we bring forth fruit, any more than the branch of the vine can unless it abide in the vine. To abide in Christ we must enjoy the Spirit of God, that our minds may be enlightened to comprehend the things of God. When I look at the history of the Church of God in these latter days I many times marvel at what has been done and how we have progressed, considering the traditions, unbelief, failings, follies and nonsense that man is heir to in the flesh. We have had a great many traditions to overcome and the opposition of the world to contend with from the beginning until today. *Brethren and sisters, we should be faithful. The Lord has put into our hands the power to build up his Zion and kingdom on the earth, and we have more to encourage us than was ever possessed by any generation that has preceded us. We have the privilege of building up a kingdom that will stand forever.* Noah and the Antediluvian world did not have this privilege. Enoch built up the Zion of God a little while, and the Lord took it away. Jesus and the Apostles came here. Jesus fulfilled his mission, preached the Gospel, was rejected by the Jews, and was crucified. His disciples had a similar fate, and the Gospel was taken to the Gentile nation, with all its gifts and blessings and power, and Paul the Apostle of the Gentiles warned them to take heed lest they, in turn, should lose it through their unbelief.

You know how it has been with them—that there has been a falling away, and that for seventeen hundred years the voice of a Prophet or Apostle has not been heard in the world; and now again, in these latter days, the Lord Almighty, remembering his promises made from generation to generation, has sent Angels from heaven to restore to man the Gospel and has given authority to administer the same. The Revelator John, says he saw an angel flying through the midst of heaven, having the everlasting gospel to preach to them that dwell on the earth, to every nation, kindred, tongue and people, Saying with a loud voice, "Fear God, and give glory to him who made the heavens, the earth, the seas, and the fountains of waters; for the hour of God's judgment has come."

Oh! ye Gentile nations, wake up and prepare yourselves for that which is to come, for as God lives his judgments are at your door. They are at the door of our nation, and the thrones and kingdoms of the whole world will fall, and all the efforts of men combined cannot save them. It is a day of warning, but not of many words, to the nations. The Lord is going to make a short work, or no flesh could be saved. If it were not for the manifestation of the power of God what would be the fate of his Zion and people? The same as in the days of Christ and his Apostles. *The Lord has had Zion before his face from before the foundation of the world, and he is going to build it up. "Who am I," saith the Lord, "that I promise and do not fulfill?" The Lord never made a promise to the sons of men which he has not fulfilled, therefore Latter-day Saints, you have all the encouragement in the world to sustain you in the faith that the Zion of God will remain on the earth. The work is in our hands to perform, the God of heaven requires it of us and if we fail to build it up we shall be under condemnation, and the Lord would remove us out of the way and he would raise up another people who would do it. Why? Because the Almighty has decreed that this work shall be performed on the earth, and no power on earth or in hell can hinder it.*

I would here say to our delegate to Congress, when you go to Washington, have no fears with regard to the opposition of men. You have every reason to go in confidence, and do your duty, knowing that the Lord will stand by you, and so has every man in the Church and kingdom of God. I care not where we are placed or what God requires at our hands. He is at the helm, and he has protected us until today. Where should we have been a few years ago when the army was sent to destroy us, if it had not been for the protection of the Almighty? We should not have been here. And so it will be in days to come. The world hate us because the Almighty has called us out from the world to proclaim his Gospel and build up his kingdom. Let us be faithful, for the Lord is going to protect us, and build up Zion. He will also gather Israel, rebuild Jerusalem and prepare the way for his second coming, in the clouds of heaven.

Then let us, Latter-day Saints, wake up to our duty. Think nothing too hard that the Lord requires of us. Let us build this Temple that we may attend to the ordinances for the living and the dead. If we do not do this we shall be sorry. When I see men who have received the word of God, and tasted the powers of the world to come, and then turn away, I think of the parable of the five wise and five foolish virgins. It will pay us to be wise and to have oil in our lamps, to have fellowship with the Holy Spirit, and to live our religion and keep the commandments of God day by day. Brethren are passing away. I have been away three or four weeks on a visit to the people in the upper settlements, and since my return I hear of this man and that man dead, whom I saw well and hale before I went away.

So it will be with us in a little while. *We shall pass away and go to the other side of the veil, and the burden of the building up of Zion will rest upon our sons and daughters.* Then rejoice in the Gospel of Christ. Rejoice in the principles of eternal life. I am looking for the fulfillment of all things that the Lord has spoken, and they will come to pass as the Lord God lives. *Zion is bound to rise and flourish.* The Lamanites will blossom as the rose on the mountains. I am willing to say here that, though I believe this, when I see the power of the nation destroying them from the face of the earth, the fulfillment of that prophecy is perhaps harder for me to believe than any revelation of God that I ever read. It looks as though there would not be enough left to receive the

Gospel; but notwithstanding this dark picture, every word that God has ever said of them will have its fulfillment, and they, by and by, will receive the Gospel. It will be a day of God's power among them, and a nation will be born in a day. Their chiefs will be filled with the power of God and receive the Gospel, and they will go forth and build the new Jerusalem, and we shall help them. They are branches of the house of Israel, and when the fullness of the Gentiles has come in and the work ceases among them, then it will go in power to the seed of Abraham.

Brethren and sisters, let us remember our position before the Lord! Let us try and keep the faith, let us labor for the Holy Spirit, that our hearts, minds and eyes may be opened, that we may live by inspiration, that when we see dark clouds rising and evils strewing our path, we may be able to overcome. The Savior was tempted, so were his Apostles, and if we have not been we shall be. As the Lord told Joseph Smith, "I will try and prove you in all things, even unto death. If you are not willing to abide my covenants unto death, you are not worthy of me." Did Joseph abide unto death? I think he did, and he with Abraham, Isaac and Jacob, will sit at the right hand of the Lord Jesus Christ, and will receive his glory and crown. He was true and faithful unto death, and his testimony is in force today, in language as loud as ten thousand thunders. Whether it is believed or rejected it will have its fulfillment on the heads of this generation.

By and by great Babylon will fall and there will be wailing, mourning and sore affliction in her midst. The sons of Zion have got to stand in holy places to be preserved in the midst of the judgments that will shortly overtake the world. We can see how fully the revelation, calling us to go to the western countries, has been fulfilled. In less than forty years, a standard has been lifted up, and people gathered here from France, England, Scotland, Wales, Denmark, Norway, Sweden, and almost all the nations of the earth in fulfillment of that revelation. When it was given no man among us knew anything about Salt Lake or the Rocky Mountains; but it has been fulfilled before our eyes. We have

Appendix B - The Signs of the Coming of the Son of Man

come up here, and in so doing have fulfilled the revelations of God so far. Let us continue, I pray God my heavenly Father that he will bless the Latter-day Saints; that he will give us his Holy Spirit and wisdom, that our eyes may be opened, that we may have faith in the things of God. Let a man lose the Holy Spirit and what faith has he? None, either in God or in his revelations, and that is what is the matter today. You may take the best friends we have outside of this kingdom, and you can hardly get them to believe that God has any thing to do with the affairs of men, or that he has power to do anything for them, either as individuals or nations. If their eyes were open one moment they would understand that God holds them all in the hollow of his hand, weighs them in the balance and that they cannot make a move without his permission. They would no longer wonder why the Latter-day Saints have faith in God if their eyes were open so that they could understand the work and things of God. They cannot understand it, they cannot even see the kingdom of God unless they are born of the Spirit of God, and they cannot enter into it unless they are born of the water and the Spirit, according to the words of Jesus to Nicodemus.

I have a desire that we may be faithful in our mission and ministry, as Elders of Israel and as Saints of God, that we may do our duty, and maintain our position before the Lord. Let our prayers go up before him. If I have any *forte* it is prayer to God. *We are not called to build up Zion by preaching, singing and praying alone; we have to perform hard labor, labor of bone and sinew, in building towns, cities, villages;* and we have to continue to do this; but while we are so engaged, we should not sin. We have no right to sin, whether we are in the canyon drawing wood, or performing any other hard labor, and we should have the Spirit of God to direct us then as much as when preaching, praying, singing and attending to the ordinances of the house of God. If we do this as a people we shall grow in the favor and power of God. We should be united together, it is our duty to be so. Our prayers should ascend before God, and I know they do. I know that President Young is prayed for—I know that his Counselors and the Twelve are prayed for, and that the

Church and kingdom of God is prayed for. We should continue this, and if we pray in faith we shall have what we ask for. The Lord has taught us to pray, and I rejoice that I have learned to pray according to the order of God, for in this we have a promise—that where two or three agree in asking for any thing that is just and right, it shall be granted unto them.

May God bless you! May he give us wisdom, and his Holy Spirit, to guide us, that we may be enabled to be true and faithful to our covenants, and be prepared to inherit eternal life, for Jesus' sake. Amen.

Cooperation

Remarks by President Brigham Young, delivered in the New Tabernacle, Salt Lake City, April 6, 1869.

Reported by David W. Evans.

I have it in my mind to say a few words upon cooperation. I will quote a saying of one, whose partial history is given to us in the New Testament. The saying is this, "my yoke is easy, my burden is light." The knowledge I have gained in my private experience proves to me that there is not a man or woman, community or family, but what, *if they will hearken to the council that God gives them, can do better in everything, spiritual or temporal, than they can if they take their own way.*

Taking up the system of our cooperative method of merchandising, it gives to the people ease and money. They are not obliged to run a mile or two through the mud to buy a yard of ribbon, they have it in their own Ward, and they can purchase it twenty or thirty percent cheaper than they ever could before. I know it is frequently said by our Elders when any new system is introduced to the people, "put down your names, hand over your money, and if you are required to pay two dollars for that which is worth only one, do it and ask no questions." I have never requested my brethren and sisters to act in any such way. I want their eyes opened and their understandings enlightened; I wish them to know and understand their business transactions and everything they do just as perfectly as a woman knows how to wash dishes, sweep a room, make a bed or bake a cake. I want it to be just as familiar to the brethren as to make a pair of shoes, to sow and gather their grain or any other portion of their ordinary labor. I do not ask any of you to go blindfolded into any matters or any system of business whatever; instead of that I prefer that you should know and understand all about it. *I wish to enlighten your minds a little with regard to the system of merchandising which has heretofore prevailed in this Territory.*

There is quite a number of the community who were acquainted with the first merchants who came here. It is true that a few of our own brethren brought a few goods; but the first merchants who came here were Livingston and Kinkead. They, to my certain knowledge, commenced by selling the goods they brought at from two to five hundred percent above cost. There were a few articles, with the real value of which everybody was acquainted, that they did not put quite so high; but just as quick as they came to a piece of goods, the value of which everybody did not understand, the people might look out for the five hundred percent. They continued their operations here until they made hundreds of thousands of dollars. I do not think I ever heard a person, professing to be a Latter-day Saint, complain of those merchants. Others followed them. They came here, commenced their trade and made money, in fact we poured it into their laps. I recollect once going into the store of Livingston and Kinkead, and there being a press of people in the store, I passed behind one of the counters. I saw several brass kettles under it, full of gold pieces—sovereigns, eagles, half eagles, etc. One of the men shouted, "Bring another brass kettle." They did so, and set it down, and the gold was thrown into it, "chink," "chink," "chink," until, in a short time it was filled. I saw this; the whole drift of the people was to get rid of their money. *I have heard more complaints the last few weeks about the cooperative movement than I ever heard before about merchandising.*

Now, I will tell you the facts about this movement. We started the cooperative system here when we thought we would wait no longer; we opened the Wholesale Cooperative Store, and since that, retail stores have been established, although some of the latter were opened before the Wholesale store was opened. I know this, that *as soon as this movement was commenced the price of goods came down from twenty to thirty percent*. I recollect very well, after our vote last October Conference, that it was soon buzzed around, "Why you can get calico down street at eighteen, and seventeen cents a yard;" and it came down to sixteen. But when it came down to sixteen cents, who had a chance to buy any? Why nobody, unless it was just a few yards that were sold to them as a favor. But when it came to the Wholesale Cooperative Store the price was put at sixteen cents, and retail stores are selling it today at seventeen and a half or eighteen cents a yard. I will tell you that which I expect will hurt the feelings of many of you: Among this people, called Latter-day Saints, *when the devil has got the crowns, sovereigns, guineas and the twenty dollar pieces, it has been all right; but let the Lord get a sixpence and there is an eternal grunt about it.*

I will relate a little circumstance in relation to cooperation at Lehi. Five months after they had commenced their retail store on this cooperative system there, they struck a dividend to see what they had made; and they found that *every man who had paid in twenty-five dollars—the price of a share, had a few cents over twenty-eight dollars handed back* or credited to him. Is not this cruel? Is not this a shame? It is ridiculous to think that they are making money so fast. Did they sell their goods cheaper than the people of Lehi could buy them before? Yes. Did they fetch the goods to them? O, yes, and yet they made money. A few weeks ago I was in the Wholesale Store in this city, and I was asking a brother from American Fork how cooperation worked there; and I learned that *three months after commencing every man who had put in five dollars, or twenty-five dollars had that amount handed back to him and still had his capital stock in the Institution*; and still they had sold their goods cheaper than anybody else had ever sold them there.

The question may arise with some how can this be? I will tell you how it is: our own merchants make a calculation of charging you just fifty percent on their staple goods, and from one hundred to five hundred on their fancy goods. Now these Cooperative Stores sell their goods for twenty percent less than they can be bought from the merchants; and although they sell at a lower rate, the reason is they recruit their stock of goods every week if necessary, while our merchants, up till very recently, did it only about once a year. These little stores at American Fork, Lehi, Provo, and other wards and places around, can drive their teams here in a day and replenish their stocks of goods, and that enables them to turn over their money quickly; and if they put on six or eight percent instead of fifty, *by turning their money over every week,* in about twelve weeks they make a dollar double itself. That comes the nearest keeping the cake and eating it of anything I know. I have heard people say you cannot do that, but those who are investing their little means in these stores are actually doing it.

I know that many of our traders in this city are feeling very bad and sore over this. They say, "you are taking the bread out of our mouths." We wish to do it, for they have made themselves rich. Take my community, three-eighths of whom are living on the labor of the remaining five-eighths, and you will find the few are living on the many. Take the whole world, and comparatively few of its inhabitants are producers. *If the members of this community wish to get rich and to enjoy the fruits of the earth they must be producers as well as consumers.*

As to these little traders, we are going to shut them off. We feel a little sorry for them. Some of them have but just commenced their trading operations, and they want to keep them up. They have made, perhaps, a few hundred dollars, and they would like to continue so as to make a few thousands; and then they would want scores of thousands and then hundreds of thousands. *Instead of trading we want them to go into some other branches of business.* Do you say, what business? Why, some of them may go to raising broom corn to supply the Territory with brooms, instead of bringing them from the States. Others may go to raising sugar cane, and thus supply the Territory with a good sweet; we have to send to the States for our sugar now. We will get some more of them to gathering up hides and making them into leather, and manufacturing that leather into boots and shoes; this will be far more profitable than letting hundreds and thousands of hides go to waste as they have done. Others may go and make baskets; we do not care what they go at, provided they produce that which will prove of general benefit. Those who are able can erect woolen factories, get a few spindles, raise sheep and manufacture the wool. Others may raise flax and manufacture that into linen cloth, that we may not be under the necessity of sending abroad for it. If we go on in this way, *we shall turn these little traders into producers, which will help to enrich the entire people.*

Another thing I will say with regard to our trading. Our Female Relief Societies are doing immense good now, but they can take hold and do all the trading for these wards just as well as to keep a big loafer to do it. It is always disgusting to me to see a big, fat, lubberly fellow handing out calicoes and measuring ribbon; I would rather see the ladies do it. The ladies can learn to keep books as well as the men; we have some few, already, who are just as good accountants as any of our brethren. Why not teach more to keep books and sell goods, and let them do this business, and let the men go to raising sheep, wheat, or cattle, or go and do something or other to beautify the earth and help to make it like the Garden of Eden, instead of spending their time in a lazy, loafing manner?

Now, if you think this is speculation, brethren and sisters, just enter into it for it is the best speculation that has been got up for a great while. I recollect the people used to say we were speculating when we were preaching the Gospel. They accused "Joe Smith," as they called him, of being a speculator and a money digger." I acknowledged then, and I acknowledge now, that I am engaged in the greatest speculation a man can be engaged in. The best business to pursue that was ever introduced on the face of the earth is to follow the path of eternal life. Why, it gives us fathers, mothers, wives, friends, houses and lands. Jesus said they who followed Him would have to forsake these things. I reckon some of us have done it already; and all who will live faithful, may have the privilege of so doing. Many of this people have sacrificed all they possessed on this earth, over and over again, for the truth's sake; and if Jesus gave us the truth in relation to this, we shall be entitled to fathers, mothers, wives, children, gold and silver, houses, lands and possessions a hundred fold. But we do not want the spirit of the world with all this. What is the advantage of following the path of life? It makes good neighbors, and fills everybody with peace, joy and contentment. Is there contention in a family that follows in the path of eternal life? Not the least. Is there quarrelling among neighbors where this course is followed? No. Any going to law one with another? Such a thing is unknown. I say praise to the Latter-day Saints, as far as these things are concerned.

What I have in my mind with regard to this cooperative business is this—There are very few people who cannot get twenty-five dollars to put into one of these cooperative stores. There are hundreds and thousands of women who, by prudence and industry, can obtain this sum. And we say to you put your capital into one of these stores. What for? To bring you interest for your money. Put your time and talents to usury. We have the parable before us. If we have one, two, three or five talents, of what advantage will they be if we wrap them in a napkin and lay them away? None at all. Put them out to usury. *These cooperative stores are instituted to give the poor a little advantage as well as the rich.* I have said to my brethren, in starting these stores in different places, "If you want help I will find means to put in to give the thing a start;" but I have only found two places in the Territory in which they were willing to sell me stock—Provo, where they wanted a wholesale store, and the wholesale store in this city. Go to this ward or the other and the answer is invariably, "we want no more means, we can get all we need." They did not think they could before starting. I recollect the Tenth Ward in this city had but seven hundred dollars to start with; in two or three weeks after they commenced I asked some of the brethren how they were prospering, and was told they had a thousand dollars' worth of goods on the shelves and money in the drawer and owed nothing. This is considered one of the poorest wards in the city, but it is not so.

Now take upon you this yoke; it is a great deal easier than to pay so much more for goods as you have been doing. I say the "yoke is easy and the burden is light" and we can bear it. *If we will work unitedly, we can work ourselves into wealth, health, prosperity and power, and this is* *required of us*. It is the duty of a Saint of God to gain all the influence he can on this earth, and to use every particle of that influence to do good. If this is not his duty, I do not understand what the duty of man is. I thank you for your attention, brethren and sisters. God bless you. Amen.

United Order—Tithing—Cooperative Labors in Brigham City

Discourse by Elder Lorenzo Snow, delivered in the Tabernacle, Ogden City, Sunday Afternoon, April 21, 1878. Reported by James Taylor.

I will read, this afternoon, a few verses of the revelation commencing on page 345 of the new edition of the Book of Doctrine and Covenants:

"1. Verily I say unto you who have assembled together that you may learn my will concerning the redemption of mine afflicted people—

"2. Behold, I say unto you, were it not for the transgressions of my people, speaking concerning the church and not individuals, they might have been redeemed even now.

"3. But behold, they have not learned to be obedient to the things which I required at their hands, but are full of all manner of evil, and do not impart of their substance, as becometh saints, to the poor and afflicted among them;

"4. And are not united according to the union required by the law of the celestial kingdom;

"5. And Zion cannot be built up unless it is by the principles of the law of the celestial kingdom; otherwise I cannot receive her unto myself.

"6. And my people must needs be chastened until they learn obedience, if it must needs be, by the things which they suffer."

I wish to remind my brethren and sisters, in the first place, that we are dependent for our information and intelligence upon the Spirit of God, which may be in us, if properly cultivated, a spirit of inspiration, of revelation, to make manifest clearly to our understanding the mind and will of God, teaching our duties and obligations, and what is required at our hands. And, on occasions of this kind, when we are assembled together to learn the will of God, it is of importance that we exercise faith, and have the spirit of prayer, that the Lord will cause something to be said that will instruct, and give us such information and knowledge as will be of use and service in our daily walk and under the circumstances that surround us.

We need assistance. We are liable to do that which will lead us into trouble and darkness, and those things which will not tend to our good, but with the assistance of that comforter which the Lord has promised his Saints, if we are careful to listen to its whisperings, and understand the nature of its language, we may avoid much trouble and serious difficulty.

We are told in these verses which I have read, that the Saints in former days were driven from the land of their possessions because they lacked that union which was necessary for their safety and salvation, and to preserve them upon this land which the Lord designed to give them for an inheritance. They were not united according to the union which was required by the celestial law. And we are told here that Zion cannot be built up upon any other principle or foundation. This is the subject that concerns every Latter-day Saint, and is well worthy of deep reflection, and we should seek the spirit of inspiration, that we may understand it properly, and how it may, perhaps, effect us in our present situation.

There are principles which are revealed for the good of the people of God, and clearly manifest in the revelations which have been given; but in consequence of not being more persevering and industrious, we neglect to receive the advantages which they are designed to confer, and we think, perhaps, that it is not necessary to exert ourselves to find out what God requires at our hands, or in other words, to search out the principles which God has revealed, upon which we can receive very important blessings. There are revealed, plainly and clearly, principles which are calculated to exalt the Latter-day Saints, and preserve them from much trouble and vexation, yet, through lack of perseverance on our part to learn and conform to them, we fail to receive the blessings that are connected with obedience to them. These principles of union, which the Latter-day Saints in former times ignored, and in consequence of disobedience to them, were driven from Missouri, are called by different names—United Order, Order of Enoch, the principles of Union of the Celestial Law, etc. When we search the revelations of God in regard to them, we see that wherever the Gospel of the Son of God has been revealed in its fulness, the principles of the United Order were made manifest, and required to be observed. The system of union, or the Order of Enoch, which God has taken so much pains to reveal and make manifest, has been, and is, for the purpose of uniting the Latter-day Saints, the people of God, and preparing them for exaltation in his celestial kingdom, and also for the purpose of preparing them here on this earth to live together as brethren, that they may become one in all matters that pertain to their worldly affairs, as well as their spiritual interests, that they may become one—one in their efforts, one in their interests—so that there shall be no poor found in the midst of the Latter-day Saints, and no moneyed aristocracy in the midst of the people of God, but that there should be a union, an equality. Before this Church was organized, in April, 1830, there were given revelations touching the United Order; and from the day the first revelation was given in regard to these principles, there have been given a great number of revelations making the principle of the United Order very plain to the understanding of those who wish to comprehend them. The principles and system have been pointed out in various revelations very distinctly, so that the Saints might not err. The Lord has shown us that he considered this order no small matter, but a subject of vast importance; so much so, in fact, that he has pronounced severe penalties on those who disobey its principles, and promised most important blessings to those who receive it and conform to its requirements. Doc. and Cov., page 327, 276, 258, 264.

The Latter-day Saints, no doubt, have made very great improvement, and advanced considerably beyond the point the Saints reached when

Appendix B - United Order

they were in Missouri, and were chastened in consequence of their not having conformed to the principles of union, as required; but when we see these sacred principles disregarded, to a certain extent, so much as they are, we wonder why it is so, and how it is that they are so much neglected, so much ignored—principles of such vast importance to our exaltation and glory, and for our safety, and on account of disobedience to which the Lord could not sustain and defend his people in the State of Missouri, but suffered them to be overcome and expelled by their enemies.

The Lord, when he counseled that Jackson County should be purchased by the Saints, was very strict in regard to the manner in which they should observe the principles of union; and he called one of his servants, and told him that he would make him an example in regard to what would be required of those who should go up to the land of Missouri to receive their inheritance. That was Martin Harris. (Doc. & Cov., sec. 58, page 203, verses 35 and 36.) The Lord said: "It is wisdom in me that my servant Martin Harris should be an example unto the church, in laying his moneys before the Bishop of the church. And also, this is a law unto every man that cometh unto this land to receive an inheritance; and he shall do with his moneys according as the law directs."

Now, here is one of the first principles of the United Order, and it was made and ordained a law by every person, and everyone was required to observe it, who should be privileged to go to the land of Missouri to receive an inheritance. But this, I think, will apply, not only to those who should go to the land of Missouri, but to the people of God in every land. Wherever there is a people of God, the principles of the United Order are applicable, if they would receive and obey them. Some have thought that the United Order was to be kept only by the people who should go up to the land of Missouri. Now this, I believe, is incorrect. It would seem very singular that the Latter-day Saints, when they receive the Gospel, should not have the privilege of uniting themselves, according to the principles of the celestial law, and that Jackson County should be the only place where this law might be observed. I shall not have time to pursue this subject so particularly as I would wish, I will simply refer to some revelations in regard to the matter.

In Kirtland, Ohio, there was a United Order established under the direct influence and instructions of Joseph Smith. He received revelations from the Lord in regard to this subject. And there was not only a United Order established in Kirtland, but there was also a United command of God to be established in a locality about fifteen or twenty miles from Kirtland, in a town called Thompson. And the Lord gave his servant, Edward Partridge, the first Bishop of this Church, revelations and important instructions in reference to organizing a Branch of the Church into the United Order in that township. And Edward Partridge needed these instructions, because it might well be understood that he, of himself, would not be able to understand the mind and will of God touching what was required according to the principles of the celestial law. Therefore, the Lord told him it was necessary that he should receive instructions in these principles. And he gave him instructions, and told him that it was necessary that the people should be organized there according to his law, otherwise they should be cut off. And he told him, furthermore, that it was their privilege to be organized according to the celestial law, that they might be united upon those principles. And also, in this revelation, he told Edward Partridge that he should have the privilege of organizing, for this was an example unto him, in all other places, in all other churches. So it was not confined to any particular locality, to Kirtland, nor to Thompson, nor to Jackson County; but in that revelation it was told the Bishop that this should be an example unto him in organizing in all Churches. So that wherever Edward Partridge should find a Church, he would have the privilege of organizing them according to the United Order, the Celestial Law, or the Order of Enoch.

Now, we might ask ourselves, would it be supposable that there could be any transgression or that we would offend God in ascertaining what the United Order is, and then conforming ourselves to its requirements, as near as possible?

In the days of the Prophet Ezra, the Jewish nation, for many years, had been in captivity, and in transgression, and been permitted to be destroyed, and driven from their locations by their enemies. Well, Ezra, on a certain occasion, saw proper to bring them together and build Jerusalem that had been thrown down. The Lord aided him in this work; and after they had been successful in building the walls, they commenced reading the laws and revelations of God; and they found that the people were in great transgression, and in disobedience to a very important and sacred law, and that was in regard to their intermarriages with aliens. They discovered that there had been a law given in the days of Moses, that they should not give their daughters to the sons of aliens, neither should they take the daughters of aliens to their sons. Well, when Ezra made this discovery, and found that the people had been intermarrying to quite an extent, he was in consternation. He sat down, plucked the hair from his head, and his beard from his face, and rent his garments; and called upon his God to forgive the people. Well, finally, the prophets, and chief men were called together and had a consultation; and then the people were called together, and they had a very grievous time in making the thing right wherein they had transgressed this holy law; and however unpleasant the requirements were in regard to making this right, it was considered absolutely important to have the blessings of God, and be approved of him. Now, I do not say, when we come back again to our subject, the principles of the United Order, that this might be our position with reference to our obedience to it. But I would say this, however, that if these principles of the United Order were so important in former days, and the Lord by some thirteen revelations or more, has made them manifest to his Saints, and the results of disobedience were such as we see, why should we not consider them of some importance at the present time? And would the Lord find fault with the people, if the Latter-day Saints would strive with all their hearts to conform to them? And would we not feel ourselves better prepared to go back and build up Jackson County, the Center Stake of Zion? Would we expect to go back unless we complied with the law in all things, and in consequence of disobedience to which, the people were expelled from that country?

It is argued by some that when the principle of tithing came in, it superseded the principles of the United Order. The law of Moses was given to be a schoolmaster, to bring the people to a knowledge of the Son of God, and induce them to obey the principles of the fulness of the Gospel. The higher law was given to the children of Israel when they were first delivered from Egyptian bondage, but in consequence of their disobedience, the Gospel in its fulness was withdrawn, and the law of carnal commandments was added. Now, do you imagine that there would have been any wrong if the people wanted to find the principles of the higher law and obey them as near as circumstances would admit? Do you suppose it would have been wrong to search out the fulness of the Gospel, while living under the Mosaic law? But, in the Book of Mormon we find this point more fully illustrated. We find that the inhabitants of this continent had a knowledge of the fulness of the everlasting Gospel and were baptized for the remission of sins, many generations before Jesus came into the world. We find that Alma was baptized in the waters of Mormon, and some four hundred and fifty other individuals. Alma, by his energy and perseverance, had discovered the fulness of the Gospel and obtained revelations from the Lord, and the privilege of observing the Gospel in all its fulness and blessings. Do you think the Lord was angry with them? They were under the Mosaic law, and yet considered it a blessing to observe the higher law.

Now I will say in regard to the matter of tithing, I think that law was given to the Latter-day Saints, one object being to prepare them for, and conduct them to, the United Order, that they might not fall into the same error as the people who were driven from the State of Missouri, but gradually be inducted into these higher principles. There is nothing more elevating to ourselves and pleasing to God than those things that pertain to the accomplishment of a brotherhood. Wise men, for centuries, have sought to bring this about, but without success. They had not the ability, the wisdom, the intelligence, nor the authority, to bring the people up to that standard, that they could become a united brotherhood. All their efforts were ineffectual. But the Lord will be successful; and he will prepare the Latter-day Saints that these principles will be in their hearts when they go back to Jackson County. Remember, while the Gospel in its fulness was observed by Alma and his brethren, and by many thousands in different ages of the world, they lived under the Mosaic Law, and cannot the Latter-day Saints under the law of tithing, observe the fulness of the gospel? If we allow that we are under the principle of the law of tithing, is there any harm in our complying with the principles of the United Order?

I am aware that it is unpleasant in the ears of some individuals, to hear about the principles of the United Order, but take the Latter-day Saints, generally speaking, throughout the various settlements of this Territory, their hearts seem to be drawn out in reference to this principle. When President Young first came into these mountain valleys, he was impressed with the importance of this principle, and he took the first steps for the accomplishment of this union. There are hundreds and thousands of individuals that came into these valleys at that time, who conformed to the first principles of this union. There are many of us that consecrated all that we possessed, and this is the first step in regard to the United Order. It is very possible that there may have been some neglect in carrying forward this principle, as, perhaps, we might have done. This I would not say particularly, but there may have been fault in us, in this matter in not carrying out what we commenced. In things that pertain to celestial glory there can be no forced operations. We must do according as the Spirit of the Lord operates upon our understandings and feelings. We cannot be crowded into matters, however great might be the blessing attending such procedure. We cannot be forced into living a celestial law; we must do this ourselves, of our own free will. And whatever we do in regard to the principles of the United Order, we must do it because we desire to do it. Some of us are practicing in the spirit of the United Order, doing more than the law of tithing requires. We are not confined to the law of tithing. We have advanced to that point that we feel to soar above this law. Now, we have thousands and tens of thousands, and I might say millions of dollars, that have been appropriated by the Latter-day Saints in various directions. We have appropriated tens of thousands of dollars for the gathering of the poor and the building of tabernacles, and for many other things that might be mentioned. When we do this, we act up to one of the principles that pertain to this United Order.

The Lord, in Kirtland, established a United Order. He called certain individuals, and united them by revelation, and told them how to proceed; and every man who would subscribe fully to the United Order will proceed in the same manner. He told those people and the Church afar off, to listen and hearken to what he required of men in this Order, and of every man who belonged to the Church of the living God—that all that they received above what was necessary for the support of their families, was to be put in the Lord's storehouse, for the benefit of the whole Church. This is what is required of every man in his stewardship. And this is a law that is required to be observed by every man who belongs to the Church of the living God. [Book Doc. and Cov., p. 234.] Now, this is one of the main features of the United Order. We are not going to stop here, in these valleys of the mountains. Many of us expect to go forth and build up the Center Stake of Zion; but before we are called, we must understand these things, and conform to them more practically than many of us do at the present time.

We are told in one of these revelations that it is necessary that we should be equal. If we are not equal in temporal things, we cannot be equal in spiritual things. Men on whom God has bestowed financiering ability are the men that are wanted at this time—that God wants, and

Appendix B - United Order

whom he would wish to call to step forth in the accomplishment of this great union. Now we call men at our conferences and send them forth to preach the gospel to the nations of the earth. They go forth in the strength and power of God, depending upon the Holy Spirit, to assist in the accomplishment of the work. In regard to the building up the kingdom of God here at home, persons who have the ability are the ones who should step forward in things that would lead the Latter-day Saints to this union. It would be of more value to them than all the things of earth. The blessings of God upon them in time and eternity would well repay them to step forth and labor for the Zion of God. **We are told that the priesthood is not called to work for money, but to establish Zion. What a lovely thing it would be if there was a Zion now, as in the days of Enoch! That there would be peace in our midst and no necessity for a man to contend and tread upon the toes of another to attain a better position, and advance himself ahead of his neighbor. And there should be no unjust competition in matters that belong to the Latter-day Saints. That which creates division among us pertaining to our temporal interests should not be. The Lord considered this union a matter of importance**, and he uses strong expressions in reference to it. Speaking in regard to those who should disobey the principles of the United Order after receiving it, the Lord says, "I have decreed in my heart that any man among you that shall break the covenant by which you are bound, he shall be trodden down by whomsoever I will." [p. 337.] And he says, in regard to some parties who turned away from this principle, "I have cursed them with a sore and grievous curse." He says in another revelation, showing the sacredness of this order, "Therefore a commandment I give unto you, and he who breaketh it shall lose his standing in the church, and be turned over to the buffeting of Satan." [p. 258.] These are severe penalties, but it is in consequence of his desire to prepare a people for celestial glory. Now, shall we say that these matters do not pertain to us, and that we shall leave them until we go back to Jackson County? I have sometimes thought that if the Latter-day Saints did not open their eyes and attend to these things very strictly, we should hardly escape these afflictions, but be persecuted as were our brethren in Missouri. After the instructions we have received during the last forty years, shall we say that we cannot conform to these principles? Shall we say that we shall ignore these glorious principles that pertain to this exalted brotherhood?

Now, we are trying to do something in Brigham City in the direction to this order; but there seems to be the greatest difficulty with ourselves, when we come to these temporal affairs. Our old ideas of things have a wonderful influence over us, that it seems a difficult matter to break the crust, and conform wholly to the requirements of the United Order. We have arrived at certain points of union in our city; but I do not wish to speak about our affairs there in any spirit of boasting, for when I consider the sacredness of these principles, and the importance of them, I feel my insufficiency and unworthiness. To engage in this labor seems to be a great and sacred undertaking. President Young used to say, "Why, up there in Brigham City Brother Snow has led the people along, and got them into the United Order without their knowing it." But I can see many things that we are very short of accomplishing. We have not entered into the fulness of the principles of the United Order, but we talk about them, and many of us try to conform to them, and get the spirit of them in our hearts. Now we number about three thousand souls, and we have moved along so far as this—I presume it is a little further than you have in Ogden—there is but one store in our city where imported goods are bought, and this belongs to the people. Now that is considered towards a union in a people of three thousand, to be agreed to do their trading in one place—that there should be one mercantile establishment. Now, you have more than one store in Ogden. Then, we have united a little further; we have but one tannery in our city of a population of three thousand. We have but one shoemakers' establishment—an association of shoemakers, consisting of about thirty persons. There is no competition in this business. I suppose you have more than one in Ogden; but you are a greater people than we are, several times over. They all purchase their boots

Appendix B - United Order

and shoes at this industrial department, and thus the men engaged in this business are sustained by the people, according to their covenants; and there are no other shoemakers in that locality. Well, we have united together on another point, that is, in a woolen factory and sheepherd. We met with a loss of some fifty thousand dollars in the burning of our factory, and the destruction of our crops by the grasshoppers. There are no rich people in Brigham City, but the people, through their union, have erected another building, much better than the one destroyed. We expect to have the factory in operation about the first of July. This shows some proof of the advancement of the people. This achievement is not in consequence of the people there having money; but this work—this amazing work, as I consider it—has been accomplished in consequence of the advancement that the people have made in this union. Well we have but one blacksmith shop in that city; some twelve or fifteen work in this establishment, and the people sustain them in their operations. Those engaged in the various branches of labor feel confident that the people will patronize them, and carry out what they have agreed in this particular, and they do not trouble themselves about any other employment, or business. There is but one furniture shop in Brigham City, and the people sustain those engaged in that business. I suppose you have more than one. There is but one tin shop, and it is patronized by all the people of Brigham City. There is but one lumbering department there, and the people sustain the parties who are employed in that business. Some eighty or one hundred persons are engaged during the lumbering season. The mills are owned by the people, and there is no competition. There is but one millinery shop in that city, and it is sustained by the people. You have more than one here; perhaps you ought to have. There is but one tailor's shop in Brigham City, and the people employed in that business are patronized by the whole people. I might mention a great many other businesses, but will leave that subject now.

Now, for the people in Ogden and the people in other settlements, it would be a good thing to unite together to supply themselves with their clothing, food, furniture, building materials, and with everything that pertains to their comfort and convenience, without being under the necessity of employing, or using, those things that are imported. You have a great many wide-awake, financiering men in Ogden, very intelligent men, who are full of wisdom and stir, and have the principles of the Gospel in them. You are ahead of the people of Brigham City in this respect, but we are ahead of you in some other respects. In proportion as a man possesses a knowledge over his brethren, we should be more anxious to accomplish good for Zion; and he should be the one to set a proper example for the union of the people. I believe if the Latter-day Saints would go forward and establish the United Order in their midst more than they do, the Lord would more abundantly sustain and bless us, and provide remedies against the evils to which we are exposed—persecution and difficulties from outside, that we will not talk about today.

The sisters here in Ogden are accomplishing considerable in regard to the United Order. They are uniting themselves together to do a great work. I do not know but what they, in connection with others, will be, more or less, the salvation of Zion; and it is a good thing for them to persevere, and for some of the brethren to follow their good example in this respect.

A great deal might be said in regard to the principles of the United Order, that I do not feel to talk about this afternoon, but I do feel to urge on those brethren who have the means and are in circumstances, to search out the mind and will of God in regard to these matters, and let us try to build up Zion. Zion is the pure in heart. Zion cannot be built up except on the principles of union required by the celestial law. It is high time for us to enter into these things. It is more pleasant and agreeable for the Latter-day Saints to enter into this work and build up Zion, than to build up ourselves and have this great competition which is destroying us. Now let things go on in our midst in our Gentile fashion, and you would see an aristocracy growing amongst us, whose

Appendix B - United Order

language to the poor would be, "we do not require your company; we are going to have things very fine; we are quite busy now, please call some other time." You would have classes established here, some very poor and some very rich. Now, the Lord is not going to have anything of that kind. There has to be an equality; and we have to observe these principles that are designed to give everyone the privilege of gathering around him the comforts and conveniences of life. The Lord, in his economy in spiritual things, has fixed that every man, according to his perseverance and faithfulness, will receive exaltation and glory in the eternal worlds—a fulness of the Priesthood, and a fulness of the glory of God. This is the economy of God's system by which men and women can be exalted spiritually. The same with regard to temporal affairs. We should establish the principles of the United Order, that give every man a chance to receive these temporal blessings. I do not say that it would be proper to give a man just baptized the fulness of the Priesthood at once. Neither would it be right to give a man who has just come from the old country the home and possessions of him who has been here and labored and toiled for years to accumulate them. It would not be right for the possessor to step out of his house, and let the one who has never labored and toiled go in and take his place; but this man who has got the blessings of God around him, should be willing to sacrifice a portion of his surplus means to establish some industry, that this poor man can work and obtain a good remuneration for his labor, that he can see comfort and convenience before him, by persevering as he has done who has been thus blessed. This is the spirit and aim of the United Order, and that we should endeavor to establish. We should employ our surplus means in a manner that the poor can have employment and see before them a competence and the conveniences of life, so that they may not be dependent upon their neighbors. Where is the man who wants to be dependent upon his neighbors or the Tithing Office? No! He is a man, and is the image of God, and wants to gather the means around him, by his own, individual exertions. Blessed of God, are we, who have surplus means, and we should be willing to employ those means whereby such individuals may have, as before mentioned. The

United Order is not French Communism. It is not required of those who possess the means of living to expend those means among those who know nothing about taking care of and preserving them. But let no man be oppressed and placed in circumstances where he cannot reach forth and help himself.

Well, I wanted to say a few things by way of suggestion to the brethren. May God bless his people in Ogden.

Take the Book of Doctrine and Covenants, trace the subject of the United Order, and you will find it explained fully. And there need not be any difficulty in regard to what is required at our hands.

May we so live as to be worthy of a standing in the presence of God. Amen.

Interest Manifested Relating To Temporal Affairs — Revelations Pertaining To Being One In Temporal, As In Spiritual Things — Consecration — Stewardship — Jackson County — Sanctification

Discourse by Elder Orson Pratt, delivered in the new tabernacle, Salt Lake City, Sunday afternoon, June 14, 1874. (Reported by David W. Evans.) Journal of Discourses, Volume 17, p.103+

There seems to be at the present time a great deal of interest manifested among the Latter-day Saints, and even among those who are connected with our Church, in regard to some instructions that have been imparted to the Latter-day Saints in relation to their temporal affairs. The instructions which have been imparted, and which the people are, in some measure, receiving, are comparatively new in their estimation, that is, it is supposed they are new, and something which we, in times past, have not practiced. But if we appeal to the revelations of God, we shall find that no new thing has been required of us. It is generally termed, however, by Latter-day Saints, the New Order. You hear of it in all parts of the Territory. What is meant by the New Order? Is it really new in the revelations of God, or is it something new for us to practice it? We have been required, in the year 1874, to come back again to an old order, as taught in ancient Mormonism. What I mean by ancient Mormonism is Mormonism as it was taught some forty-three or forty-four years ago. There is a generation now living on the earth who seem to be comparatively ignorant of the doctrines which were taught some forty years ago to men who are now old and have grey heads and gray beards. Since that time a new generation has arisen; and they begin to think that something new, something that will turn things upside down, is being introduced into Mormonism. I will say to all who have such ideas, you are entirely mistaken, it is not so; we are trying to get the people to come back again to the old principles of Mormonism, to that which God revealed in the early rise of this Church.

Every man, whether he is or is not a Latter-day Saint, when he comes to study our written works, the written revelations which God has given, will acknowledge that the Latter-day Saints cannot be the people they profess to be, they cannot be consistent with the revelations they profess to believe in and live as they now live; they have got to come into the system which the Saints call the New Order, otherwise they cannot comply with the revelations of God.

I believe that I will quote a few revelations this morning, in order to show you what God said in relation to property or temporal things, in the early rise of this Church. The first revelation that now occurs to my mind will be found in the Book of Doctrine and Covenants, on page 217; it was given in March, 1831, forty-three years ago last March. In the third paragraph of this revelation we read these words:

"For, behold, the beasts of the field and the fowls of the air, and that which cometh of the earth, is ordained for the use of man for food and for raiment, and that he might have in abundance; but it is not given that one man should possess that which is above another, wherefore the world lieth in sin."

Do you believe this revelation, Latter-day Saints? "Oh, yes," says one—"we believe Joseph Smith was a Prophet." Have you practiced it? Oh, that is another thing. How, then, are we to know that you believe this revelation if you do not practice it? How are the world to know you are sincere in your belief, if you have a revelation which you profess to believe in, and yet give no heed to it. I do not wonder that the world say that the Latter-day Saints do not believe their own revelations. Why? Because we do not practice them. "It is not given that one man should possess that which is above another, wherefore the world lieth in sin." There may be some strangers here, and they do not believe this book, but I will tell you what they would say as men of reason, they would say that if you Latter-day

Saints call this your book of faith, and doctrines, and covenants, to be consistent you ought to comply with it. That is what they would say, and it is really a true saying, and consistent and reasonable. If we believe this, let us practice it; if we do not believe in it, why profess to believe in it?

I will now refer you to a revelation given on the second day of January, 1831, it is on page 120 of the Book of Doctrine and Covenants. I will tell you how this revelation was given, for I was present at the time it was given. The Church, then, was about nine months old. The Prophet Joseph, who received all the revelations contained in this book, was then living in the State of New York, in the town of Fayette, Seneca County. He called together the various branches of the Church that had been organized during the nine months previous in that State, and they assembled together in the house in which this Church was organized, namely, Father Whitmer's house. You will recollect, in reading the Book of Mormon, that the sons of Father Whitmer, young men, are noted as witnesses of the Book of Mormon, David Whitmer having seen the angel, and the plates in the hands of the angel, and heard him speak, and the hand of the angel was placed on his head, and he said unto him—"Blessed be the Lord and they that keep his commandments." And he heard the voice of the Lord in connection with three other persons testifying out of the heavens, at the same time that the angel was administering, that the Book of Mormon had been translated correctly by the gift and power of God, and commanding him to bear witness of it to all people, nations and tongues, in connection with the other three that were with him. These were some of the individuals also who saw the plates and handled them, and saw the engravings upon them, and who gave their testimony to that effect in the Book of Mormon. It was in their father's house where this Church was organized, on the 6th of April, 1830; it was in their father's house where this little

Conference was convened on the 2nd of January, 1831, and this Conference requested the Prophet Joseph Smith to inquire of the Lord concerning their duties. He did so. He sat down in the midst of the Conference, of less than one hundred, I do not know exactly the number, and a scribe wrote this revelation from his mouth. One item contained therein, in the fifth paragraph, reads thus:—

"And let every man esteem his brother as himself, and practice virtue and holiness before me. And again I say unto you, let every man esteem his brother as himself; for what man among you having twelve sons, and is no respecter of them and they serve him obediently, and he saith unto the one, Be thou clothed in robes and sit thou here; and to the other, Be thou clothed in rags and sit thou there, and looketh upon his sons and saith, I am just. "Behold this have I given unto you a parable, and it is even as I am: I say unto you, be one; and if ye are not one ye are not mine."

Perhaps the Saints may think that this has reference to spiritual things alone, and means to be one in doctrine, principle, ordinances, faith, belief, and so on, and that it has no reference whatever to temporal things; but in order to show you that this has reference to temporal as well as to spiritual things, let me quote that which God said a few months after this in another revelation. I have not time to turn to all these revelations, but I will quote them. The Lord says—"Except ye are equal in the bonds (or bands) of earthly things, how can you be made equal in the bands of heavenly things?" Here was a question put to us: How can you be made equal in the bands of heavenly things, unless you are equal in the bands of earthly? Surely enough, we can not be made equal. If we are unequal in this life, and are not one, can we be entrusted with the true riches, the riches of eternity? I believe I will read to you a small portion of another revelation that was given on stewardships. The Lord commanded certain ones among his servants to take charge of these revelations when they were in manuscript, before they were published, that they might be printed and sent forth among the people, and he also gave them charge concerning the Book of Mormon, and made them stewards over these revelations and the avails arising from them. And the Lord said— "Wherefore, hearken and hear, for thus saith the Lord unto them, I, the Lord, have appointed them and ordained them to be stewards over the revelations and commandments which I have given unto them, and which I shall hereafter give unto them; and an account of this stewardship will I require of them in the day of judgment; wherefore I have appointed unto them, and this is their business in the Church, to manage them and the concerns thereof, and the benefits thereof, wherefore a commandment give I unto them that they shall not give these things unto the Church, neither unto the world, nevertheless, inasmuch as they receive more than is needful for their necessities and their wants, it shall be given into my storehouse and the benefits shall be consecrated unto the inhabitants of Zion, and unto their generations, inasmuch as they become heirs according to the laws of the kingdom.

Now, you notice here, the Lord did not intend those individuals whom he named to become rich out of the avails of the sale of the Book of Mormon and the Book of Doctrine and Covenants, and other revelations and the literary concerns of his Church, he never intended that they should become rich while others were poor, that was not the order; but inasmuch as they received more than was needful for their support what should they do with it? Should they aggrandize themselves while their poor brethren were destitute? No, not at all; they were to give all the surplus, over and above what was really necessary to support them, into the Lord's storehouse, and it was to be for the benefit of all the people of Zion, not only the living but for their generations after them, inasmuch as they became heirs according to the laws of the kingdom of God.

There was a certain way to become heirs according to the laws of the kingdom of God. Heirs of what? Heirs of the avails arising from the sale of the revelations which all the inhabitants of Zion were to be benefited by. Says one—"But perhaps that was limited to those six individuals who are here named, and did not mean the whole Church." Wait, let us read the next sentence—"Behold, this is what the Lord requires of every man in his stewardship, even as I the Lord have appointed or shall hereafter appoint." From this we learn that all the stewards which the Lord had appointed; and all that he should appoint, in a future time, to stewardships, were to hand over all their surplus—all that was not necessary to feed and clothe them—into the Lord's store house. None who belonged to the Church of the living God are exempt from this law. Does that law include us? It includes all who belong to the Church, not one is exempt from it. Have we been doing this, Latter-day Saints, for the last forty-three years, since this revelation was given? Have we been complying with the order we undertook in the year 1831, to enter into? This old order is not a new order that you talk so much about.

Iu [In] the year 1831, we commenced emigrating to the western part of the State of Missouri, to a county, quite new then, called Jackson County; most of the land at that time was Government land. When we commenced emigrating there the Lord gave many revelations. The Prophet Joseph went up among some of the earliest to that county, and God gave many revelations contained in the Book of Doctrine and Covenants, in relation to how the people should conduct their affairs. Among the revelations then given was the commandment that every man who should come up to that land should lay all things which he possessed before the Bishop of his Church. Another revelation, given before we went up to that land, speaking of a land which the Lord, at some future time, would give us for an inheritance, commanded that we should consecrate all our property into his store-house. If we had wagons, horses, mules, oxen, cows, sheep, farming utensils, household furniture, gold and silver, jewelry, wearing apparel, it mattered not what it was, the Lord said, in a revelation given in February, 1831, that it should all be laid before the Bishop of his Church, and that it should be consecrated to the Lord's storehouse. This reduced us all on a level. If a man had a million dollars when he gathered up to Jackson County, if he complied with the law, he would be just as rich as the man who had not one farthing. Why? Because he consecrated all he had, and the poor man could not do any more than that, hence all who complied with the law were equally poor or equally rich.

What was the next step after this consecration? In those days we had but one Bishop—his name was Edward Partridge, and he was called by revelation—and the next step after this general consecration, the Lord commanded the Bishop and his two counselors to purchase all the land in Jackson County, and in the counties round about, that could conveniently be got, the general price being one dollar and a quarter an acre. And what next? After purchasing these lands as far as they had the means to do so, every man that had consecrated his property was to receive an inheritance. Now recollect, none except those who consecrated, none who disobeyed that law, were to receive an inheritance or stewardship; but all who consecrated their properties according to this law were to receive their stewardship.

What is the meaning of a stewardship? A steward is one who is accountable to somebody for the property that he manages, and that is his stewardship, whether it be landed property, farming utensils, wagons, cows, oxen, horses, harness, or whatever may be committed to him. To whom were the brethren in Jackson County accountable for the stewardship committed to them? To the Bishop. The Bishop was called in these revelations a common judge in Zion, ecclesiastically speaking, not according to the civil laws; so far as our ecclesiastical laws were concerned he was to be a common judge, and each person was to render an account of the stewardship which he had to the Bishop. I do not know how often; perhaps once a year, perhaps longer than that, perhaps oftener. I do not know that there was any specified time given in these revelations about how often these accounts should be rendered up. But how were the people to live out of the avails of the stewardship committed to their charge? They were to have food and raiment, and the necessary comforts of life. Well, of course, a wise and faithful steward, having health and strength, and perhaps a good deal of talent, might so take charge of a stewardship that he might gain more than he and his family needed, and keeping an account of all these things, and rendering the same when required, some of them would have a considerable surplus above that which they and their families needed. What was to be done with that? Why, as stewards, they would have to consecrate it into the Lord's storehouse, the Lord being the owner of the property and we only his stewards.

There were some men who were entrusted with a larger stewardship than others. For instance, here was a man who knew nothing about farming particularly, but he might be a master spirit as far as some other branch of business was concerned. He might understand how to carry, on a great cloth manufactory and everything in the clothing line necessary for the inhabitants of Zion. Such a man would require a greater stewardship than the man who cultivated a small farm, and had only himself and a wife and two or three children to support. But would the fact of one man having a greater stewardship than another make one richer than another? No. Why not? Because, if one received fifty or a hundred thousand dollars to build and stock a large manufactory for the purpose of manufacturing various kinds of fabrics for clothing, although he might have a surplus of several thousand dollars at the end of the year, he would not be any richer than the farmer with his few acres of land, and let me show you how they would be equal. The manufacturer does not own the building, the machinery, the cotton or the flax, as the case may be, he is only a steward, like the farmer, and if, at the end of the year, he has five, ten, or fifty thousand dollars surplus, does that make him a rich man? By no means, it goes into the Lord's storehouse at the end of each year, or as often as may be required, thus leaving him on the same platform of equality with the farmer and his small stewardship. Do you not see the equality of the thing? In temporal matters it is not given that one man shall possess that which is above another, saith the Lord.

Now did the people really enter into this, or was it mere theory? I answer that, in the year 1831, we did try to enter into this order of things, but the hearts of the people had been so accustomed to holding property individually, that it was a very difficult matter to get them to comply with, this law of the Lord. Many of them were quite wealthy, and they saw that on that land a great city called Zion, or the New Jerusalem, was to be built; they understood that from the revelations, and they said in their hearts—"What a fine chance this will be for us to get rich. We have means and money, and if we consecrate according to the law of God we can not get rich; but we know that people by thousands and tens of thousands will gather up here, and these lands will become very valuable. We can now get them at the government price, a dollar and a quarter an acre, and if we lay out a few thousands in land, we can sell it out to the brethren when they come along at a thousand per cent. profit, and perhaps in some cases at ten thousand per cent., and make ourselves wealthy, so we will not consecrate, but we will go ahead for ourselves individually, and we will buy up the lands to speculate upon." These were the feelings of some who went up to that country; but others were willing to comply with the word of God, and did just as the revelation required, and they laid everything they had before the Bishop, and received their stewardship.

After he had organized these things, Joseph the Prophet, in August of the year 1831, went back to Kirtland, about a thousand miles east, and while there the Lord revealed to him that the inhabitants of Jackson County were not complying with his word; hence Joseph sent letters up to them containing the word of the Lord, chastening them because of their disobedience and rebellion against the law of heaven. He did this on several occasions, and one occasion, especially, as you will find recorded in the history published in some of our periodicals. I think you will find it in the fifteenth volume of the Millennial Star, in language something like this—"If the people will not comply with my law, which I have given them concerning the consecration of their property, the land shall not be a land of Zion unto them, but their names shall be blotted out, and the names of their children and their children's children, so long as they will not comply with my laws, and their names shall not be found written in the book of the law of the Lord."

In another revelation, published in the Book of Doctrine and Covenants, the Lord says—"The rebellious are not of the blood of Ephraim, wherefore they shall be plucked up and shall be sent away out of the land." When this revelation was given all was peace in Jackson County. We had no enemies there any more than we had elsewhere, wherever the Church might be located; all was comparative peace. But the Lord said that the rebellious should be plucked up and sent away out of the land. The people thought there was no prospect whatever of that revelation being fulfilled. All was peace, and to say that they were to be plucked up and driven out of the land was out of the question. They did not repent, that is all of them, but continued in their disobedience, neglecting to consecrate their properties, according to the requirements of the law of the Lord; and hence, when they had been there about two years and five months from the time of their first settlement or location, they were literally plucked up and cast away out of the land. You have the history before you. Their enemies arose upon them and began to tear down their houses, and they burned two hundred and three of the dwellings our people had built in that land. They burned down their grain stacks, hay stacks and fences, and chased the Latter-day Saints around from one part of the county to another, sometimes tying them up to trees and whipping them, in some instances until their bowels gushed out. They tore down the printing office and destroyed it, also one of our dry goods stores, and scattered the goods through the streets; they went into houses and, taking therefrom the bedding and furniture, piled them up in the streets and set fire to them, and thus they continued their persecutions until, finally, they succeeded in driving the Latter-day Saints from the county, and thus the word of the Lord was fulfilled which said—"I will pluck them up and send them away out of the land, for none but the obedient shall eat of the good of the land of latter Zion in these latter days."

Another revelation God gave, to warn the people, in which he told them to remember the Book of Mormon, and the new covenant which he had revealed, and which, if they did not observe, he said—"Behold, I the Lord have a scourge and a judgment which shall be poured out upon your heads." This was given between one and two years before we were driven out of that county, in Kirtland, Ohio, through the Prophet Joseph, and sent up to them to warn them. Another revelation said if the people did not do thus and so, they should be persecuted from city to city, and from synagogue to synagogue, and but few should stand to receive an inheritance—meaning those who had gone into that county.

Now go through this Territory, from one end thereof to the other, hunt up the greyheaded and grey-bearded men and the old ladies, who were once in Jackson County, and see how many you can find who lived there then, and you can judge whether the word of the Lord has been fulfilled or not. I guess that you will find but very few if you hunt, all through the Territory.

Let us read a little further in the revelations, and see whether God has cast us entirely off or not. In one of the revelations, given after we were driven out across the Missouri River into Clay County, and into the surrounding counties, the Lord said, concerning the people who were scattered and driven—"Behold, I have suffered these things to come upon them because of their sins and wickedness; but notwithstanding all these afflictions which have come upon my people, I will be merciful unto them, and in the day of wrath I will remember mercy, wherefore I, the Lord, will not utterly cast them off."

Though but few should stand to receive an inheritance, the Lord said he would not utterly cast them off.

What next? He gives an inferior law, called the law of Tithing, suited and adapted to us. After we had been driven for neglecting to comply with the greater law of consecration of all we had, he thought he would not leave us without a law, but he gave us an inferior law, namely, that we should give in one-tenth part of our annual income. This law was given in May, 1838, I do not remember the exact date, and I believe that we have tried to comply with it; but it has been almost an impossibility to get the people universally to comply with it.

There is another item connected with this law of Tithing that has but seldom been complied with, namely, the consecration of all surplus property. Now go round among the Saints, among the emigrants who have gathered up from time to time, and there has been only now and then a man who had any surp[l]us property, let him be the judge. If a man had fifty or a hundred thousand dollars, he said in his own heart—"I really need all this, I want to speculate, I want to buy a great deal of land to sell again when the price of land shall rise; I want to set up a great store in which to sell merchandise to the people, and if I consecrate any of this it will curtail my operations, because it will diminish my capital, and I cannot speculate to the extent I should if I retained it all, and I shall therefore consider that I have no surplus property. Now an honest-hearted individual would have a little surplus property, and he would put it in; but from that day until the present time I presume that the tenth of their annual income has been paid by the majority of the people. I do not really know in relation to this matter, at any rate the Lord has not utterly forsaken us, hence I think we have kept his law in some measure, or in all probability he would have cast us off altogether.

But how is it that we have been smitten, driven, cast out and persecuted, and the lives of our Prophet and Patriarch and hundreds of others destroyed by rifle, cannon, and sword in the hands of our enemies? How is it that such things have been permitted in this free republic? "Oh," says one, "It is because you practiced polygamy." I answer that we did not practice polygamy in the days of the persecutions which I have named, they came upon us before we began that practice, for the revelation on polygamy was not given until some thirteen years after the rise of this Church, and that was after we had been driven and smitten and scattered to and fro, here and there by the hands of our enemies, hence, it was not for that that we were persecuted. But if we take the printed circulars written by our enemies, we can give you their reasons for persecuting us. One of their reasons was that we believed in ancient Christianity, namely, speaking in tongues, interpretation of tongues, healing the sick, etc.; and our enemies did not believe in having a community in their midst who claimed to have Apostles and Prophets and to enjoy the gifts of the Gospel the same as the ancient Saints. Our enemies said they would not have such a people in their society, and if we did not renounce these things they would drive us from our homes. You can read this with the names of the mob attached to it, in connection with a great many priests and ministers of different denominations. The Rev. Isaac M'Coy and the Rev. Mr. Bogard, and many others who might be named, were among the leaders of the mob who persecuted the Latter-day Saints.

Now, why is it, Latter-day Saints, that we have been tossed to and fro and smitten and persecuted for these many years? It is because we have disobeyed the law of heaven, we have not kept the commandments of the Most High God, we have not fulfilled his law; we have disobeyed the word which he gave through his servant Joseph, and hence the Lord has suffered us to be smitten and afflicted under the hands of our enemies.

Shall we ever return to the law of God? Yes. When? Why, when we will. We are agents; we can abide his law or reject it, just as long as we please, for God has not taken away your agency nor mine. But I will try to give you some information in regard to the time. God said, in the year 1832, before we were driven out of Jackson County, in a revelation which you will find here in this book, that before that generation should all pass away, a house of the Lord should be built in that county, (Jackson County), "upon the consecrated spot, as I have appointed; and the glory of God, even a cloud by day and a pillar of flaming fire by night shall rest upon the same." In another place, in the same revelation, speaking of the priesthood, he says that the sons of Moses and the sons of Aaron, those who had received the two priesthoods, should be filled with the glory of God upon Mount Zion, in the Lord's house, and should receive a renewing of their bodies, and the blessings of the Most High should be poured out upon them in great abundance.

This was given forty-two years ago. The generation then living was not only to commence a house of God in Jackson County, Missouri, but was actually to complete the same, and when it is completed the glory of God should rest upon it.

Now, do you Latter-day Saints believe that? I do, and if you believe in these revelations you just as much expect the fulfillment of that revelation as of any one that God has ever given in these latter times, or in former ages. We look, just as much for this to take place, according to the word of the Lord, as the Jews look to return to Palestine, and to re-build Jerusalem upon the place where it formerly stood. They expect to build a Temple there, and that the glory of God will enter into it; so likewise do we Latter-day Saints expect to return to Jackson County and to build a Temple there before the generation that was living forty-two years ago has all passed away. Well, then, the time must be pretty near when we shall begin that work. Now, can we be permitted to return and build up the waste places of Zion, establish the great central city of Zion in Jackson County, Mo., and build a Temple on which the glory of God will abide by day and by night, unless we return, not to the "new order," but to that law which was given in the beginning of this work? Let me answer the question by quoting one of these revelations again, a revelation given in 1834. The Lord, speaking of the return of his people, and referring to those who were driven from Jackson County, says—"They that remain shall return, they and their children with them to receive their inheritances in the land of Zion, with songs of everlasting joy upon their heads." There will be a few that the Lord will spare to go back there, because they were not all transgressors. There were only two that the Lord spared among Israel during their forty years travel—Caleb and Joshua. They were all that were spared, out of some twenty-five hundred thousand people, from twenty years old and upwards, to go into the land of promise. There may be three in our day, or a half dozen or a dozen spared that were once on that land who will be permitted to return with their children, grand-children, and great-grand-children unto the waste places of Zion and build them up with songs of everlasting joy.

But will they return after the old order of things that exists among the Gentiles—every man for himself, this individualism in regard to property? No, never, never while the world stands. If you would have these revelations fulfilled you must comply with the conditions thereof. The Lord said, concerning the building up of Zion when we do return— "Except Zion be built according to the law of the celestial kingdom, I can not receive her unto myself." If we should be permitted, this present year, 1874, to go back to that county, and should undertake to build up a city of Zion upon the consecrated spot, after the order that we have been living in during the last forty years, we should be cast out again, the Lord would not acknowledge us as his people, neither would he acknowledge the works of our hands in the building of a city. If we would go back then, we must comply with the celestial law, the law of consecration, the law of oneness, which the Lord has spoken of from the beginning. Except you are one you are not mine. Query, if we are not the Lord's who in the world or out of the world do we belong to? Here is a question for us all to consider. There is no other way for us to become one but by keeping the law of heaven, and when we do this we shall become sanctified before God, and never before.

Talk about sanctification, we do not believe in the kind of sanctification taught by the sectarian religion—that they were sanctified at such a minute and such an hour and at such a place while they were praying in secret. We believe in the sanctification that comes by continued obedience to the law of heaven. I do not know of any other sanctification that the Scriptures tell about, of any other sanctification that is worth the consideration of rational beings. If we would be sanctified then, we must begin to-day, or whenever the Lord points out, to obey his laws just as far as we possibly can; and by obedience to these laws we continually gain more and more favor from heaven, more and more of the Spirit of God, and thus will be fulfilled a revelation given in 1834, which says that before Zion is redeemed, let the armies of Israel become very great, let them become sanctified before me, that they may be as fair as the sun, clear as the moon, and that their banners may be terrible unto all the nations of the earth. Not terrible by reason of numbers, but terrible because of the sanctification they will receive through obedience to the law of God. Why was Enoch, and why were the inhabitants of the Zion built up before the flood terrible to all the nations around about? It was because, through a long number of years, they observed the law of God, and when their enemies came up to fight against them, Enoch, being filled with the power of the Holy Ghost, and speaking the word of God in power and in faith, the very heavens trembled and shook, and the earth quaked, and mountains were thrown down, rivers of water were turned out of their course, and all nations feared greatly because of the power of God, and the terror of his might that were upon his people.

We have this account of ancient Zion in one of the revelations that God has given. What was it that made their banners terrible to the nations? It was not their numbers. If, then Zion must become great it will be because of her sanctification. When shall we begin, Latter-day Saints, to carry out the law of God, and enter upon the process necessary to our sanctification? We are told by the highest authority that God has upon the earth that now is the accepted time and now is the day of salvation, so far as entering into this order which God has pointed out is concerned. Shall we do it? Or shall we say no? Shall there be division among the people, those who are on the Lord's side come out and those who are against the law of God come out? I hope this division will not be at present. I hope that we shall take hold with one heart and with one mind. The time of the division will come soon enough. It will be in the great day of the Lord's power, when his face shall be unveiled in yonder heavens, and when he shall come in his glory and in his might. Then the heavens will be shaken and the earth will reel to and fro like a drunken man. "Then," saith the Lord, "I will send forth mine angels to gather out of my kingdom all things that offend and that do iniquity." That will be time enough for this great division. Let us not be divided now, Latter-day Saints, but let us manifest our willingness to comply with the word and law of the Most High, and be prepared for the blessings which he has in store for us

Our Traditions—Receiving Counsel

Discourse by Elder George Q. Cannon,
delivered in the Tabernacle, Ogden City, Nov. 13, 1870.
Reported by David W. Evans.
Source: Journal of Discourses, vol.13, pp.368-376.

[NOTE: This article is included because it discusses both Zion and cooperation, and suggests what holds the Saints back from embracing both. Many may not know that George Q. Cannon was a member of the First Presidency under three prophets, Young, Taylor, and Woodruff. This author suspects he also penned the "Encyclical Letter Upon Co-operation" found in Appendix C.]

[W]hen I look at the progress that the brethren and sisters are making I feel gratified. There are times, perhaps, when I feel as others do—that we are not making the progress that we should do; that we are more careless and harder in our hearts and less under the influences of the Holy Spirit and the counsels of the servants of God than we should be. This is my feeling sometimes; but when I look calmly at the Saints, and consider the many difficulties with which they have to contend and the vast amount of tradition that has to be uprooted and overcome, I am gratified at the progress which they make, and feel comforted in the prospects that are before us, and before the Zion of God with which we are connected.

It is these traditions that we have to contend with that are so difficult for us to overcome, that interfere so seriously with the progress of the people in the things of God. They cling more closely to us than many of us imagine, and it is only when the Spirit of God rests upon us and we realize its power to a greater extent that we can understand and comprehend the power of tradition over our minds and conduct. This is the great obstruction to the teachings of the Elders and to the reception of and obedience to counsel; and that prevents the people being united as the heart of one man. It is this which prevents us entering upon the more perfect order that God has revealed, and that gives our enemies more power in our midst than they otherwise would have. It should be the aim of every one of us to seek, as far as possible, to put these things away from us. It is our privilege to have power from God, to have sufficient faith bestowed upon us through His Holy Spirit, to overcome these traditions. The writers in the Book of Mormon, in speaking of the veil of darkness that rested upon the minds of the people, alluded to it as a veil which can be rent asunder by the exercise of faith and by the blessing of God upon His Saints. There is a veil over our minds in consequence of the Fall, and our being shut, as it were, through that, from the presence of God. He can see us, but to us He is invisible, and we can know Him only through His Holy Spirit, as He reveals Himself to us from time to time. In consequence of this the adversary has great power over the hearts of the children of men; and it is only by exercising faith, by seeking earnestly for that Spirit which He bestows, that we are enabled to counteract this darkness and the influence which Satan seeks to exercise over our hearts.

I rejoice in one fact which God has revealed; it comforts my heart when I think of our condition and circumstances and of His kingdom, and that is that we live in the day when, according to the words of the prophets and according to the revelations which God has given to us in this dispensation, the power of Satan is becoming less and less, and the power of God is to increase and to be made more and more manifest, to the exposing of the works of darkness and to the breaking of the yoke which the enemy of all righteousness seeks to fasten upon the minds and understandings of the children of men.

It is a glorious thought for us to reflect upon that we live in a day and at a time in which God has promised to exercise His power in our behalf; when He and Jesus and the holy angels and the spirits of just men made perfect are all engaged with us in hastening the great work of redemption, and in banishing from the earth the power of evil which has so long held it in thralldom. God has given us this promise, and if we will labor with the zeal and industry which should characterize His Saints in carrying out His purposes He will bestow upon us every blessing that we need, and will give us power, as I have said, to overcome our traditions, to see the things of God in their true light, and to behold the truth in all its splendor and beauty.

There is one great truth that we have to learn. Brother Carrington alluded to it in his remarks; and all the Elders allude to it more or less when addressing the Saints, and that is, that the Gospel offers every advantage to those who obey and are faithful to it that God can bestow upon His children. There is no advantage to be gained outside of this Church or outside this Gospel; there is no blessing that we can seek for or desire, or that would be proper for us to receive under our present circumstances that we cannot obtain inside the Gospel, or inside the truth; or that we can obtain outside the Gospel, or by departing from the servants of God. You may let your minds run, if you please, over all there is pertaining to the earth and man, or that will contribute to the happiness of man on the earth, and you cannot conceive of any blessing or advantage that is not within your reach legitimately, if you pursue the path God has marked out and by abiding the counsels He makes known from time to time. A great many do not comprehend this; and this is one of the traditions that we have to contend with, and it arises from the lack of faith in our hearts, and the unbelief that we have received from our forefathers. And we have to contend with it when counsel is given to us in relation to our temporal circumstances and other matters. It is frequently the case that we cannot see any particular advantage in that counsel; it does not strike us favorably. We imagine that some other course would be better for us to pursue, and that by adopting some other line of policy or conduct greater advantages would accrue unto us. But we have to learn, if we have not already learned it, that obedience to counsel is the policy for us to pursue; and that when we indulge in thoughts of an opposite character we suffer ourselves to be led astray by the power of the adversary. Hence it has become almost proverbial among the Saints that the path of counsel is the path of safety. Those who have had years of experience in the Church have arrived at the conclusion that the path marked out for us to walk in by those who have authority to counsel and dictate is invariably the path of safety to those who adopt it. But our traditions interfere with this.

You look back over the policy that has been taught us for the past few years. I refer more particularly to this because, having been at home in the midst of the Saints, I have been more familiar with the counsels given. I can cast my eyes back for that time, and see, and doubtless you can when you reflect upon it, that there have been many items of counsel given that the Saints have been reluctant to obey or adopt, and which, if they had been carried out in the spirit in which they were given, would have resulted in great advantage to us as a people, and doubtless as individuals. I will refer to one item, that has been talked about a great deal—namely, sustaining our enemies. Now it seems that a moment's reflection on this point would satisfy every individual that the policy foreshadowed in this counsel was the best that could be adopted by a people surrounded with such circumstances as those surrounding us. But how difficult it has been to induce the people to carry that counsel out; why it has been so difficult that in some instances men have actually run the risk of losing their standing in the Church of Jesus Christ rather than forego the gratification of traditions and desires, which, seemingly, have taken entire possession of them—namely, to do as they please in relation to these matters.

Now, as I have said, a moment's reflection ought to satisfy everybody that this is the true course for us to pursue; that if we intend to build up the Zion of God and to become a great people, it is essential that we should concentrate our means in one channel; that we should sustain those who are friendly to and whose whole interest is centered in the cause of Zion; and that, instead of spending our means in fostering a power in our midst that is opposed to the work of God, we should be willing, rather than do this, to forego what may seem to be an advantage to us, and even deprive ourselves of comforts and submit to privation if necessary to carry out this policy. If our minds were not blinded by tradition we should see at once that it would be an advantage to us as a people to put our means in one direction, and not allow it to go outside the kingdom of God any more than it is absolutely necessary; and that we should never use the influence which God has given us, or the means which He has bestowed upon us to foster or maintain any man or anything that is opposed to His cause. Why, the security that we have here in these mountains depends upon our taking this course to a very great extent.

We are engaged, as has been remarked, in a warfare. The enemy that we have to oppose is one that does not relent in the least degree; he does not yield or show the least sign of mercy or even to give us fair play; but continually shows a disposition to crowd us to the wall and take every advantage, and to overwhelm us in every possible manner. God has brought us to this land; He has given it unto us and has made it a blest land for our sakes. He has sustained us in a wonderful manner for a great many years, and has given unto us the means whereby we could surround ourselves with those things necessary for our convenience and comfort. For long years the effort has been incessant on the part of God's servants to induce us to become a self-sustaining people. Now that the railway is completed we can see God's Spirit and His wisdom in this, impelling His servants to dwell upon this theme. Year after year, conference after conference, and meeting after meeting were the Saints instructed and continually urged to establish home manufactures, and to develop the resources which they had in their own midst, so that they might become self-sustaining. There was a providence in this. As I now view it, I can see its force more clearly than ever, although I always saw the force and necessity of the counsel; but now that events have worked out the results that we see around us, I can see the propriety in God inspiring His servants to give this counsel so many years ago. He could see in His divine wisdom that a day was coming when we should be, so to speak, overwhelmed, or when attempts would be made to overthrow us, and when there would be a greater necessity, apparently, than at that day, that we should be able to sustain ourselves, and to keep our means within ourselves, and not be under the necessity of fostering those from abroad who might come amongst us to acquire fortunes from our means and labors. For years has counsel on these subjects been reiterated in our ears, and scarcely a meeting has been held by the First Presidency, the Twelve Apostles, or any of the Elders of Israel in which this subject has not been prominently dwelt upon, the Elders feeling in their spirit and in their entire being that it was essentially important that the Latter-day Saints should carry out this policy strictly. We can now begin to see, if this counsel had not been given, and the Saints had continued to spend their money with anybody and everybody, no matter if it were the greatest enemy of the kingdom of God, what would have been our position today. Our enemies would have been in our midst, numbering hundreds where they now only number tens; and the efforts to disintegrate the kingdom of God might have been attended with a degree of success, whereas they have been entirely abortive.

You may trace the counsels that have been given to us from the beginning, one step following another in natural order and succession; one principle leading to another, and one important truth engendering, as it were, another important truth, revealing it and bringing it more forcibly home to our minds, until finally cooperation and its necessity have been brought to our attention and enforced upon us. Here tradition has come up again and has had its effect; and it has required days, weeks, and it may be said years of preaching to bring this principle home to the minds of the Latter-day Saints, so that they could see and understand its beauty and propriety, and the advantages which would result from its adoption in our midst. If we had not these traditions to contend with, cooperation would be sustained with hardly a dissentient. We should grasp the idea at once, and see beauty in it. We would say, "That is a principle I can recognize; I see its force and its advantages, and I am ready to adopt it and carry it out." But no, there are these traditions; there is this unbelief, this reluctance on the part of the people to part with their old systems and to adopt the principles of the Gospel and the revelations of Jesus Christ, as they are given unto us. There is that terrible tradition, that has such strong hold of all our minds, that the Priesthood of God and the religion of Jesus Christ have nothing to do particularly with temporal matters. It is a tradition almost as old as Christianity. It has come down to us for generations and centuries, and is fully interwoven in the hearts, minds and feelings of the children of men, and it is an exceedingly difficult thing to get them to comprehend that temporal things and spiritual things are alike in the sight of God; that there is no line of demarcation between the two; that the religion of Jesus Christ applies to one as much as another, and comprehends within its scope, temporal equally with spiritual matters.

This has made it difficult to enforce upon us the necessity of practically carrying out the principle of cooperation. "O," say men, "that is a temporal matter, pertaining merely to the buying and selling of goods; it is not particularly connected with life and salvation or with eternal glory in the kingdom of God." But there they mistake. I look upon that principle, though it may be subordinate in some respects, as divine, as coming through revelation, and as necessary in its place as any other principle that can be mentioned which is connected with the Gospel of Jesus Christ. They are all alike to me—all alike necessary and divine. Divine wisdom has prompted their practice, and has inspired the servant of God who presides and whom God has chosen to be His mouthpiece in our midst, to reveal them, one as much as another, unto us as a people.

When we have practiced this principle long enough, and are sufficiently advanced in it, there are other principles, now ahead, which we shall be prepared to enter upon and practice. But we must get rid of this tradition that envelopes us and which lies in our pathway, and which is so serious an obstacle to our progress. As fast as we overcome our traditions there will be other principles revealed to us, and thus it will go on, law after law and principle after principle being revealed until we shall be prepared to enter into the glory of our God, and to dwell in the presence of God and the Lamb.

It is essentially necessary then, in view of these things, that we should exercise faith. Our minds should be drawn out and our faith exercised. It may be but little in the beginning. As the Prophet Alma said, when addressing the people on one occasion, and referring to the word of the Lord, it was like seed planted in the heart; its influence and effect at first were not very powerful; but if it were planted in the heart, by and by it began to germinate and grow and the possessor of it said, "Why it is a good seed, I feel it growing!" And if it were nourished, and cherished it would continue to grow until, to use a figure, it would become a great tree, and fill the whole man with light, knowledge and wisdom, and with the gifts and qualifications necessary to make him perfect before the Lord. Our faith may be small in the beginning, but if we cultivate it, it will grow; if we do not it will die out, noxious weeds will spring up and choke it. But if we exercise it as we should, the veil of darkness that separates us from God, and which prevents us comprehending the things of His kingdom, will grow thinner and thinner, until we see with great distinctness and clearness the purposes of God our heavenly Father, and comprehend them as He designs we should, and carry them out in our lives.

This should be our aim as a people and as individuals, every day living so near to God that we shall have more of His Spirit and power, and more of the gifts and endowments of the holy Gospel of the Son of God. If we take and continue in this course we shall feel and understand that we are progressing in the knowledge of God and in the comprehension of truth. And let me tell you, my brethren and sisters, if we thus live, when counsel is given, no matter what it may be, or what principle it may refer to, it will be plain and simple, and as clear unto our minds as the

Appendix B - Our Traditions

light we now see; and our understandings will be enlightened by it and we shall see beauty in it.

If it be to stop trading with our enemies, we will adopt it. We shall feel, "That principle is true, it recommends itself to my understanding; the Spirit of God bears witness to my spirit that it is true, and I will adopt it." And then, after awhile, when cooperation is taught unto us we will receive that also in a like spirit and faith; and if our minds are possessed of the Spirit of God we will say, "There is light in this principle; I see its advantages, I will sustain it by carrying it out myself, and I will try and exercise influence with my friends and induce them to do the same, that it may become universally practiced in the midst of the Saints." It will be thus, if we live our religion, not only with every principle that God has revealed, but that He may hereafter reveal. We shall know for ourselves concerning them; they will be plain and simple and in harmony with our feelings. There will be no disturbance of mind, no difficulty in carrying them out. This will go on under the leadership of him whom God has chosen to be our guide, and we shall progress step by step, week by week, gaining power, knowledge, influence, territory and wealth, until we shall emancipate this land and redeem it from the thralldom of sin and from the power of Satan; and the kingdom of Satan will recede before the light, faith and power of the Saints of the kingdom of God.

This is the work in which we are engaged. It is not a work to occupy our attention for one day, and then have it diverted from it for a week; but it is the work of our entire lifetime, all that we have to do. It is a mission that God has given to us here on earth. We can't be engaged in anything more noble than this work, for it is the work of God—a work in which He, Himself, is engaged—a work that occupies the attention and labors of Jesus, and every holy apostle, prophet, and Saint that has ever lived on the earth. These things are not gained without exertion; they require industry, zeal and attention on our part; and when we thus bestow attention on the work in which we are occupied, why God is with us, angels around about us, the heavens are open to us, the Spirit of God is poured out upon us, and our lives are a pleasant flowing stream, full of peace, joy and heaven. We feel that we have heaven indeed, here below; and wherever we go we carry this holy influence with us and diffuse it around us; and thus the power of Satan is weakened on the earth, and the power of God is increased.

There are some of the brethren and sisters, doubtless, who cannot see these things in this light. You will hear them very frequently say, "I cannot see this counsel, I can't comprehend it, it don't strike me;" but there is no fault in the counsel. They would, by their words, reflect on the counsel; they would convey the idea to those who listen to them, that there is something at fault; they are right, but the counsel is wrong. Now, it may be given as a rule, I believe, to the Latter-day Saints, that in every such case, whether it be man or woman, he or she has got to repent and seek unto the Lord for faith and for the light of His Holy Spirit to be given unto them.

How was it with us when we first heard the truth? Oh! How sweet and delightful the sound of the Elder's voice when he proclaimed that God had spoken from the heavens; that angels had come to the earth again, and that the holy Priesthood was bestowed upon men! How sweet, when he said that the Church was organized with its ancient power and purity and pristine fullness; that the Holy Ghost, with its wealth of gifts, and blessings, had been bestowed upon men! How was it with those who were prepared for these tidings when they heard them proclaimed? Their hearts burned within them and they were filled with joy when the testimony of the truth came to them; and when other principles were taught unto them, O, the joy that filled them in listening to them, and they knew by the testimony of Jesus and by the Spirit and power of God that rested upon them that these things were true! They could get up in their meetings and testify "I know this is true." When they heard the gathering preached they had the testimony that it was true; and some had it before it was preached. They knew it was from God and that God established His Zion, and their hearts burned at the thought that they would soon be with the Saints of God in Zion. They yearned for the land of Zion and for the society of the people of God. This was their testimony, and they had it in the States, Europe, Africa, Asia, islands of the sea, and in every land where the Gospel has been preached and the people have been prepared to receive it.

This has been the testimony, and if this spirit has continued to rest upon them every principle that has been taught has been plain and delightful to them. Is not this our experience, brethren and sisters? We can all bear testimony to it. Then whence come this darkness and these doubts respecting counsel? Whence comes this query about cooperation? Whence comes this distrust about other counsel in relation to temporal matters? Why, it is very easy to understand whence it comes and what its origin is. It can be traced to neglect of duty, to the hardening of the heart, to the indulgence of a spirit of unbelief, to the neglect of prayer, to becoming selfish and sordid, and to the commission of sin. There are causes for all this, for let me tell you, and testify to you today, that the Latter-day Saint who lives near to God, and has the Spirit of God constantly resting upon him or her, never has any doubts about any principle that God has revealed. When the gathering was taught they were prepared for it; when the payment of tithing was taught they were prepared for it; when consecration was taught they were prepared for it; when the move South was taught they were prepared for it; when the move back was taught they were prepared for it; when celestial marriage was taught they were prepared for it; when the word came, "Cease to trade with our enemies," they were prepared for it; and when cooperation was taught they were prepared for it. There was no doubt in their minds, because the same Spirit that taught them that this was the truth in the beginning, and that God had spoken from the heavens, taught them also that all these things were true. But when you have doubts respecting counsel given by the servants of God, then be assured, my brethren and sisters, there is room for repentance; we are not living as near to God as we should do; we have not the Spirit of God as we once had it, and we should seek unto God with full purpose of heart, that the light of His Spirit may be bestowed upon us again. Then, when the servant of God stands up and teaches us concerning the things of the kingdom, his words will find a lodging place in our hearts; his counsels will be clear and sweet unto us, and there will be no dubiety, no distress, neither any disposition to repel these counsels or to feel offended at them. And if the word come to us to go on a foreign mission, to go to "Dixie," to Bear Lake, or any other place to perform this or that labor, we shall be ready to obey, for the Spirit will reveal to us beforehand what we have to do and prepare us for its performance.

These are the privileges of the Latter-day Saints. I talk not of something that is theory, or away off, or that happened years ago; I talk not of that which is out of our reach, but I speak of that which is within our reach, within the reach of all: it is practical. We can obtain and possess and enjoy it; and if we do not, we do not live up to our privileges as Latter-day Saints. O! I feel sometimes, I wish I had the tongue of an angel to proclaim to the children of men the glad tidings of salvation that God has revealed to us in the day in which we live. This blessed time! This time of times, when God in His mercy has restored His Church to the earth, and has given us prophets and Apostles and the Holy Ghost and its gifts; and in His great mercy has brought us to this land, where we can dwell in peace, where we can go out and in before the Lord without any to molest or make us afraid.

My brethren and sisters, what blessed privileges we do enjoy when compared with the Saints in former days; and even when compared with our own circumstances in the early history of the Church, what blessed privileges God has given us in this glorious land! We have rulers of our own choice—men whom God has chosen; we have the voice of God in our midst, so that we need not walk in darkness and doubt. There is no uncertainty in all the land of Zion concerning the purposes of God. It need not be said of us as it was of Israel, "There is no Urim and Thummim; there is no dream or vision, and no prophet in the land." We have the prophet of God; we have the visions of the Almighty; we have the Spirit of God descending upon us like sweet dew; we have the gifts of the Spirit of God; we have the Gospel in the fulness and plenitude of its power. We have all this, and we have the promises of God concerning us and our posterity; and, as I have said, we have this glorious land of freedom and liberty, where we can build up the kingdom of God in power and great glory; where we can be a free people, if we so choose. If this is not the case, it is because we are wicked, because we disobey counsel; because we harden our hearts and have placed ourselves in a position to be scourged. It is not God's will that we should be, or that our enemies should have power over us. It is His good will and pleasure to give unto us the kingdom and dominion, and to strengthen and uphold us.

Let us then be faithful! Let us live day by day, from morning until night, in the moments of business and when perplexed with its cares, with our thoughts on the kingdom, and our prayers ascending to the God of our fathers, yea, unto our Father, for His blessings upon us; and that He may fill us with His spirit and prepare us for the things that await us, and help us to be faithful even unto the end.

That we may all be thus faithful and overcome, and be counted worthy to sit down with our fathers, Abraham, Isaac and Jacob, and with all the holy ones in the presence of God and the Lamb, and be crowned with glory, immortality and endless lives, is my prayer in the name of Jesus. Amen.

Appendix C

"An Encyclical Letter Upon Co-operation And The Social System."

Source: Tullidge's Quarterly Magazine, Volume I. 1881, pp.389-392

[NOTE: This remarkable letter was sent out in 1875 <u>under the signatures of the First Presidency and the Twelve Apostles</u>. Pay particular attention to the second paragraph, and the very last sentence.]

To The Latter-Day Saints:-

The experience of mankind has shown that the people of communities and nations among whom wealth is the most equally distributed, enjoy the largest degree of liberty, are the least exposed to tyranny and oppression and suffer the least from luxurious habits which beget vice. Among the chosen people of the Lord, to prevent the too rapid growth of wealth and its accumulation in a few hands, he ordained that in every seventh year the debtors were to be released from their debts, and, where a man had sold himself to his brother, he was in that year to be released from slavery and to go free; even the land itself which might pass out of the possession of its owner by his sale of it, whether through his improvidence, mismanagement, or misfortune, could only be alienated until the year of jubilee. At the expiration of every forty-nine years the land reverted, without cost, to the man or family whose inheritance originally it was, except in the case of a dwelling house in a walled city, for the redemption of which, one year only was allowed, after which, if not redeemed, it became the property, without change at the year of jubilee, of the purchaser. Under such a system, carefully maintained, there could be no great aggregations of either real or personal property in the hands of a few; especially so while the laws, forbidding the taking of usury or interest for money or property loaned, continued in force.

One of the great evils with which our own nation is menaced at the present time is the wonderful growth of wealth in the hands of a comparatively few individuals. The very liberties for which our fathers contended so steadfastly and courageously, and which they bequeathed to us as a priceless legacy, are endangered by the monstrous power which this accumulation of wealth gives to a few individuals and a few powerful corporations. By its seductive influence results are accomplished which, were it more equally distributed, would be impossible under our form of government. It threatens to give shape to the legislation, both State and National, of the entire country. If this evil should not be checked, and measures not be taken to prevent the continued enormous growth of riches among the class already rich, and the painful increase of destitution and want among the poor, the nation is liable to be overtaken by disaster; for, according to history, such a tendency among nations once powerful was the sure precursor of ruin. The evidence of the restiveness of the people under this condition of affairs in our times is witnessed in the formation of societies of grangers, of patrons of husbandry, trades' unions, etc., etc., combinations of the productive and working classes against capital.

Years ago it was perceived that we Latter-day Saints were open to the same dangers as those which beset the rest of the world. A condition of affairs existed among us which was favorable to the growth of riches in the hands of a few at the expense of the many. A wealthy class was being rapidly formed in our midst whose interests, in the course of time, were likely to be diverse from those of the rest of the community. The growth of such a class was dangerous to our union; and, of all people, we stand most in need of union and to have our interests identical. Then it was that the Saints were counseled to enter into co-operation. In the absence of the necessary faith to enter upon a more perfect order revealed by the Lord unto the church, this was felt to be the best means of drawing us together and making us one. Zion's Co-operative Mercantile Institution was organized, and, throughout the Territory, the mercantile business of the various Wards and Settlements was organized after that pattern. Not only was the mercantile business thus organized, but at various places branches of mechanical, manufacturing and other productive industries were established upon this basis. To-day, therefore, co-operation among us is no untried experiment. It has been tested, and whenever fairly tested, and under proper management, its results have been most gratifying and fully equal to all that was expected of it, though many attempts have been made to disparage and decry it, to destroy the confidence of the people in it and have it prove a failure. From the day that Zion's Co-operative Mercantile Institution was organized until this day it has had a formidable and combined opposition to contend with, and the most base and unscrupulous methods have been adopted, by those who have no interest for the welfare of the people, to destroy its credit. Without alluding to the private assaults upon its credit which have been made by those who felt that it was in their way and who wished to ruin it, the perusal alone of the telegraphic dispatches and correspondence to newspapers which became public, would exhibit how unparalleled, in the history of mercantile enterprises, has been the hostility it has had to encounter. That it has lived, notwithstanding these bitter and malignant attacks upon it and its credit, is one of the most valuable proofs of the practical worth of co-operation to us as a people. Up to this day Zion's Co-operative Mercantile Institution has had no note go to protest; no firm, by dealing with it, has ever lost a dollar; its business transactions have been satisfactory to its creditors and yet its purchases have amounted to fifteen millions of dollars! What firm in all this broad land can point to a brighter or more honorable record than this? During the first four years and a half of its existence it paid to its stockholders a dividend in cash of seventy-eight per cent and fifty-two per cent, as a reserve to be added to the capital stock, making in all a dividend of one hundred and thirty per cent. The Institution declared as dividends, and reserves added to the capital stock, and tithing, during those four and a half years, upwards of half a million of dollars. So that the stockholder who invested one thousand dollars in the Institution in March, 1869, had by October 1st, 1873, that stock increased to $1.617.00, and this without counting his cash dividends, which in the same space of time would have amounted to $1,378.50! In other words. a stockholder who had deposited $1000.00 In the Institution when it started, could have sold, in four years and a half afterwards, stock to the amount of $617.00, collected dividends to the amount of $1,378.50, thus making the actual profits $1,995,50, or within a fraction ($4.50) of two hundred per cent upon the original investment, and still have had his $1,000 left intact! This is a statement from the books of the Institution, and realized by hundreds of its stockholders. And yet there are those who decry co-operation and say it will not succeed! If success consists in paying large dividends, then it cannot be said that Z. C. M. I. has not succeeded. In fact, the chief cause of the trouble has been, it has paid too freely and too well. Its reserves should not have been added, as they were, to capital stock; for, by so doing, at the next semi-annual declaration of dividends a dividend was declared upon them, which, as will be perceived, swelled the dividends enormously and kept the Institution stripped too bare of resources to meet whatever contingencies might arise.

It was not for the purpose alone, however, of making money, of declaring large dividends, that Zion's Co-operative Mercantile Institution was established. A higher object than this prompted its organization. A union of interests was sought to be attained. At the time co-operation was entered upon, the Latter-day Saints were acting in utter disregard of the principles of self-preservation. They were encouraging the growth of evils in their own midst which they condemned as the worst features of the systems from which they had been gathered. Large profits were being concentrated in comparatively few hands, instead of being generally distributed among the people. As a consequence, the community was being rapidly divided into classes, and the hateful and unhappy distinctions which the possession and lack of wealth give rise to, were becoming painfully apparent. When the proposition to organize Zion's Co-operative Mercantile Institution was broached, it was hoped that the community at large would become its stockholders; for if a few individuals only were to own its stock, the advantages to the community would be limited. The people, therefore, were urged to take shares, and large numbers responded to the appeal. As we have shown, the business proved to be as successful as its most sanguine friends anticipated. But the distribution of profits among the community was not the only benefit conferred by the organization of co-operation among us. The public at large who did not buy at its stores derived profits, in that *the old practice of dealing which prompted traders to increase the price of an article because of its scarcity, was abandoned*. Zion's Co-operative Mercantile Institution declined to be a party to making a corner upon any article of merchandise because of the limited supply in the market. From its organization until the present it has never advanced the price; of any article because of its scarcity. Goods therefore in this Territory have been sold at something like fixed rates and reasonable profits since the Institution has had an existence, and practices which are deemed legitimate in some parts of the trading world, and by which, in this Territory, the necessities of consumers were taken advantage of--as, for instance, the selling of sugar at a dollar a pound, and domestics, coffee, tobacco and other articles at an enormous advance over original cost because of their scarcity here-have not been indulged in. In this result the purchasers of goods who have been opposed to co-operation, have shared equally with its patrons.

We appeal to the experience of every old settler in this Territory for the truth of what is here stated. They must vividly remember that goods were sold here at prices which the necessities of the people compelled them to pay, and not at cost and transportation, with the addition of a reasonable profit. The railroad, it is true, has made great changes in our method of doing business. But let a blockade occur, and the supply of some necessary article be very limited in our market, can we suppose that traders have so changed in the lapse of a few years that, if there were no check upon them, they would not put up the price of that article in proportion as the necessities of the people made it desirable? They would be untrue to all the training and traditions of their craft if they did not. And it is because this craft is in danger that such an outcry is made against cooperation. Can anyone wonder that it should be so, when he remembers that, from the days of Demetrius who made silver shrines for the goddess Diana at Ephesus down to our own times, members of crafts have made constant war upon innovations that were likely to injure their business?

Co-operation has submitted in silence to a great many attacks. Its friends have been content to let it endure the ordeal. But it is now time to speak. The Latter-day Saints should understand that *it is our duty to sustain co-operation and all in our power to make it a success.* At a meeting of the stockholders of the Institution at the time of the General Conference a committee of seventeen was chosen to select and arrange for the purchase of a suitable piece of ground for a store and to proceed to erect upon it such a fireproof building as would answer the purposes of the Institution. The objects in view in this proceeding were to concentrate the business and thereby lessen the cost of handling and disposing of the goods and to decrease rent and insurance. The saving in these directions alone, not to mention other advantages which must result from having such a store, will make a not inconsiderable dividend upon the stock. A suitable piece of ground has been secured. and upon terms which are deemed advantageous, and steps have been taken towards the erection of a proper building. But the Institution, to erect this building and carry on its business properly, needs more capital. The determination is still to sell goods as low as possible. By turning over the capital three or four times during the year they can be sold at very low figures, and at but a slight advance over cost and carriage, and yet the stockholders have a handsome dividend. To purchase goods to the greatest advantage the Institution should have the money with which to purchase of first hands. To effect this important result, as well as to unite in our mercantile affairs, the Institution should receive the cordial support of every Latter-day Saint. Everyone who can should take stock in it. *By sustaining the Co-operative Institution, and taking stock in it, profits that would otherwise go to a few individuals will be distributed among many hundreds.* Stockholders should interest themselves in the business of the Institution. It is their own, and if suggestions are needed, or any corrections ought to be made, it is to their interest to make them.

The Institution has opened a retail store within a few weeks, one of the old-fashioned kind, in which everything required by the public is sold. This should receive the patronage of all the well-wishers of co-operation. In the settlements, also, the local co-operative stores should have the cordial support of the Latter-day Saints. Does not all our history impress upon us the great truth that in union is strength? Without it, what power would the Latter-day Saints have? *But it is not in doctrines alone that we should be united, but in practice and especially in our business affairs.*

Your Brethren,

BRIGHAM YOUNG,	ERASTUS SNOW,
GEORGE A. SMITH,	FRANKLIN D. RICHARDS,
DANIEL H. WELLS,	GEORGE Q. CANNON,
JOHN TAYLOR,	BRIGHAM YOUNG, JUN.,
WILFORD WOODRUFF,	ALBERT CARRINGTON.
ORSON HYDE,	
ORSON PRATT,	SALT LAKE CITY, UTAH TERRITORY
CHARLES C. RICH,	JULY 10TH, 1875.
LORENZO SNOW,	

ABOUT THE AUTHOR

I'M NOBODY

I'm not the prophet and I'm not a member of the Seventy, in fact, I've never even been a bishop. Currently, I serve as a ward librarian in my Utah ward. I'm no one in the LDS Church.

HOWEVER...

I've been fascinated with the idea of Zion since I first read about it at age 15. I suppose I might have *heard* about Zion in Sunday School between the time my family joined the LDS Church in 1970 and when I first read about it in 1977. That spring my sister married a man from Salt Lake City and for a wedding gift, she gave me a novel entitled, "Added Upon" by Nephi Anderson.

Reading a description in that novel about life in the New Jerusalem lit a fire in my soul that has endured over four decades. The idea of participating in a Zion society makes living in the most abundant nation in history rather bland by comparison. America achieved what no other nation has done – a society built on political, economic, and social freedoms. In spite of this, I still yearn for Zion, which I expect will be ten times what America was at her peak: A Celestial City -- A light to the world -- The literal capital of God's Kingdom on Earth. I ACHED TO LIVE THERE.

TRAGEDY AND HOPE

Then I forgot about her. I was preoccupied for six years while I served a mission, enrolled at BYU, and got married. I had forgotten lady Zion; I was out to become a success! Then, I came across and read Hugh Nibley's speech (now a chapter in the book Approaching Zion) entitled "Work We Must, But the Lunch is Free". It threw me for a huge loop – rocked my world – challenged all my economic assumptions. I realized that I had been suckered by the "delicacies" of the prostitute Babylon. But what hurt more was that I soon came to realize that most of my fellow Mormons apparently had only a vague notion of what Zion was and appeared to have little or no interest in building it in the here and now. Imagine my joy when an occasional conference talk referenced quotes by modern prophets that indicate that the goal of building Zion had not been abandoned. Imagine my joy when a few full-length talks were given over the past dozen or so years indicating that the vision of building a latter-day Zion still lights a few hearts.

SO, I'VE BEEN WAITING...

Waiting for my fellow Saints to catch the vision. Waiting for the Brethren to give us directions. I have been biding my time the past three decades gathering examples of human institutions that more readily approximate Zion's organizational principles
(like cooperatives and freedom-based schools). I've studied the history of the LDS Church's economic experiments and discovered many remarkable things of which the general membership is apparently unaware.

AND NOW...

...I'm tired of waiting.

So, I'm taking personal responsibility and becoming a "Ziontist" -- one who studies and applies Zion principles in their life and encourages others to do so. It makes sense that God will call those to build the "official" Zion who are already moving in that direction, those who by their actions demonstrate to Him that Zion is in their hearts. I choose to be among them.

I invite all who read this, and find it compelling, to get "anxiously engaged in [this] good cause, and do many things of their own free will, and bring to pass much righteousness."

Made in the USA
San Bernardino, CA
20 November 2019